Adirondack Memories and Campfire Stories

A jolly crowd enjoy a cookie
and tea break following their outing.
Courtesy Jane Ritz

Compiled, Edited and with
Written Commentary by

William J. O'Hern

Adirondack Memories and Campfire Stories

Edited and with Written
Commentary by William J. O'Hern

First Paperback Edition, June 2014

The book and cover design and typesetting
were created by Nancy Did It! (www.NancyDidIt.com)

Cover: The Flume Fall, West Branch of the Ausable River,
Adirondack Park and Forest Preserve, N.Y.
©Mark Bowie, Outdoor Images • www.markbowie.com

Back cover color inset: Photo S. R. Stoddard.
Colorized by and courtesy of the Maitland D. DeSormo Collection

For permission to reprint the following material, grateful
acknowledgement is made to the New York State Conservationist for:
"Long Lake" by Roland B. Miller
"Blue Mountain Lake" by Roland B. Miller
"Pit Burning Charcoal" by David B. Carl and Roland B. Miller
"Cy Brown" by Barnett Fowler
"Indian Lake" by Gretchen H. Fish
"Life on an Adirondack" by John Wilkins

In the
Adirondacks

Camden, NY 13316 • www.adkwilds.com

Printed in the United States of America by Versa Press, Inc.
ISBN 978-0-9890328-3-4

IN APPRECIATION

Courtesy Special Collections, Feinberg Library, SUNY College at Plattsburgh

George Glyndon Cole
June 6, 1909–March 21, 2004

George Glyndon Cole's quest to document and preserve historical content brought people together. The archivist-publisher-educator, nevertheless, would have been the first person to say success would not have come about without a dedicated team of volunteer associate editors, the cooperation of publishers, the subscribers, and contributors who selflessly offered stories and poems without remuneration—all for the love of history and folklore.

This compilation recognizes the volunteer spirit of everyone who contributed to *North Country Life* and *York State Tradition* and to all ages who have a curiosity about New York State's rich historical past.

A special note of gratitude goes to the volunteer-collaborators whose work made this book possible. I would like to acknowledge posthumously those who were sharing and selfless. Each person's spirit lives through their writing.

CONTENTS

Collection V:
ADIRONDACK THRILLERS

PART TWO: CAMPFIRE STORIES

Collection VI:
STORIES TOLD AROUND THE CAMPFIRE

PREFACE

One of the most popular regional magazines from 1946 through 1974 was George Glyndon Cole's *North Country Life*, later called *York State Tradition*, compiled and edited by the historian-folklorist-archivist. Throughout New York and across the United States, fans made the quarterly digest a much-anticipated periodical, keeping it in publication for twenty-eight years.

The reason was simple: People were as smitten then as they are now with the magic of the Adirondacks and the North Country, and Cole's quarterly gave them a delicious dose of that magic in the form of stories, articles, poetry and folklore.

Cole delighted his readers with personal recollections and informative histories about the Adirondack waters and mountains, legends and lore. He included poetry, literature, and interesting reprints of old newspaper and periodical stories, true backwoods tales, pioneer stories, military history, among other topics.

Cole's "light touch" style of editing was appropriate fine for what he was doing. As long as a given passage was grammatically correct and clear in its meaning, he didn't change it, although for a different style of magazine it might have been said with a bit more sophistication. But, sophistication wasn't the goal here, so he chose not to impose it. The point was to have Adirondack and North Country history and its peoples' way of life documented.

I want to keep Cole's tone and "editorial voice" intact. Along the same lines I believe we can accept most facts as "what the writer knew at the time," so I questioned very few and only the most significant facts, for example, the likely confusion of the Adirondack Park and Forest Preserve.

Cole was inspired by the compulsion, shared by many others at roughly the same time, to document everyday life in upstate New York before all traces of it disappeared.

"The same impulse drove Marjorie Lansing Porter to record folk songs in the farms and lumber camps," Anthony F. Hall pointed out in an article titled "A Journey Through Our Back Pages: Re-discovering *North Country Life*," in the June 14, 2013, issue of *The Lake George Mirror*. "And Richard W. Lawrence to create the Adirondack Center Museum in Elizabethtown, Harold Hochshild to begin Township 34 (out of which the Adirondack Museum in Blue Mountain Lake emerged) and Carl Carmer, Harold Thompson and Louis Jones to collect folk tales."

Hundreds of readers asked Cole to assemble a collection of stories from his magazine in book form. If all of their requests were laid end to end, they might well stretch to the peak of Cloud Splitter, the translation of the putative Native-American name for Mount Marcy—New York State's highest mountain.

Cole never did compile a book-length collection, but with so few of the magazines still in existence, now seemed the time for me to take the project on. When I met Cole in 1989, I found him to be humble, kind, and extremely intelligent. He shared my imagination and gave his blessing to my proposal that one day I would like to represent his years of work in anthology form.

Adirondack Memories and Campfire Stories is like a narrated map: it explores Adirondack places and little-known villages and towns as well as those that are now tourist centers. There are remembrances of some representative trades and industries and stories about Adirondack thrillers and some memorable adventures in the mountains. The second part of the book relates tales and stories of the sort heard around an evening campfire as the loons call, the frogs croak, and little children's eyes grow large with amazement.

Adirondack Memories and Campfire Stores further fulfills Cole's readers' wishes that twenty-eight years of articles, stories and poems about their beloved Adirondacks and North Country be brought together in one place. It continues the anthology begun in *Adirondack Kaleidoscope: Culture, Lifestyles and North Country Characters.*

North Country Life, opposite, was published by George Glyndon Cole from 1946–1974, although the name changed to *York State Tradition*, above, beginning with the Spring 1963 issue.

INTRODUCTION

Glyndon Cole's *North Country Life* and *York State Tradition* stories, along with my Adirondack travels, are a tapestry of Adirondack history and folklore. They are a compilation of the experiences, imagination, and curiosity of old-timers, friends of Cole's and readers who contributed to his magazine. In *Adirondack Memories and Campfire Stores* I have gathered interesting and sometimes unusual information about Adirondack and North Country places. By "unusual" I mean things like searching for lost mines and sea serpents, being chased by a panther or pack of wild dogs, or finding out about a West Canada Lake treasure. The second part of this book includes a collection of stories, tales and legends.

The less contact one has with urban society, the more distinctive one's character becomes. This is true with communities as well as with people. Rural, hard-scrabble North Country communities without paved roads were even more isolated after heavy snowfalls in the pre-diesel snowplow days. Little outside entertainment existed for people living in out-of-the way localities—other than what they made for themselves. All winter long, snow blanketed the ground. Activity was reduced for months.

Everyday living centered on tending farm animals, felling trees and sawing blocks. Splitting and chopping the billets into fire and stove wood dimensions was routine. Some men and women trapped. Residents frequently scrutinized and culled spoiling fruits and vegetables stored in cool root cellars, and something was always being repaired or built in the woodworking shop. At night a family sat together reading, penning letters, playing instruments and singing, playing cards and board games and *talking*—a glowing concept!

Spring was a busy time in the north. Crop farmers were eager to plant, livestock were turned out to greening pastures, and as the waterways thawed, ice-imprisoned logs rolled to pulp mills and the first "sports" flocked to the North Country to fish the icy waters. Once school was out, families journeyed to campgrounds and resorts in Tupper Lake, Lake Placid, Saranac Lake, and hundreds of other places. The luckiest owned summer cottages. While most would get only a brief respite from the cities, North Country magic did its work swiftly, and most longed to return from the moment they left.

If they were lucky, there might be some excitement in the little town where they bought their groceries and fishing tackle and bait. There could well be a fireworks display on July 4th, maybe even a parade, and the county fair drew hundreds to view prime livestock and find out who made the first-prize pies and pickles, but mostly to ride the rides and overeat unhealthy but delicious foods.

This cabin, with log walls and hemlock bark roof, stood at Bassesett's Carry on Utowana Lake, between Eagle Lake and Raquette Lake. *Photo S. R. Stoddard. Courtesy Special Collections, Feinberg Library, SUNY College at Plattsburgh*

Early tourists relied on steamers such as this one plying the Saranac River near the lower lake. *Photo S. R. Stoddard. Courtesy Special Collections, Feinberg Library, SUNY College at Plattsburgh*

The native-born as well as the cottagers and campers enjoyed evening campfires. It's been that way all over the world for centuries. And when people sit around campfires, it is very likely that a few tales—true or slightly embellished or intentionally tall—will be part of the conversation. The country store, with its traditional potbelly stove, was another gathering place where tales were enjoyed.

I began to learn about storytellers during my childhood. I was raised in the little rural hamlet of Fairmount, New York. There I blended with the wildlife, woods and water, as well as with the oldsters, from whom I heard stories about living in the times of pre-electric farming. But when I sat through years of taping interviews during all the seasons of the Adirondacks, I discovered the universal thread that stitches a present-day storyteller with an African tribal *griot*: the telling of the tale.

★ ★ ★

There is little enough of storytelling today. So just when does a fellow have the time to sit and let his imagination fly freely? Anyone who earnestly enjoys the younger generation can generously share the age-old custom of oral tradition from a pleasant lookout, surrounded by wild expanses, be it from a boulder, a mountaintop, fire tower, warm sandy bank above water or a lawn chair with a pleasant urban view. Any berth from which we can view everyday scenery will do. Positioned long enough, with no clock to remind us of the time and with a little mix of oral history, geography, myth or legend, we may frame scenarios, putting old happenings into present-day context.

The stories that tale-spinners bring to us are the stuff of dreams. We may not believe—even for a minute—every tall tale, but in our secret minds we live them. We all are great adventurers in our dreams. We claw through snake-infested swamps and impenetrable cripple brush, or grapple for safe finger-holds on a sheer rock face while all in the outing party but us are in desperation. We struggle in raging whiteout snowstorms, triumph against tumultuous spring-fed rivers, defeat killing temperatures with subzero polar-guard sleeping bags, heft the most amazing loads up endless slopes, pedal mountain bikes down mud-caked trails and over miles of demanding terrain in the most amazingly small amount of time, wrestle alligators and thwart grizzlies, dive for sunken treasure in dangerous cross currents, and explore eerie ocean bottoms. In the end a reality check takes over from fantasy, and behold, the protected scenic land: the preserves, parks and other biodiverse wild land, leisurely trails, the eroding-rock hoodoos, sand ridges and sagebrush slopes—even better marvels than we fantasized.

When Chinooks flog the trees and rattle our thermo-pane windows, or snowpiles hide driveways and clog highways so that urban dwellers do not want to venture out, flatlanders snug in warm houses may wonder how the poor backwoods people of early American history ever got by, struggling against all odds in shacks and log cabins. They may, however, feel a little wistful envy of the world's greatest explorers, pioneers and adventurers who braved frigid temperatures and arctic blizzards, who conquered mountains.

Then on a fine day the sight of backpackers, rock climbers, and speleologists (the cave-plungers who grope into darkness), or of picnickers and sightseers who seek no less worthy destinations, or the smell of an aromatic balsam pillow from a distant forest or even a gnarly-shaped bit of driftwood art picked up from a shoreline, may give us a sting of envy for all who find adventure. I can only hope my selection of Cole's stories does some of these wonders justice.

Wednesday night story hour, 1888. Adirondack Lodge, Heart Lake. Built 1878–79. Burned on September 3, 1903. *Photo S. R. Stoddard. Courtesy of the Mailtland C. DeSormo Collection*

PART ONE

Adirondack Memories

Adirondack Memories teems with curious nooks and crannies and unique places that distinguish New York's Adirondack-North Country.

Here you'll find everything from curious places to Adirondack communities to bootleggers, early trades and industries, and Adirondack thrillers actually experienced by early North Country folks. Did you know that Rouse's Point was a champion tale-spinning town, or that Big Moose Lake was the scene of a real American tragedy? Are these tales true—at least partly? It's all in the telling, and the reader must decide. At any rate, they make for amusing and sometimes electrifying reading, and if you pass some of these tales along at a future campfire, you'll be part of a long and important tradition.

A gathering of guests at the fabulous Loon Lake House. 1889. *Courtesy Special Collections, Feinberg Library, SUNY College at Plattsburgh*

As in other rural areas of America, early North Country folks were involved in the business of survival through farming, logging, hunting, trapping, and an almost perpetual preparation for long winters. The country store, with its traditional potbelly stove, provided a place to socialize, exchange information, and tell stories. In the summertime, evening campfires served the same purpose. Old salts loved to "put one over" on listeners. Storytelling, a universal thread that ties humanity together from its beginning to the present—is the focus of the first part of *Adirondack Memories and Campfire Stories.*

PART ONE

Adirondack Memories

Corduroy road between Eagle Bay and Inlet, NY. Pre-1917. *Courtesy Jane Ritz*

MOUNTAIN LONGINGS

By William J. O'Hern

The Adirondack Mountain country is a land of high mountains and rolling hills with more lakes and streams than can easily be counted, on the top of the northeastern section of New York State, just below the St. Lawrence River, east of the Tug Hill plateau, and west of Lake George and Lake Champlain. It is a diverse country of dense unlumbered tracts, broken by bogs and swamps where tangling alders and the black spruce grow. There are stands of virgin timber, white pine, big hemlocks, and dwarf spruce on mountainsides with gnarled branches that point eastward—the direction the prevailing wind blows. Thousands of square miles are covered with a green canopy which attracts a wide variety of people. And everywhere you go there are plenty of spruce and balsam, the trees that provide the forest scent, the healthful potpourri that does strange things to one's mind.

Once part of that wholesome mixture were the Adirondack wayside springs, a part of the landscape along the winding mountain highways. The wooden open-faced pipes, darkened with the moisture of many seasons, and the moss-covered troughs were positioned near dirt roads. Overflowing their brims, these man-made basins' crystal-clear waters once reflected leafy patterns overhead, the whooshing shadows of birds, and drifting cloud formations. Cool, much-loved landmarks along dusty roads and major turnpikes, most have fallen into disuse or been tagged as no longer potable—a loss in more ways than one.

But there is still much to enjoy on one's way to a favorite Adirondack place. A heavy mantle of snow on roadside trees, withered leaves flickering, still attracts attention, as do the avenues of forest foot trails of pure autumn colors, a-sparkle with dancing sunbeams reflecting from morning dewdrops. The hush of utter solitude envelops the lone backpacker. The peace of an Adirondack scene seems other-worldly.

No greater benefits can these ancient Adirondack wild lands give to man than the bonus that comes with the whispered hush that steals from the forest in winter, or the lush green hues in mid-summer, when the trees are alive with the songs of birds and the trails call one to follow. The beauty of fall heals and invigorates, and nothing compares to the

Bette and Jay O'Hern. Two peaceful adults caressed by the merest trace of a breeze and absorbed in soft-voiced dialog of the rewarding Adirondack beauty stand in the moment.
Photo by Roy Reehil

sounds and smells of greening spring, when an early-season wanderer pauses on the forest trail or roadside overlook for precious moments of utter privacy.

The mountains have a way of doing strange and surprising things to a person who stays away from the wooded slopes for a long time. When you're gone for longer than you'd like, time begins to seem like an old-fashioned water dipper with a hole in the bottom. You can scoop up water with it, but it leaks out before you can drink all of it. Maybe that's why people like to write about their beloved mountains. It's not always possible to go back when the yearning strikes, but you can maintain a kind of connection by reading and writing about the places you long to be…and that's all that's needed for a while.

It's possible that's how many of Cole's contributors felt and the reason he used their works, as average as they might be. They all tried to tell what the Adirondacks is like, although of course there is a lot more to it than what one group of people had to say.

No matter how old they were, or how far away Cole's contributors moved from the mountains, not a one could be satisfied to live out the rest of his or her life without some kind of contact with the Adirondacks. In answer to their longings, the writers immersed themselves in recollections of the natural beauty of the region, its fascinating history, and its many faces. And Cole's readers, no matter how far they roamed, could open an issue of one of his magazines and renew their Adirondack connection.

It's difficult to nail down the common denominator that unites Cole's writers, and later North Country writers like me. I do know it's safe to say that there is a shared love for the North Country, a realization that for us it is the most special place on earth. There is no doubt that the landscape is stunning, but it is the people—the natives and individual characters in the landscape that make it so interesting. To me Frances Seaman, who lived a lifetime at Long Lake, makes a lot of sense. No one can know everything there is to know about the mountains, or whether the famous well-polished writers are better prepared to tell about the Adirondacks. We do know that the contributors Glyndon Cole chose to highlight brought a great deal of joy to readers who needed an Adirondack connection. What writer could ask for more satisfaction than that?

SEAGULLS IN THE ADIRONDACK MOUNTAINS

Now what do sea gulls want with mountain lakes
Where woodland shadows dance on every shore?
No briny billow shatters here and breaks
The silence of the mountains with its roar.
They are not here in flocks as by the sea,
But glide around alone or as a pair
And stay through balmy season, then they flee,
Content with bounty nature gave them there.
Now what do sea gulls want away from home?
There is an answer, and no doubt it's true,
That birds as well as men will always roam
To quiet havens known to but a few.

—John Van Brakle, *North Country Life*, Summer 1960

I recall the congenial events of this day—like many similar pleasurable Adirondack experiences. We were either outdoors on a sundrenched beach, taking a woodland walk, climbing a mountain, rowing against the wind over a choppy lake or inside camp, playing board games on a rainy day, enjoying a taffy pull, making fudge and popping corn. All were ordinary life events, as real as any centuries-old hemlock tree—and the memories as sizable as its spreading branches. It's difficult to explain how badly I sometimes miss those days when life had such a simple beauty. *Courtesy Leigh Portner, Sr.*

FISHING PISECO IN 1850

By Robert V. Anderson, *North Country Life*, Summer 1960

Every Adirondack fisherman must have looked, on some occasion, at the forest about him and wondered how the fishing was in "the good old days." Just how true is the common conception that the streams and lakes were filled fin-to-fin with big ones just begging to be hooked?

I recently found a partial answer to this question and some additional information on Adirondack recreation of more than a hundred years ago in a batch of old papers. In two manuscripts dated 1849 and 1850, the secretary of the Piseco Trout Club related the activities of a group of gentlemen from Troy, New York City and Medford, Massachusetts, when they came to Piseco on prolonged fishing trips.

The name of the club indicates a degree of formality which apparently was not present in the organization, for it seems to have been merely a group of kindred spirits who annually spent about two weeks together fishing at Piseco Lake. The reports show that they continued to gather for this purpose for at least the nine years from 1842 to 1850, in that time, taking 6,407 pounds of trout. The 1850 vacation may have been the last time they fished Piseco, for some dissatisfaction with the results—only 383 pounds of trout—was indicated.

Much of the rather flowery language of the reports had a special implication for the members; the modern reader can only guess what was intended. However, there are some passages which convey the spirit of the events so well that they are well worth quoting. For example, the 1849 account opens with a description of their arrival at the boarding house:

> *On the memorable 29th of May under the care of the veteran Brundage the following gentlemen, members of the Piseco Trout Club, were safely put down at Walton Hall, viz., Vail, Warren, Duane, Gibson, Trott and Brooks. Our reception was of that cordial character which usually marks the advent of good cheer, good intentions & good pay. fter the interchange of*

A Piseco Lake catch. *Courtesy Edward Blankman (The Lloyd Blankman Collection)*

this hearty welcome, the improved appearance of the premises attracted our attention: a piazza had been constructed the whole length of the main building, affording shelter to both person & rod, and an unfinished kitchen adjoining attested Mr. Rude's growing appreciation of comfort; where cleats for the repose of rods were insufficient, the spirited Mr. Trott soon supplied them, he having a peculiar eye on all occasions to order and elegance.

Brundage apparently drove his vehicle over a road from Northville or Lake Pleasant to the boarding house they called Walton Hall. This road probably was the same route which appears on Colton's railroad and township maps of the 1850s as a post road running from Lake Pleasant to Piseco and on to Morehouse. The route would be much the same as that we now follow.

The facilities seem to have been a far cry from a modern motel, and in some ways may have been more primitive than those presently available at a state campsite. But the fishermen had the same attitude we do as indicated by not wasting any time in getting out on the lake, for the account continues:

To the true angler an afternoon is regarded something like a fat codicil to a will—not to be neglected or overlooked—consequently three of the party, the Pres't, Vice Pres't, & Secretary ordered their oarsmen to prepare for business, the two former, going down, the latter, going up the lake…

It is probably worth pointing out that in that day before outboard motors a proper lake trout fisherman had someone to row for him so that he could give his entire attention to "trailing" for fish. The report includes the names of the oarsmen for this group, recording them as A. Dunning, M. Dunning, Mr. Lobb, Dan Rude, Henry Rude, "Eli" Rude and John Nichols. Presumably they were all local people.

Since to a fisherman the weather is likely to be an item of prime importance, much of the record concerns the weather. Our climate may be changing, but the Adirondack weather of late May and early June in 1849 seems to have been much the same as that which we observe today.

Those familiar with the area may recall similar days like that of Sunday, June 3rd, when the weatherman "threw the book at them":

> *The night preceding the Sabbath was full of heaviness and rain—the morning was moist and somber in the extreme; the mountains smoked as if a thousand fires were raging at their bases—detachments of fog crept lazily up their huge sides, now & then pausing, as if expecting recruits which were at hand of all sizes and shapes—the trees seemed to weep from every pore & the whole vegetable world bore the impress of some sad bereavement. It was a goodly sight in such a region & at such a time to see the knots of people approaching the Hall, where Sabbath service was about to be offered, but the scene was greatly heightened when the small multitude were assembled—it was sublime & touching; for when heaven's artillery was speaking outwardly... we were inwardly engaged in imploring its protection & seekikng its blessing...*

The evening was measurably serene:

> *If a convention of weatherologists had been summoned here this day, it would have collected matter enough for a volume. The last object that attracted our attention and which appears at great intervals was the Lunar Rainbow—even Mistress Rude was moved to look at it & if she had had a yard stick she might have attempted its measurement.*

The weather this day had not been a hardship to the fishermen since, unlike modern fishermen, they did not fish on Sunday; the fact that a minister was a member might have had something to do with it. On the other occasions when the weather was unfavorable, their diversions included chess. Letters and newspapers also came to them there in the woods whenever anyone went to the nearest post office.

The club held more formal meetings than their conventions on the lake. At one they resolved to wear distinctive costume and the next year duly wore an imported Scotch tartan. At another the wives at home were remembered by making them honorary members. Still it was not too serious, for the fish elected the officers, he who caught the most pounds of fish becoming the next year's president. And the secretary lamented—in that day before photography—that since none of them were artists the scenes of their activities could not be depicted other than by the pen so that "the great fish of '47, of which we are justly proud, is only embalmed in charcoal..."

Food claimed much of their attention. A special day was chowder day. Fried fish can be tiresome as a steady diet even for a fisherman. A moose steak dinner was recorded, and one of the members paid five dollars to have a hind quarter delivered to him the following January. (Moose became extinct in the Adirondacks about 1860.) One of the honorary lady members contributed a punch bowl the year after her election, and it was much appreciated, the modern convenience of canned beer not being available. A very special event was the time they caught a buck on the lake and so contributed a nonpiscatorial catch to the larder. The secretary described the event for us:

> *The 7th with its soft southwest wind filled us all with hope—but with nothing else. The trout would not respond as in times past under a similar influence & among the more ambitious competing members, a sense of weariness & dissatisfaction was apparent. Fortunately a truce occurred ... All of a sudden, the quiet but vigilant and observing Dan espied afar off what proved to be a young Buck making the transit of the lake. No incident is so inspiriting to an oarsman as a discovery of this*

nature & he turns his boat round like a saucer & irrespective of lines, reels, and hooks, makes for the spot, which he reaches in hot haste; and engages in the capture. Dan took to this active and deadly scene our adventurous and enthusiastic Vice Pres't who was as much at home in such an encounter as he is in the 'sweating room' of his Troy Bank. Here was an Offering too large to discount & the pleadings of the prey only hastened his downfall ... This opportune, triumphant act prepared for us a repast, rich for all time and there under the shade of the 'Prunus Canadensis,' we discussed the comparative excellence of young liver and young venison. Departing from his usual habit, the junior member from New York, who had been an efficient ally in the recent capture, offered a playful toast to 'The day ever deer' in the recollection of the Club.

But they were interested mostly in fish. Before and after their annual meeting some of the members used the hotel at Lake Pleasant as a headquarters from which to take short trips into the adjacent territory. However, Piseco was a group endeavor and competition, so the secretary duly kept a record of what they caught there. From 1842 to 1850 the members took 6,407 pounds of trout from that lake. This was shared among seven or eight persons, none of whom probably fished more than eighty days in that period. President Vail took 1,601¼ pounds and Vice President Warren 1,495¼ pounds to entitle them to their offices.

Some of the larger fish were also recorded. Most of these ranged between 4 and 6 pounds. Warren in 1848 caught the largest, a 16 ¾ pound monster; Brooks had a 13½ pound catch in 1849, but the top fish of 1850 was a mere 10¼ pound trout. Apparently the biggest fish caught was in 1847, but the record does not show its weight. And while some favored fishing spots such as Tree Tops and Steep Rocks, there is not much guidance to be found in the report for the modern Piseco angler.

The 1849 report had a very happy tone. The members were well satisfied with their sport. The 1850 report, by contrast, shows rumblings of discontent. The secretary indicated a feeling that the lake was depleted and made an early-day plea for conservation:

> *If we could do anything to arrest the wanton & utter depletion that awaits our richest trout lakes through the barbarous habit of killing the fish at improper seasons, we should confer a benefit on the public—but the voice of both law & reason is totally unheeded, and is likely to be for a century to come.*

A large factor in their discontent was the drop in their catch from 866¾ pounds in 1849 to only 383 pounds in 1850, and the size of the record fish had also decreased. One of these might have been forgiven, but not both. So Secretary Brooks wrote that he was resigning, that he would look no more on Benton's Cove, Pork Barrel, Steep Rocks, or Sandy Point. By implication he suggested that the Piseco Trout Club disband and join him at a new unspoiled frontier at Saranac Lake. Lesser men could take the places of these pioneers of Piseco fishing—as we have.

HOW EAGLE LAKE GOT ITS NAME

By Gilbert Hagerty, *North Country Life*, Winter 1958

American place names that had their origin in the bark houses and tepees of the Native Americans, names that carried the pomp and circumstance of the courts of Europe, names that were cast carelessly by *coureurs des bois*, by gamblers and by land speculators—all are romantic and colorful, and all have left their marks, but the more interesting names are those that have been earned because of some tale or event that has been long forgotten.

Of the many Eagle Lakes that dot the maps of America, there is one in the heart of the Adirondacks that came by its name with all the romance of heraldry. E. R. Wallace, in his *Descriptive Guide to the Adirondack Wilderness* in 1872, described it as lying alone in the forest, a woodsman's

Mountain backpackers usually sight grouse, a few rabbits, squirrels and chipmunks, fisher, and sometimes bear. And there are always plenty of deer in the woods. The mountain scrambler will find peaks with their elevation of 4,000+ feet impressive if they climb via the herd paths to the summit rock outcrops. On an Adirondack clear day, lakes and rivers can be seen through the forest winding below and far off panoramas of distant ranges can be viewed. *Courtesy Earl M. Kreuzer*

two miles due west of Eighth Lake of the Fulton Chain. Less than a mile long and perhaps a half mile wide, it is nearly surrounded with sheer rock walls rising from 25 to 100 feet—a veritable punch bowl hewn in the solid rock. This Eagle Lake was admirably named in the 1840s.

It all came about as a result of a search by two curious gentlemen of scientific bent for a small lake which had been described by Ebenezer Emmons while engaged in conducting a geological survey in this area in 1836. Emmons was a professor of natural history at Williams College and one of the earlier explorers of the Adirondack Wilderness.

The two men had been struggling thru the dense Adirondack underbrush for more than five hours in search of Emmons's elusive lake and had fought their way up steep ridges, over sprawling windfalls, and around impenetrable forest tangles. Finally they won a position on a high ridge interlaced with a thick stand of spruce so dense and dark that only a trickle of light filtered down to the forest floor.

Entirely exhausted, the two invaders found a comforting cushion of moss on an old log and removed their packs for much-needed respite.

In this state of exhaustion, the restful minutes fled by, and the wilderness silence lent a dignity too great to be broken by any small talk. They were content to let the green silence engulf them.

Then the sharp crack of a dry stick came like an explosion out of the deeper shadows. In a moment they were alert.

"There it is again!" whispered one. "Listen."

It seemed to be coming closer. The dry brush crackled. All was quiet again.

"Can you see anything?" the other whispered.

"The brush is so heavy I can't make anything out."

"There—over there! Behind that big spruce!"

Then, in an avalanche of snapping twigs, the dim dark hulk of a bear lunged out of the shadows. He stopped, sniffed, spotted the two, and with inquiring eyes and bared teeth, raised himself high on his ample haunches.

The only weapon available, an old pistol, antiquated to the state of being considered, even then, a family relic, was hurriedly whipped out and fired in the general direction of the curious bear. His curiosity being at an end, he dropped to all four feet and with a grunt of disgust and slid into the dark shadows again.

Realizing that this was no place to tangle with other possible invaders, the two startled explorers decided it might be the better part of valor to get out of there and head for another ridge.

The taller of the two volunteered to climb one of the tall trees and take a bird's eye look to see if he could find one. In a few moments he was out of sight in the thick boughs above . The other waited below with an anxious eye cocked upward and his archaic pistol cocked for more wilderness prowlers.

"I'm nearly at the top!" the climber shouted from about sixty feet up.

Just then an eerie shriek from above set the tree tops quivering. A billow of feathery thunder echoed thru the forest. Dead branches snapped.

Screams rose like thunder out of China. A scattering of short dry sticks came hurtling down on the head of the one who waited.

"What's wrong?" the one below anxiously called.

There was no immediate answer except for the sharp crunch of brittle wood. Then the climber's hat plopped to the ground. Tense, hoarse screeches slashed thru the air once more. Indeed there was no time for an answer; the climber, straddling a limb, with both hands busy, was in mortal combat. He had unknowingly invaded the private aerie of an enraged eagle!

Blood trickled into his eyes from the deep gashes etched into his forehead by the eagle's sharp talons. His fingers were white and numb from gripping the branches for support. While the huge bird wheeled around for another attack, he risked a look down over a span of green branches. He gasped and swayed back, frantically clutching tighter the frail supports. He felt a tingling sensation race down his legs to his very toes. A feeling of desperation seized him now, for there directly below him at a dizzy distance was an oval patch of dark water, for the most part surrounded by an almost perpendicular wall of rock! The tree he clung to grew on the very edge of this overhanging precipice!

The eagle came plummeting at him again with sickening speed, but this time he managed to protect his head under the nest of the thickly woven mass of sticks, whose ragged ends dug mercilessly into his flesh. There was a miniature whirlwind for a moment from the formidable pounding of the creature's wings. Cruel, razor-sharp talons were poised open and ready. But unable to pounce on its quarry, the eagle banked sharply for another attack.

During this brief interim the man frantically swung down to a lower branch, freed himself from his awkward position, and made his precarious descent.

Once on the ground, the tree climber wiped the blood from his forehead and inspected his wounds.

"What did you see?"

"An eagle—a damned big eagle!"

"Nothing else?"

"An eagle and a lake."

"Lake—where?"

"About spitting distance away from you and down about a hundred feet."

"Must be one that's not on the map."

"If it isn't, it ought to be—Eagle Lake!"

It was drawing toward dusk, and we had the pack baskets full of trout. The card game and "wet goods" [booze] were over and gone and most were comparing stories and tackle and fish-hooks tied to green dragon flies' tails in the late summer afternoon. Earle had family responsibilities. Riley wanted to beat everyone in one last game, but no one would play with him anymore and Hiram and Yankee Ira were suffering, you might say, from a lack of Sweet Acorn chewing tobacco—a constant complaint. *Courtesy Earl M. Kreuzer*

THE FABULOUS LOON LAKE HOUSE

By Melinda Ryan, *York State Tradition*, Summer 1971

The magnificence that had been the Loon Lake House appeared to me on a silent, snowy night as I sat in awe on a snowmobile in front of the sleeping giant. The reflected lights of the snowmobiles made every room blaze with an inner light. Decades reversed their march, and I saw it reincarnated!

Time could not stand still just for me. It cruelly rushed on again as the other snowmobilers turned away. My own insignificant light revealed merely an enormous old building, long abandoned and lonely.

Few people have stopped in the modern pace of life to remember a slower and grander era. Sheer size may stop a few and make them wonder a bit. Those who are impressed enough to delve deeply into the past never fail to be disillusioned. A study of the history of the Loon Lake House reveals an almost legendary story as big as its material remains.

The Loon Lake House was located in some of the wildest and most romantic country in the Adirondacks. It was in one of the last regions to be explored and settled. The lake itself is about two and a half miles long and three-fourths of a mile wide. At its "narrows," the banks are separated by a mere ninety feet of ever-moving water. The shore is rocky and irregular. Two small islands are situated just off shore, each with a lone pine tree in the center of it. The area around the lake is the highest point between Lake Champlain and the St. Lawrence River. This high elevation (1800 feet) provides a majestic view of the mountains of Northern New York and Canada.

Back in 1878, the game was more plentiful than it is now. Deer, ducks, ruffed grouse and speckled trout were abundant. The untouched forest offered life and beauty to anyone who was farsighted enough to take advantage of it. Two such farsighted people were Ferd W. Chase and his wife, Mary.

Ferd Chase was born in Vermont in 1840. In the Civil War he served in the Union Army, after which he worked as an expressman on the Central

Vermont Railroad for several years. Then he became a clerk at the Central House in Essex Junction and worked his way up to manager. It was during this time, in 1874, that he married Mary H. Howe, also a native Vermonter.

She was born in 1843. Being a talented musician, she taught piano and voice in her home town of Jericho and in adjoining communities. She made her rounds to the homes of her students on horseback, riding sidesaddle, as was proper for an accomplished young woman. After her marriage to Ferd Chase, she aided him in managing the Central House, which they ran together for four years.

Essex Junction had an infamous reputation for train delays. Many bitter thoughts were written about this place, but the hotel was often the subject of appreciative comments, of which this is an example: "The hostelry of Landlord Chase fully atones for Essex Junction!"

During these prosperous four years, they made several vacation trips to Hunter's Home, a small hunting and fishing camp on the north branch of the Saranac River. About a mile and a half from there the Chases found "their" spot. This was a commanding plateau on the southeast shore of Loon Lake. They promptly leased ten acres and returned to Vermont to make plans for a final trip.

They arrived at Loon Lake in October 1878 and began laying a foundation. On May 19, 1879, their hotel was opened for guests. The building was a three-story, 31-room log house with verandas on all four sides.

The first five guests were a Mr. Bixby of Plattsburgh, C. Turner of Schuyler Falls, Henry Wetherby of Burlington, E. Hubert Allen of New York, and Jasper Kane of St. Albans, Vermont. A total of 455 guests signed in during that first season. Many requests for accommodations had to be refused.

In the early 1800s, besides accommodating hunters and fishermen, the Chases catered to people with tuberculosis. Mrs. Chase was known to have instinctive nursing skill, and her ability to inspire courage helped many to regain their health.

The first years were hard. Mrs. Chase did all the housework herself and helped in the management of the hotel. At one time, they were almost out of provisions as well as cash. The guests had to be fed somehow. Finally, as a last resort, Ferd hitched up the buckboard, and the Chases headed for the nearest grocery store, which was in Ausable Forks. The trip took one day and half a night. An obliging storekeeper trusted them for a barrel of flour and other provisions.

By much hard work and personal "going without," in thirty years the Chases had expanded their hotel into an enterprise which was valued at well over a million dollars and was rated second to none. A living legend had been born on ten acres and a dream.

Expansion and excellence became a necessity and a tradition.

Business continued to grow, and the Chases expanded accordingly. By 1882 an annex was added to the original building, which eventually became the kitchen of the bigger structure. None of the older buildings were ever torn down, but were simply added on to, creating a huge, rambling and surprisingly efficient establishment. The first big separate annex was built in 1893, an impressive building in itself.

The Chases also added to their landholdings until they owned 3500 acres of lake shore and wilderness. Later, much of this was leased to campers who were willing to pay for privacy.

A nine-hole golf course was cleared. Fifty-three cottages were built at strategically beautiful spots. An acetylene lighting plant and a laundry provided the conveniences of a town, which Loon Lake gradually became.

The main building, built in 1883, was an impressive structure, full five stories high plus one story underground. The pillars of the porch were two stories high, and there was a balcony on the roof of the porch. The rooms were all large and airy and furnished with the best pieces of the day. They were steam heated and several had fireplaces.

Loon Lake was "the" place to spend the hot summer months. In the early years the only means of transportation to this vacation spot was the horse and buggy or stage coach. Later, the Delaware and Hudson Railroad came in from the east and southeast. The Adirondack and St. Lawrence Railroad came in from the north, west and south. Still later the New York Central serviced the area.

From Plattsburgh it was a two-hour trip via the Chateaugay Railroad to the Loon Lake station. Morning papers and passengers were met by a stage. The three-mile ride to the hotel was a hectic yet beautiful one on the dirt road along the shore of the lake.

Ferd Chase died in November 1916, at the age of 77. Mrs. Chase lived until January 1933.

The hotel died with Mrs. Chase. It went into receivership, and the property has since had several different owners. In 1956 the main building was destroyed by fire.

The material remains of the once-tremendous Loon Lake House are fast disappearing. The ornate first annex was torn down in 1968–69, and a huge liquidation auction was held. Local people say the property has been sold again, but no one knows for sure to whom. Winter snows close in on a few dilapidated old cottages; the golf course feels the treads of snowmobiles. Spring will bring new owners and a new face to the timeless land that once held the Loon Lake House.

PROSPECT HOUSE: ONE-TIME MECCA OF HIGH SOCIETY

Author unknown, *North Country Life*, Summer 1960. Reprinted from *Ziyara Bugle*

In the magnificent Central Adirondacks, 85 miles north of Utica on route 8, stands Blue Mountain with its peak reaching towards the clouds. It looks down upon one of the most charming landscapes of mountains, forests and lake to be found anywhere. Indeed, world travelers have pronounced the vista to be unsurpassed anywhere, here or abroad.

Here on Prospect Point, extending into the blue waters of Blue Mountain Lake, there was built in 1882 a strange-looking building resembling in part the United States Hotel and the Grand Union Hotel of Saratoga fame. It was known as Prospect House.

It was six stories in height with a piazza 370 feet in length and 20 feet wide. Inside there were many baths and fireplaces. It even had an elevator run by steam from burning logs cut upon the premises.

The nearest railroad station was 30 miles away at North Creek, later made famous when Theodore Roosevelt came out of his hunting lodge in the wilderness to board a waiting special train with steam up to carry him to Washington and to the Presidency, following the assassination of President McKinley at Buffalo in 1901.

Guests of the hotel, after arriving at North Creek, boarded a coach usually drawn by six horses and were driven over a rough mountain road to Prospect House. The road was rocky enough to have deterred any guest from coming a second time, but such was not the case. Women passengers were usually strapped in to avoid being tossed about or out, a forerunner of the present automobile safety belt.

But when the guests arrived at Prospect House, the hardships of the ride were forgotten. They found at their destination one of the finest resort hotels in the entire country. Moreover, it was the first hotel ever built with an electric light in every room. In addition there was running water and a mild form of steam heat in every room.

Prospect House, Blue Mountain Lake. "Once known for the 'ungainly pile of piazzas' on its shoreline, now perhaps the most beautiful of Adirondack lakes." —Roland B. Miller.
Courtesy Special Collections, Feinberg Library, SUNY College at Plattsburgh

The electric light had been invented only five years before by Thomas A. Edison, and here in a little stone building electricity was being generated with the help of two dynamos run by steam arising from a wood fire.

And more than that! There was a two-story outhouse reached from the second floor piazza so that guests on the upper floors would not be obliged to go all the way down.

For more than a decade and a half, Prospect House was the Mecca of high society from the Millionaire's Row of New York City and elsewhere. The New York papers gave liberal space to the hotel's social events, which were graced by the Tiffanys, the Astors, the Biddles, and others of like prominence. Witness what one New York society editor wrote in 1883:

> *The Grand Masquerade Ball at the Prospect House was one of the greatest events of the season. The large and magnificent parlor was brilliantly illuminated with a thousand electric lights and filled to repletion with the Elite from every clime. Such an amount of dazzling beauty, such brilliant figures robed in costly attire, such a brilliant flow of wit and humor, seldom grace the halls of Prince or Potentate.*

Wines of world famous brands and vintages were to be had. The meals were of the finest foods and served by Negro waiters. It was indeed a hotel of distinction noted for the charm of its atmosphere, service, and splendid isolation.

In summer it was usually filled to its capacity of 600 guests, all of whom enjoyed a full round of concerts, dances, billiards, bowling, water sports, and other amusements of the day with a competent social director in charge. Rates for this luxury hotel were $25.00 per week in the summer months; $15.00 per week in off seasons!

In time, a new method of approach to Blue Mountain was offered. It was indeed a most novel one. Dr. William Seward Webb Sr. loved the Adirondack wilderness and accumulated eventually 250,000 acres, of which 70,000 were set aside as a private preserve from which the public was barred. He foresaw the possibilities of the Adirondack Mountains eventually becoming a rendezvous not only for millionaires but for others of lesser income. For that purpose, he financed the building of a new railroad running from Herkimer to the north. On July 1, 1892, the first train left Herkimer for the Fulton Chain of Lakes. Soon the railroad was extended to Malone, with a spur over to Raquette Lake. The road was known as the Adirondack and St. Lawrence Railroad.

At Raquette Station, tourists could board a small steam yacht and travel northward thru Raquette Lake, Marion River, Utowana and Eagle Lakes into Blue Mountain Lake.

It so happened, however, that the Marion River for three quarters of a mile was not navigable because of shoals. To bypass this, one of the most unique railroads in the world was built.

The tracks were of standard gauge. The only train consisted of a locomotive and three open-side coaches that had originally been part of the equipment of the horse drawn Brooklyn, New York, Street Railroad Company. Two of the coaches could carry 125 passengers. The third coach was for their baggage. The original locomotive and one of the coaches are now on exhibition at the Adirondack Museum, located on the former site of Blue Mountain Hotel.

At the Marion River railroad terminal, the passengers would disembark and board a second yacht to take them to their destination.

This little railroad was unique in another respect. It had for a Board of Directors Collis P. Huntington, president of the Santa Fe Railroad, Dr. Webb, J. Pierpont Morgan, William West Durant, Chauncey Depew and others.

The popularity of Prospect House continued until about 1900. Then typhoid fever appeared in the neighborhood. Two cases developed among the guests. In those days the fear of contagion lingered after the disease had passed. So it was with Prospect House. Guests began to go elsewhere. The number of patrons decreased to such an extent that the hotel was obliged to close its doors forever.

Prospect House remained standing, alone, empty and ghostly, until 1915, when it was demolished. Today only the former electric plant building remains to remind passersby of the old landmark. But in its place have arisen fourteen modern housekeeping cottages calling upon the weary traveler to tarry for a good night's rest and to enjoy the beauties of the island-studded lake and the mountains.

The old stagecoach and steamboat days are over. The speedboat, automobile and airplane have taken their place. Where once it took 26 hours to go from New York to Blue Mountain, the modern auto by means of the Thruway and connecting highways cuts the time to perhaps seven or eight hours.

But the pristine beauty of the blue Mountain country still remains, and the "forever wild" policy of the New York State Adirondack Park continues to furnish rest and relaxation to the thousands of tourists who travel northward to the wilds each summer.

Camp Nit on Beaver Lake in the Moose River Plains. 1915. Wellington Kenwell built this structure for Charles Chapin in the late 1890s. *Courtesy George Blakeman*

KILROY WAS NOT HERE

By David H. Beetle, *North Country Life*, Spring 1947
Reprinted from the Utica *Observer-Dispatch*

In 1947 North Country Life *presented a description and something of the historical background of the Adirondack wilderness site of the proposed Higley and Panther Mountain dam sites about which a tug-of-war was raging in the State Legislature when the article was first published. The ten-year battle ended with the Forest Preserve being saved from the destructive flooding of hundreds of Adirondack wild lands in the vicinity of the Moose River [Plains] Recreation Area.*

The lengthy legal battle is fully covered in Paul Schaefer's The Forest Preserve: 1945–1955. *The March 1985 issue of* Adirondack Life *magazine carried a full page color photo of Schaefer's relief map of the Adirondacks, together with the story of its building. The dams as proposed are shown on that map.*

Schaefer was a leading opponent of the dam projects. His eloquent voice echoed what so many opponents felt. He wrote in 1947: "... To preserve this land in its natural wild state is to bequeath to the youth of tomorrow a heritage of incalculable value, for the combination of forest, waters and wildlife as presently contained in this Moose River region is a combination that is vanishing swiftly from America..."

In 1985 I wrote Paul. I told him I was born during those years he spent on the Moose River Committee fighting for the "Plains'" continued existence. I was in fact his "youth of tomorrow." I thanked him for his efforts in saving the remote territory from becoming "a graying cemetery of stumps, mudflats and desolation, devoid of wildlife." My historical research on the informal history of the Moose River Plains means much more when the land still exists to explore and enjoy in all its beauty.

Paul responded to my letter with a book that outlined the Moose River Committee's efforts and a note penned on the front inside jacket:

To Jay O'Hern, who has crystallized into a reality the splendid dreams I once had of the Moose River region in the Adirondacks. —Paul Schaefer, Dec. 13, 1985

Over time, Beetle took his original reconnaissance story and converted it into "The South Branch and the League Club." It became Chapter XI of his classic book, Up Old Forge/West Canada Creek *published by North Country Books, Inc.*

★ ★ ★

There are thousands of people who will tell you that the Higley or Panther dams shouldn't be built because they would be bad for the hunting and fishing, or that they would ravish the last big chunk of Adirondack wilderness.

There are as many others—especially in the Black River valley—who disagree. They are the mill owners, who want more electricity; the river-bank farmers, who want fewer floods; and Watertown residents, who think the dams would improve the city water.

Somewhere in the middle just now (a bad spot to be) is the State Legislature, which finds the Panther-Higley dam question one of the current session's biggest headaches.

Among those doing the shouting, though, there are few who have ever visited the place where the dams may be built. Fewer still know anything of the history of the place. This, therefore, is intended as a description of the battlefield; as an answer to the question of what the country they're fighting over is like—a story of its past and of its present.

First, in case you'd like to know where they're talking of putting the dams, a little geography may help.

Briefly, if they're built, they will be on the South Branch of the Moose, though that's not much help to most people. Anyway, your best chance of encountering the Moose is at McKeever—the horseshoe-shaped hamlet on the Utica-Old Forge road where the state is building a new bridge. From there the Moose flows about fifteen miles to Lyons Falls, where it runs into the Black River, a busy commerce-lined stream that glides by eighteen pulp and paper mills before pouring into Lake Ontario at Sackets Harbor.

Upstream from McKeever the Moose divides, with one branch curving around and crossing the highway again just below Old Forge. It is the other branch, however, that is now getting everyone's attention. Here it is that the Black River Regulating District (similar to a fire or sewer district except that this one was set up to regulate a river) wants to build at least one dam—maybe someday, two. And, it seems, the benefiting downstream taxpayers are willing to pay the shot.

The first of these proposed dams (as you go up the river from McKeever) would be about fifty miles from the bridge and would create a lake, slightly smaller than Hinckley, stretching back another seven miles. Halfway along, the great bulk of 2200-foot Panther Mountain would nose out into the waters.

Sporting camps were familiar places to gather and spin yarns.
Courtesy of the Maitland C. DeSormo Collection

The second (and this, because it seems the more imminent, is the one which sportsmen are fighting tooth and nail) would begin from two to three miles beyond the lapping waters of the first and would create at the foot of Higley Mountain a sprawling five-mile-long lake with an island in the middle and long fingers going up the Indian and Red rivers.

This area, generally, of course, lies between Route 8 to Speculator and Route 28 to Blue Mountain Lake. Both of these highways start from Deerfield Corners, but by the time they've reached Inlet and Piseco, respectively, they're 24 wilderness miles apart. In fact, a line drawn between the two villages would just about hit Higley Mountain at a point eight miles from Inlet. And, if you were to take a compass and try to find the place in New York State from which you could swing the biggest circle without having it cross highway or railroad, you'd put the point on West Canada Lakes, just over the divide from the place they want to build Higley Dam.

Into this vast wilderness then, and down a valley lined with such mountains as Higley, Little Moose, Indian Lake, Stink Lake, Rose, Panther, and Woodhull flows the South Branch of the Moose.

The Higley area is the more fascinating. Right across an 800-foot wide arm of the proposed Higley Reservoir would be one of the state's famous old survey lines—the one laid in 1772 by a determined surveyor, Archibald Campbell, and by a task force of less determined Indians who, when the whiskey gave out, quit cold, leaving the V-shaped 110-mile trail of blazes dangling in the wilderness.

For years these blazes served as a sort of coat hanger for draping later surveys. Called the Totten-Crossfield Line, it puts on today's maps the names of a couple of obscure Manhattan ship's carpenters who served as a front for land speculators seeking to buy the Adirondacks from the Indians. To press the venture, they started Campbell & Co. out from Sir William Johnson's hunting lodge on the Sacandaga with instructions to proceed bee-line through the wilderness 30 degrees west of north until he came to a point which he calculated was due west of a curiously-shaped boulder on Lake Champlain. Somewhere near a big pine on the South

Branch of the Moose, he decided he had reached that point, drove in a copper spike, and turned east. Thirty-five miles from Champlain came the sit-down strike.

Probably Campbell and the Indians didn't look around much, but if they had they would have found a rock cut at a point where today's river regulators hope to put in the two million dollar, 100-foot-high, 800-foot-long Higley Dam. Beyond that (and slated to be flooded out) are three little lakes, currently known as Ice House, Hell-Diver, and Beaver. On one side of the river for about a mile rise the Moose River cliffs. And opposite them are the Moose River Plains—a wide stretch covered with foot-high blueberry bushes and flanked by what the sportsmen call "virgin forest," although there's more than gossip to indicate that a century after Campbell left, a lumberman by the name of Rousseau moved in, cut down some whopping big pines, and sent them floating down the Moose to the Black.

A slight mound of earth and possibly an old gravestone (one was put there once) remains as the chief monument to this era. Told that there was an old road down the river to McKeever (there still isn't one, even today), a Negro, Tom Hynes, wandered finally into a lumber camp on the Plains. Then, while trying to back-track through waist-deep February snow, he fell into the Moose and dragged himself back to the camp again—this time with both legs frozen. Thawed out, he sang songs and entertained the lumbermen around the fire. That night gangrene set in. He died and was buried in a grove of poplars.

Next, hunters began to trek into the Plains to get venison for the Saratoga resort trade—storing the deer at times in an ice house they threw together for the purpose (that, of course, is where Ice House Lake gets its name).

Amazingly, about the same time a Piseco settler (in the 1870s you might think he would have been satisfied to get that far) named Moore got the idea of going into the Upper Moose just beyond the Plains and trying to "farm it." He arrived with wife, two daughters, two oxen, and a cow, but a winter and a summer later he got discouraged and withdrew. Later-comers found the plow and his small clearing.

Ghost and stories of the supernatural go hand in hand with the Adirondacks. The spirit of Fred Hynes is reported to still be active around Ice House Pond in the Moose River Plains where this wooden marker once stood before it was destroyed in a volley of gunfire in the late 1890s. *Taken from the front page of "The Governors" last complimentary club supper menu given in honor of guides Dick Burch and Tom Savage held at The Pafraets Dael in Troy, New York, December 31, 1894.*

Not until 1891 did the Plains threaten to become a Broadway and 42nd Street. That spring there rumbled in the wagons of Wellington Kenwell. Son of a Johnsburg farmer, Young Wellington, a five-foot nine, 185-pounder, straight as a ramrod, eschewed tilling submarginal Adirondack soil for hunting, guiding (his clients included Grover Cleveland), and hotel-keeping. He was, in fact, running a hostelry on Little Moose Lake when a physician told his erstwhile Indian Lake schoolteacher-wife that she needed to go where there were a lot of balsams in order to get over her bronchitis.

Well, Wellington—from his Saratoga hunting days—knew there were a lot of balsams bordering the Plains and, while getting to them was not the easiest way of filling the doctor's prescription, it was at least one way—and he took it. So also did his wife, a six-month-old daughter, Laura (now Mrs. Edward LaFountain of Syracuse), a four-year-old son, Gerald (lately an Inlet guide, Mexico, N.Y., farmer, and skipper of the Fulton Chain excursion boat "Osprey"), a hired man, two or three carpenters, and eventually a tutor for the children (for a time this was Dr. John Hun, later Princeteon University math professor and founder of the Hun School).

It was quite a trek. Even after hauling supplies 34 miles from the railroad at North Creek to Headquarters House on the Cedar River, he still had nineteen miles of tote road laid by Saratoga hunters to negotiate. The party arrived safely, though, and taking advantage of the Plains (the land didn't have to be cleared), threw up a two-story hunting lodge for thirty guests, a barn for the cattle, and maybe a woodshed or two.

There the Kenwells lived for ten years, sometimes going out winters, but not always. Guests included Governor Black, Civil War General Tillinghast, Corning glass and Troy shirt tycoons, New York Times reporter Robert Lanier, a man who later invented the airplane compass, and a car wheel manufacturer from Rochester by the name of Chapin.

Fabulous folk, the Kenwells, as you might imagine! Wellington spent all his spare time reading the classics. It is said of him that if you read a passage from the Bible, he'd tell you the chapter and verse; if you read the first line of "Thanatopsis," he'd recite the rest from memory; if you mentioned an Adirondack lake, he'd tell you who surveyed it first and when. An ascetic pioneer, he neither chewed, smoked, nor drank.

Mrs. Kenwell, apparently a nurse and doctor by intuition, once fixed an injured guest with two broken ribs and a fractured collarbone so effectively that when he finally got out to an Albany hospital, the doctors said they couldn't have done better themselves. The bones didn't even have to be reset.

Best of the traditions about Wellington is one about a guest who asked him what was the worst noise he ever heard in the woods.

He cocked his head thoughtfully. Wolves? No—although he'd heard plenty. Panthers? No—nothing like that.

"It was a funny scraping noise I heard one morning when I woke up," he said. "A dreadful scraping noise. Worse than any animal I've ever heard. It was Mrs. Kenwell scraping the bottom of the flour barrel and I knew I had to go eleven miles in a spring thaw to Inlet to get more."

Inlet, by the way, was his own personal shortcut. When the Adirondack Railroad went through to Old Forge, he abandoned the Saratoga hunters' route to North Creek and built a tote road to the Fulton Chain on Sixth Lake. That's the road that's still used today to get into the Upper Moose country, although now it cuts over and starts at Limekiln Lake.

About three years after Kenwell built his hotel, a neighbor moved in briefly, picked a place halfway between the Plains and a small waterfall called Rock Dam, and put up a hunting cabin. Beecher by name, he was the son of Henry Ward Beecher, famed Brooklyn clergyman, and the nephew of authoress Harriet Beecher Stowe. Both places were there when the U.S. Geological Survey men came through; hence the names Kenwell and Beecher appear on today's maps, although neither place is standing.

After ten years, his wife cured, Wellington went into the more prosaic job of running resort hotels like the Arrowhead, and sold his place to Stewart L. Woodford, ambassador to Spain just prior to the war over Cuba. Three years later Woodford found the property too much of a burden and burned it down. Kenwell's pump remains. So does Beecher's fireplace. That's all.

When the Kenwells left, the population dropped sharply. Since 1901 it has wavered from zero to two. Recently it's been mostly zero.

Today most folks agree that the Upper Moose is a pretty lovely place—if you like wilderness. Fire—except for the carefully chaperoned burning of the old Kenwell place—has come no nearer than little Indian Lake. There a few years ago 130 men battled a nasty 400-acre blaze for four days. But around the Plains themselves the pine that escaped the early lumbermen are now four feet across and 125 feet tall. It takes six men to reach around them.

An Adirondack Mountain Club party, snowshoeing in last winter [1946], covered fifty miles, found lots of deer and plenty of signs of mink, but no human beings or fresh chewing gum wrappers and not even the sign, "Kilroy was here." They emerged mouthing such adjectives as "wonderful," "grand," and "magnificent."

At Kenwell's South Branch of the Moose River hostelry. Louis Porter guided and packed for Wellington and Eliza Kenwell. *Courtesy Louise Porter Payne*

Ausable Pass from the Beebe House. In the early afternoon as they tracked over the wooden boardwalk, the casual trampers found other guests sitting under the covered porch or perched upon the giant boulders in a relaxed manner not unusual in the Adirondacks—where Beebe House customers enjoyed lounging on warm summer days, smoking pipes and peering into the distance with binoculars. Summer in the mountains was spectacular.
Photo S. R. Stoddard Courtesy Special Collections, Feinberg Library, SUNY College at Plattsburgh

HEAD FOR THE HILLS

By Dorothy O. Haeusser, *North Country Life*, Date unknown

Are you suffering from red pencil fever, textbookitis, or classtrophobia? Let me prescribe hiking as a remedy. This hobby may be engaged in by people of any age, is an inexpensive as you care to make it, and pays big dividends in peace of mind and good health. When your nerves are getting a little frayed from over-work, a day in the woods will relax you and make you forget completely the problems that you have been turning over and over in your mind.

The essential equipment needed for hiking is a pair of sturdy, comfortable, water-tight shoes. A knapsack containing a plastic raincoat, windbreaker, and warm sweater will prepare you for any kind of weather.

You may be as ambitious a hiker as you wish. There are all kinds of possibilities—short, local hikes for some. ascents up peaks with marked trails for the more energetic, climbs up trailess peaks for the adventurous, and sheer cliffs for the skilled rock climber who uses ropes and crampons.

Hiking is year round recreation. people who say that they wouldn't be able to stay out all day in the winter find that they do not mind it al all if properly dressed for the weather. Some prefer to ski through the woods, but the on skier can have a lot of fun snowshoeing. It takes no time at all to get used to walking on snowshoes, and you can climb on snowshoes where it is too steep to use skis. how exciting it was to discover I could walk with confidence on deep snow! Trail markers that were a couple of feet above my head in summer were only about a foot above the snow.

"HEAVEN UP-H'ISTEDNESS"

Unknown author, *North Country Life*, Winter of 1948

> *Mountain climbing in the Adirondacks is becoming a favorite pastime among vacationist.* —G. Glyndon Cole

"Rat-I-ron-taks! (Tree Eaters!)" Scoffed the Iroquois, derisively referring to the Algonquians who roamed the mountains of Northern New York. And so the Adirondacks were named. In recent years a more meaningful interpretation has evolved, "They of the high rocks." This makes sense to the ever-increasing number of outdoor enthusiasts who yearly pick this for their vacationland. Mountain climbing in the Adirondacks is fast becoming a popular outdoor activity.

In the Adirondack Park there are more than 2000 mountain peaks to climb. Varying in size, they provide all types of biking experience, from sauntering to some windswept knoll to "random scooting" to some high and rocky summit. A big attraction is to "climb the 46"—and thereby hangs a tale!

"The 46" are those Adirondack mountains in the High Peak region of Essex and adjoining Franklin counties, which are 4000 feet or over in elevation. Two of them are over 5000 feet and when the climber takes into consideration that 21 of the 46 are still untrailed and must be climbed with map and compass, the adventure of climbing these summits becomes a greater challenge. Until 1946 only 31 recorded persons had ever stood atop all 46.

The first persons known to have climbed the mountains did so for scientific purposes in 1836 while mapping the region, measuring distances and heights and making meteorological studies. But 15-year-old Esther McComb, who lived at the foot of 4872-foot Whiteface Mountain was the first person on record to climb for fun, and the peak on which she landed in 1838 is known as Esther. Esther started something back in 1838—the idea of climbing mountains for fun—and today thousands take to the woods for various types of climbing.

Old Mountain Phelps was a guide in the Keene Valley region, in the period 1849–69, and his mountain climbing trips grew to be favorite pastime for summer vacationists. To be among the high peaks of the Adirondacks he called "heaven up-h'istedness" and his picturesque terms are used and loved today by outdoor folk as being strictly Adirondack. To hike without a trail, in Phelps' parlance, was "random scooting," and a tight place in the woods became a "regular random scoot of a rigmarole."

Gradually the mountains became known to more of those who wanted to ascend high places. One of the favorite love stories of the region centers around Heart Lake's Adirondack Loj, a hiking center nine miles from Lake Placid.

The building of the original lodge dates back to 1877 when Henry Van Hoevenberg and Josephine Scofield climbed Mount Marcy, the highest summit, and from the top picked out a clear blue lake nestled among the peaks to the north. Here they planned to return and build their future home, which was to be a house of entertainment for friends among the mountains they loved so much.

Old Mountain Phelps. *A Stoddard Photo. Courtesy of the Mailtland C. DeSormo Collection*

Unfortunately Josephine died within a year, but the following summer Henry returned to the woods, purchased the land surrounding the lake and the little mountain towering over it, and built a mountain lodge. The mountain he called "Jo" in memory of his sweetheart, and the lake, resembling a heart as one looks down upon it from Mount Jo, he called Heart Lake. Van Hoevenberg, an indefatigable climber, caused more than 50 miles of trails to be built.

Mountain climbing in the Adirondacks received a big impetus when a group of enthusiasts got together with the New York State Conservation Department in 1922 and organized the Adirondack Mountain Club, which celebrated its 25th anniversary November 15. The club built miles of trails, erected wooden lean-tos and embarked on an ambitious program to promote good camping manners, which greatly aided the Department in its development of recreational resources. This program has been expanded until now the Conservation Department maintains 453 miles of hiking trails in the Adirondack Park and 121 miles in the Catskill Park.

As in other sports, specialists soon developed in mountain climbing. Back in 1918, Bob and George Marshall, who summered at Saranac Lake, decided they would climb all the mountains in the Adirondacks with an elevation of 4000 feet or over. Pouring over their topographic maps, they counted 46, of which 30 had no trails. Eight of these had never been climbed by anyone.

Since the Marshalls finished the 46 back in 1924 with Herb Clark, their friend and guide on all trips, other climbers have become imbued with the desire to "do the 46." Mountain climbers from other states have joined the assault on the high peaks and are checking them off.

In 1946 fifteen people became 46ers. In 1947 seven more were recorded, making the present total 53. There are four aspiring 46ers that have climbed 40 or more of the peaks; sixteen others have reached or passed the 30 mark.

Mountain climbing is not restricted to any season in the Adirondacks. The hardier climbers consider the ski ascent of Mount Marcy, the State's 5344-foot rooftop, one of New York's great winter attractions. Lesser peaks are also climbed on skis or snowshoes. The record for winter ascents of Marcy on skis is held by P. F. Loope of Oswego, who has climbed more than 25 times.

The New York State Department of Commerce is prepared to furnish information to those who write to the Division of State Publicity, 112 State Street, Albany 7, N.Y. The trails are officially marked with yellow, blue or red disks to guide the neophyte or experienced hiker to lean-tos, campsites, mountain ponds, waterfalls, streams, fishing waters, or mountain country generally.

If a prospective climber wishes a sample of what's in store for him, he may drive his car up the 8-mile serpentine road, which leads to the Castle on Whiteface Mountain, and walk the few hundred steps to the summit or take the elevator. Standing on that windswept peak he will see the amazing panorama of mountains and lakes, which reward those hardy folk who tote their packs along Adirondack trails.

JOURNEY TO THE SKIES

Author unknown, *North Country Life*, Summer 1955

The Whiteface Mountain Memorial Highway has become one of the top attractions of North America. Since its official opening in 1935, millions of visitors from every state in the Union and almost every country in the world have driven their cars to the Castle near the top of the mountain and thrilled to unequalled scenic beauty.

On September 11, 1929, Franklin D. Roosevelt, then governor of New York, turned the first shovelful of earth to start the construction of this Memorial Highway. Actual work began on Christmas Day, 1931.

The road was opened to traffic on July 20, 1935. On September 14 of that year, President Roosevelt dedicated the completed highway as a memorial to the World War dead of New York State.

Driving one's own car to the peak of Whiteface Mountain has been aptly called "the supreme scenic thrill of the North American continent."

Mt. Marcy. *Courtesy Edward Blankman (The Lloyd Blankman Collection)*

The trip is an easy drive over a modern macadam highway 24 feet wide with two-foot shoulders. The average grade is 8% and at no point exceeds 10%. From the entrance to the highway in the village of Wilmington on Route 86, 13 miles from Lake Placid to the Whiteface Castle, a panoramic view of the vast Adirondack Forest Preserve unfolds as one drives the eight miles to the upper terminal.

The remaining distance to the summit, 4272 feet above the sea, may be traversed by a modern electric elevator or by the one-fifth-mile footpath. It is from the summit that scenery of unforgettable beauty greets those who make this memorable trip. More than 100 lakes and streams, bordering states, the mighty St. Lawrence River, Mt. Royal in Canada, Montreal, and countless other points are often visible from this mountain peak.

This is a spot that must be visited to be appreciated, for no word or picture can portray the grandeur of this scenic view. Only a trip to the top of the mighty monarch of the Adirondacks can tell the true story of this amazing journey to the skies.

AMPERSAND

By Henry Van Dyke, *North Country Life*, Summer 1961.
Abridged from *Little Rivers* (1903)

From time to time publisher-editor Glyndon Cole included in what he called his "not a profit-making North Country Life *project" articles and stories worked from noteworthy books previously published by bona fide publishers whose copyrights had expired. "Ampersand" is an essay that was first published in Harper's for July 1885, and was later a part of the author's* Little Rivers, *from which it is here reprinted in a slightly abridged form. Cole was an admirer of many of the mid-19th century authors of nostalgic books, books for readers who liked to tag along with the Adirondack writers. Perhaps Cole also felt a close connection with Henry Van Dyke, who said, "Many a treasure besides Ali Baba's is unlocked with a verbal key."*

The right to the name of Ampersand, like the territory of Gaul in those *Commentaries* which Julius Caesar wrote for the punishment of schoolboys, is divided into three parts. It belongs to a mountain, and a lake, and a little river.

The mountain stands in the heart of the Adirondack country, just near enough to the thoroughfare of travel for thousands of people to see it every year, and just far enough from the beaten track to be unvisited except by a very few of the wise ones, who love to turn aside. Behind the mountain is the lake, which no lazy man has ever seen. Out of the lake flows the stream, winding down a long, untrodden forest valley, to join the Stony Creek waters, and empty into the Raquette River.

Which of the three Ampersands has the prior claim to the name, I cannot tell. Philosophically speaking, the mountain ought to be regarded as the head of the family, because it was undoubtedly there before the others. And the lake was probably next on the ground, because the stream is its child. But man is not strictly just in his nomenclature, and I conjecture that the little river, the last-born of the three, was the first to be christened Ampersand, and then gave its name to its parent and grandparent. It is such a crooked stream, so bent and curved and twisted upon itself, so fond of turning around unexpected corners and sweeping away in great circles from its direct course, that its first explorers christened it after the eccentric supernumerary of the alphabet which appears in the old spelling-books as "&—and per se, and."

But in spite of this apparent subordination to the stream in the matter of a name, the mountain clearly asserts its natural authority. It stands up boldly, and not only its own lake, but at least three others—the Lower Saranac, Round Lake, and Lonesome Pond—lie at its foot and acknowledge its lordship. When the cloud is on its brow, they are dark. When the sunlight strikes it, they smile. Wherever you may go over the waters of these lakes you shall see Mount Ampersand looking down at you, and saying quietly, "This is my domain."

I never look at a mountain which asserts itself in this fashion without desiring to stand on the top of it. If one can reach the summit, one becomes a sharer in the dominion. The difficulties in the way only add to the zest of the victory. Every mountain is, rightly considered, an invitation to climb. And as I was resting for a month one summer at Bartlett's, Ampersand challenged me daily.

Did you know Bartlett's in its palmy time? It was the homeliest, quaintest, coziest place in the Adirondacks. Away back in the antebellum days, Virgil Bartlett had come into the woods, and built his house on the bank of the Saranac and Round Lake. It was then the only dwelling within a circle of many miles. The deer and bear were in the majority. At night one could sometimes hear the screams of the panther or the howling of wolves. But soon the wilderness began to wear the traces of a conventional smile. The desert blossomed a little—if not as the rose, at least as the gillyflower. Fields were cleared, gardens planted; half a dozen log cabins were scattered along the river; and the old house, having grown slowly somewhat irregularly for twenty years, came out, just before the time of which I write, in a modest coat of paint and a broad-brimmed piazza. But Virgil himself, the creator of the oasis—well know of hunters and fishermen, dreaded of lazy guides and quarrelsome lumbermen—"Virge," the irascible, kind-hearted, indefatigable, was there no longer. He had made his last clearing, and fought his last fight; done his last favor to a friend, and thrown his last adversary out of the tavern door. His last log had gone down the river. His campfire had burned out. Peace to his ashes. His wife, who had often played the part of Abigail towards travelers who had unconsciously incurred the old man's mistrust, now reigned in his stead; and there was a great abundance of maple syrup on every man's flapjack.

The charm of Bartlett's for the angler was the stretch of rapid water in front of the house. The Saranac River, breaking from its first resting place in the Upper Lake, plunged down through a great bed of rocks, making a chain of short falls and pools and rapids, about a half mile in length. Here, in the spring and early summer, the speckled trout—

Edmonds Pond from the west. The sun was shielded by an overcast sky, but it was still a pleasant day to leave footprints in the dirt track. It was summer, a time for walking, to hear sounds and unwind. Alone among the woods and forest it was easy to feel so alive—like a lord on a beautiful manor. *Photo S. R. Stoddard. Courtesy of the Mailtland C. DeSormo Collection*

brightest and daintiest of all fish that swim—used to be found in great numbers. As the season advanced, they moved away into the deep water of the lakes. But there were always a few stragglers left, and I have taken them in the rapids at the very end of August. What could be more delightful than to spend an hour or two, in the early morning or evening of a hot day, in wading this rushing stream, and casting the fly on its clear waters? The wind blows softly down the narrow valley, and the trees nod from the rocks above you. The noise of the falls makes constant music in your ears. The river hurries past you, and yet it is never gone.

The same foam-flakes seem to be always gliding downward, the same spray dashing over the stones, the same eddy coiling at the edge of the pool. Send your fly in under those cedar branches, where the water swirls around by that old log. Now draw it up toward the foam. There is a sudden gleam of dull gold in the white water. You strike too soon. Your line comes back to you. In a current like this, a fish will almost always hook himself. Try it again. This time he takes the fly fairly, and you have him. It is a good fish, and he makes the slender rod bend to the strain. He sulks for a moment as if uncertain what to do, and then with a rush darts into the swiftest part of the current. You can never stop him there. Let him go. Keep just enough pressure on him to hold the hook firm, and follow his troutship down the stream as if he were a salmon. He slides over a little fall, gleaming through the foam, and swings around in the next pool. Here you can manage him more easily; and after a few minutes' brilliant play, a few mad dashes for the current, he comes to the net, and your skillful guide lands him with a quick, steady sweep of the arm. The scales credit him with an even pound, and a better fish than this you will hardly take here in midsummer.

Ampersand waited immovable while I passed many days in such innocent and healthful pleasures as these, until the right day came for the ascent. Cool, clean, and bright, the crystal morning promised a glorious noon, and the mountain almost seemed to beckon us to come up higher. The photographic camera and a trustworthy lunch were stowed away in the pack-basket. The backboard was adjusted at a comfortable angle in the stern seat of our little boat. The guide held the little craft steady while I stepped into my place; then he pushed out into the stream and we went swiftly down toward Round Lake.

A Saranac boat is one of the finest things that the skill of man has ever produced under the inspiration of the wilderness. It is a frail shell, so light that a guide can carry it on his shoulders with ease, but so dexterously fashioned that it rides the heaviest waves like a duck, and slips through the waters as if by magic. You can travel in it along the shallowest rivers and across the broadest lakes, and make forty or fifty miles a day, if you have a good guide.

Everything depends, in the Adirondacks, as in so many other regions of life, upon your guide. If he is selfish, or surly, or stupid, you will have a bad time. But if he is an Adirondacker of the best old-fashioned type—now unhappily growing more rare from year to year—you will find him an inimitable companion, honest, faithful, skillful and cheerful. He is as independent as a prince, and the gilded youths and finicking fine ladies who attempt to patronize him are apt to make but a sorry show before his solid and undisguised contempt. But deal with him man to man, and he will give you a friendly, loyal service which money cannot buy, and teach you secrets of woodcraft and lessons in plain, self-reliant manhood more valuable than all the learning of the schools. Such a guide was mine, rejoicing in the Scriptural name of Hosea, but commonly called, in brevity and friendliness, "Hose."

As we entered Round Lake on this fair morning, its surface was as smooth and shining as a mirror. It was too early yet for the tide of travel which sends a score of boats up and down this thoroughfare every day; and from shore to shore the water was unruffled, except by a flock of sheldrakes which had been feeding near Plymouth Rock, and now went skittering off into Weller Bay with a motion between flying and swimming, leaving a long wake of foam behind them.

At such a time as this you can see the real color of these Adirondack lakes. It is not blue, as romantic writers so often describe it, nor green, like some of those wonderful Swiss lakes; although of course it reflects the color of the trees along the shore; and when the wind stirs it, it gives back the hue of the sky, blue when it is clear, gray when the clouds are gathering, and sometimes as black as ink under the shadow of storm. But when it is still, the water itself is like that river which one of the poets has described as "Flowing with a smooth brown current." And in this sheet of burnished bronze the mountains and islands were reflected perfectly, and the sun shone back from it, not in broken gleams or a wide lane of light, but like a single ball of fire, moving before us as we moved.

We landed on a sand beach at the mouth of a little stream, where a blazed tree marked the beginning of the Ampersand Trail. This line through the forest was made years ago by that ardent sportsman and lover of the Adirondacks, Dr. W. W. Ely, of Rochester. Since that time it has been shortened and improved a little by other travelers, and also not

Bartletts, Saranac Lake. *Photo S. R. Stoddard. Courtesy Special Collections, Feinberg Library, SUNY College at Plattsburgh*

a little blocked and confused by the lumbermen and the course of Nature. Nor when the lumbermen go into the woods, they cut roads in every direction, leading nowhither, and the unwary wanderer is thereby led aside from the right way, and entangled in the undergrowth. And as for Nature, she is entirely opposed to continuance of paths through her forest. She covers them with fallen leaves, and hides them with thick bushes. She drops great trees across them and blots them out with windfalls. But the blazed line—a succession of broad axe marks on the trunks of the trees, cannot be so easily obliterated, and this is the safest guide through the woods.

Our trail led us first through a natural meadow, overgrown with waist-high grass, and very spongy to the tread. Then through a tangle of old wood-roads my guide led me safely, and we struck one of the ridges which sloped gently from the lake to the base of the mountain. Here walking was comparatively easy, for in the hardwood timber there is little underbrush. The massive trunks seemed like pillars set to uphold the level roof of green. Great yellow birches, shaggy with age, stretched their knotty arms high above us; sugar maples stood up straight and proud under their leafy crowns; and smooth beaches—the most polished and park-like of all the forest trees—offered opportunities for the carving of lovers' names in a place where few lovers ever come.

After about an hour of easy walking, our trail began to ascend more sharply. We passed over the shoulder of a ridge and around the edge of a fire-slash, and then we had the mountain fairly before us. There were places where we had to haul ourselves up by roots and branches, and places where we had to go down on our hands and knees to crawl under logs. It was breathless work, but not at all dangerous or difficult. Every step forward was also a step upward; and as we stopped to rest for a moment, we could see already glimpses of the lake below us. But at these I did not much care to look, for I think it is a pity to spoil the surprise of a grand view by taking little snatches of it beforehand.

The character of the woods through which we were now passing was entirely different from those of the lower levels. On these steep places the birch and maple will not grow, or at least they occur but sparsely. The higher slopes and sharp ridges are always covered with softwood timber. Spruce and hemlock and balsam strike their roots among the rocks and find a hidden nourishment. They stand close together; thickets of small trees spring up among the large ones; from year to year the great trunks are falling one across another, and the undergrowth is thickening around them, until a spruce forest seems to be almost impassable. The constant rain of needles and the crumbling of the fallen trees form a rich, brown mould, into which the foot sinks noiselessly. Wonderful beds of moss, many feet in thickness and softer than feathers, covers the rocks and roots. There are shadows never broken by the sun, and dark, cool springs of icy water hidden away in the crevices. You feel a sense of antiquity here which you can never feel among the maples and birches.

The higher one climbs, the darker and gloomier and more rugged the vegetation becomes. The pine trees soon cease to follow you; the hemlocks disappear, and the balsams can go no farther. Only the hardy spruce keeps on bravely, rough and stunted, with branches matted together and pressed down flat by the weight of the winter's snow, until finally, somewhere about the level of four thousand feet above the sea, even this bold climber gives out, and the weather-beaten rocks of the summit are clad only with mosses and Alpine plants.

Thus it is with mountains, as perhaps with men, a mark of superior dignity to be naturally bald.

Ampersand, falling short by a thousand feet of the needful height, cannot claim this distinction. But what Nature has denied, human labor has supplied. Under the direction of the Adirondack Survey, some years ago, several acres of trees were cut from the summit; and when we emerged, after the last sharp scramble, upon the very crest of the mountain, we were not shut in by a dense thicket, but stood upon a bare ridge of granite in the center of a ragged clearing.

I shut my eyes for a moment, drew a few long breaths of the glorious breeze, and then looked out upon a wonder and a delight beyond description. A soft, dazzling splendor filled the air. Snowy banks and drifts of

Bartletts on Upper Saranac Lake was a small and remote hotel established in 1856 by Virgil Bartlett. The site was knows as Bartlett's Carry. The Saranac Lake Club took over the property in 1899. *Photo S. R. Stoddard. Courtesy Special Collections, Feinberg Library, SUNY College at Plattsburgh*

clouds were floating slowly over a wide and wondrous land. Vast sweeps of forest, shining waters, mountains near and far, the deepest green and the palest blue, changing colors and glancing lights, and all so silent, so strange, so far away, that it seemed like the landscape of a dream. One almost feared to speak, lest it should vanish.

Right below us the Lower Saranac and Lonesome Pond, Round Lake and the Weller Ponds were spread out like a map. Every point and island was clearly marked. We could follow the course of the Saranac River in all its curves and windings, and see the white tents of the haymakers on the wild meadows.

Far away to the northeast stretched the level fields of Bloomingdale. But westward all was unbroken wilderness, a great sea of woods as far as the eye could reach. And how far it can reach from a height like this! That faint blue outline far in the north was Lyon Mountain, nearly thirty miles away as the crow flies. Those silver gleams a little nearer were the waters of St. Regis.

The Upper Saranac was displayed in all its length and breadth, and beyond it the innumerable waters of Fish Creek were tangled among the dark woods. The long ranges of the hills about the Jordan bounded the western horizon, and on the southwest Big Tupper Lake was sleeping at the base of Mount Morris. Looking past the peak of Stony Creek Mountain, which rose sharp and distinct in a line with Ampersand, we could trace the path of the Raquette River from the distant waters of Long Lake down through its far-stretched valley, and catch here and there a silvery link of its current.

But when we turned to the south and east, how wonderful and how different was the view! Here was no widespread and smiling landscape with gleams of silver scattered through it, and soft blue haze resting upon its fading verge, but a wild land of mountains, stern, rugged, tumultuous, rising one beyond another like the waves of a stormy ocean—McIntyre's sharp peak, and the ragged crest of the Gothics, and, above all, Marcy's dome-like head, raised just far enough above the others to assert his royal right as monarch of the Adirondacks.

But grandest of all, as seen from this height, was Mount Seward—a solemn giant of a mountain, standing apart from the others and looking us full in the face. He was clothed from base to summit in a dark, unbroken robe of forest. *Ou-kor-lah*, the Indians called him—the Great Eye; and he seemed almost to frown upon us in defiance. At his feet, so straight below us that it seemed almost s if we could cast a stone into it, lay the wildest and most beautiful of all the Adirondack waters—Ampersand Lake.

On its shore, some five-and-twenty years ago, the now almost forgotten Adirondack Club had their shanty—the successor of "The Philosophers' Camp" on Follensbee Pond. Agassiz, Appleton, Norton, Emerson, Lowell, Hoar, Gray, John Holmes, and Stillman, were among the company who made their resting-place under the shadow of Mount Seward. They had bought a tract of forest land completely encircling the pond, cut a rough road to it through the woods, and built a comfortable log cabin, to which they purposed to return summer after summer. But the Civil

War broke out, with all its terrible excitement and confusion of hurrying hosts: the club existed but for two years, and the little house in the wilderness was abandoned.

In 1878, when I spent three weeks at Ampersand, the cabin was in ruins, and surrounded by an almost impenetrable growth of bushes. The only philosophers to be seen were a family of what the guides quaintly call "quill pigs." The roof had fallen to the ground; raspberry bushes thrust themselves through the yawning crevices between the logs; and in front of the sunken door-sill lay a rusty, broken stove, like a dismantled altar on which the fire had gone out forever.

After we had feasted upon the view as long as we dared, counted the lakes and streams, and found that we could see without a glass more than thirty, and recalled the memories of "good times" which came to us from almost every point of the compass, we unpacked the camera and proceeded to take some pictures.

It has been my good luck to climb many of the peaks of the Adirondacks—Dix, the Dial, Hurricane, the Giant of the Valley, Marcy, and Whiteface—but I do not think the outlook from any of them is so wonderful and lovely as that from little Ampersand; and I reckon among my most valuable chattels the plates of glass on which the sun has traced for me (who cannot draw) the outlines of that loveliest landscape.

The downward journey was swift. We halted for an hour or two beside a trickling spring, a few rods below the summit, to eat our lunch. Then, jumping, running, and sometimes sliding, we made the descent, and reached Bartlett's as the fragrance of the evening pancake was softly diffused through the twilight. Mark that day, Memory, with a double star in your catalogue!

Ampersand continues to be one of the most popular roadside Adirondack mountains to climb for both casual and serious climbers. The 365 degree view from the top can only be described as superb.

GEOLOGY OF THE HUDSON

By Richard F. Ward, *North Country Life*, Fall 1959

Far up the south slopes of New York's lofty Mt. Marcy there's a blue-green gem called Lake Tear of the Clouds. Fed by thawing snows, summer showers, and bubbling springs, this tiny lake wells into a little speckled trout rill, Feldspar Brook, a tributary of the Opalescent River—all small trickles at this stage, but destined for greatness, for this is the beginning of the magnificent Hudson River.

As this cold mountain water rushes down from the Adirondack wilderness, it is joined by thousands of brooks and creeks that flow from the Green Mountains, the Taconics, the Catskills and the Ramapos. In their collective might, they form the Hudson, which travels, more leisurely now, out of the farms and meadows and mountains, down the

Day trippers along the trail to Mt. Marcy. When it's summertime in the Adirondacks, it's playtime for everyone. You're apt to meet your friends along the trails and waterways, at the wilderness camps and beaches, and at any point where sport and recreation prevail. Lake Tear of the Clouds, the source of the Hudson, is found below Marcy's summit.
Courtesy Edward Blankman (The Lloyd Blankman Collection)

broad valley, past New York City's teeming millions and into the Atlantic. Even at sea, the river maintains its identity for nearly 100 miles until it finally plunges off the Continental Shelf thru a sub-surface gorge, which rivals the Grand Canyon.

Many rivers are longer than the Hudson, drain larger areas and carry far more water, but for diversity of terrain it has few rivals. The geologic history of the rocks along the banks of the Hudson and of the course by which the river makes its way from the Adirondacks to the sea, reaches back over a billion years into the dimmest geological past.

The rocks and topographic forms along the course of the river as it flows thru New York State contain the records of life and events of a large portion of the earth's history: of former shallow seas teeming with life, of the great mountain chains raised out of those seas, and of the long periods of erosion during which the great mountains were reduced to low rolling hills.

The Adirondacks, where the Hudson rises, are made up of ancient granites and other crystalline rocks, which lay at the roots of a mountain chain a billion-odd years ago. Those mountains have long since been eroded away, leaving behind a faint record of events, which took place in the primitive crust. In the Adirondacks the Hudson flows over some of the oldest known rocks on earth.

Farther south, the river skirts the Catskills and is joined by water from streams flowing over much younger rocks. These rounded mountains are carved in nearly flat-lying sediments which preserve the great delta of a huge west-flowing river which carried debris out of a New England mountain chain some 350 million years ago. A little searching through these sediments will yield ripple marks, mud, cracks, fossils of shellfish which live in shallow waters and even stumps and fragments of primitive woody plants, which grew in mud flats and swamps.

Southward the Hudson flows through what some feel is the most beautiful scenery along its course: High Tor, Storm King, Dunderberg, and Bear Mountain. These are held up by igneous and metamorphic rocks whose age (a matter of dispute) is about midway between that of the Adirondacks and of the Catskills.

Downstream from the Highlands, a sheer gray cliff rises along the west bank and forms a wall 300 to 500 feet high, stretching for nearly 40 miles. This is the Palisades, which was intruded as a great sheet of lava between layers of shale in the Triassic period some 160 million years ago. The Triassic was an epoch of widespread volcanic activity in eastern North America and in a few places lavas which poured out on the surface are still visible. The red shales which lie above and below the Palisades contain the fossil bones and footprints of early dinosaurs.

An ancestral Hudson River appears to have been in existence by the beginning of the Tertiary period, something over 60 million years ago. Its evolution from then until the beginning of the Great Ice Age, which started a million-odd years ago, is poorly known, and what is known is a matter of dispute, but it appears to have been this:

The river flowed southward over a relatively subdued, possibly nearly flat topography over the sedimentary rocks south of Albany and the crystalline rocks of the Highlands. It veered westward at Sparkill Gap at the northern end of the Palisades, then across the Watchung Mountains in the vicinity of Paterson, New Jersey, and finally out into the Atlantic somewhere in the vicinity of the Raritan River. The land along the river's course in this area was uplifted quite slowly, but the river managed to cut down at about the same rate as the uplift, thereby maintaining its course through the crystallines. Had the uplift taken place more rapidly than the river was able to cut it down, it would have been "defeated" and its course would have changed, leaving only a few high-level valley remnants as a clue to its former course. Meanwhile, a small stream was working its way north in the soft rocks along the present site of the Hudson at the Palisades. When this stream intersected the old Hudson at Sparkill, the small stream "captured" the Hudson, the old lower course was abandoned and its present lower course past New York City established. Remains of the former course can still be seen at Paterson and Millburn gaps in the Watchiung Mountains in New Jersey.

The final events in the river's history are those of the Great Ice Age or Pleistocene, which covers the last million years. During the Pleistocene epoch great continental ice sheets four times advanced south into the United States and then each time retreated to the north as the climate became warmer. At the peak of the most recent advance (a mere 15,000 years ago) the glacier completely covered the Hudson Valley. The position of the glacier's southern edge is marked by a moraine (a ridge of glacial debris), which crosses the river at its mouth, forming the Narrows in New York Harbor.

The history of the Hudson during the Pleistocene is far too complicated to permit a coherent account here, but some of the major events are both significant and interesting.

The actual modifications made by the ice are not profound, but the thousand-foot-thick ice sheet did round off sharp corners and scrape away soils, producing the rocky, rounded hills so characteristic of the Hudson Valley. As the glaciers moved down the riverbed, considerable deepening took place as a result of the scouring of the bedrock by the ice. The surface of the bedrock under the river passes below sea level near Albany and increases its depth gradually until at Storm King the bedrock surface is some 900 feet below sea level. Such an ice-deepened valley is comparable to the fjords of Norway and New Zealand. That the Hudson Gorge is entirely a fjord formed by the action of the ice has been questioned by some, who claim it is more likely that the glaciers merely deepened a valley which had been cut by the river at a time when the land stood much higher or sea level much lower.

As warmer weather drove the glacier back, the Hudson carried huge amounts of melt water laden with silt, sand, and gravel, which had been frozen in the ice. The deep fjord became filled with these sediments, and still larger amounts were deposited on the continental shelf in the Atlantic Ocean.

When the ice sheets retreated toward the northern border of the state, the depressions, which are now occupied by Lakes Erie and Ontario, began to fill with water which could not escape to the ocean thru the St. Lawrence, because that river's course was still blocked by ice. Eventually the lakes overflowed into the Mohawk River, which in turn flows into the

Hudson, and so for some time the Hudson drained the eastern Great Lakes. In time, of course, the rate of melting so exceeded the accumulation of snow that the St. Lawrence Valley became free of ice and the Great Lakes drained into the Atlantic by that route, leaving the Hudson with only one major change to undergo in order to become the river which we know today.

The weight of the thick sheet of glacier ice, which covered the St. Lawrence-Lake Champlain region, depressed the earth's crust in that area some distance below sea level, so that a tongue of the ocean occupied the St. Lawrence Valley and what is now Lake Champlain. The narrow divide which today separates Lake Champlain from the upper Hudson was also below sea level, forming a natural Hudson-Champlain-St. Lawrence seaway. Slowly the crust rebounded in the Hudson-Champlain region (it is still rising measurably), cut off the sea-level route from Albany to the St. Lawrence, and the modern Hudson River was born.

WHAT IS THE NORTH COUNTRY?

By Wilma Cummins, *York State Tradition*, Spring 1969

The North Country? What is the North Country? You read it in the newspapers: Governor Rockefeller visits the North Country. North Country has record snowfall.

On television you hear the North Country news: North Country man visits Congressman in Washington.

Geographically the North Country is apparently the area from Syracuse, or the Mohawk Valley, north to the Canadian border. There are persons who consider Buffalo a part of the North Country, but this must be an error. Buffalo is a city, and cities can't possibly be North Country. It used to be that North Countrymen themselves considered their native heath to be that broad belt stretching from Boonville to the St. Lawrence River. Maybe everybody's wrong, and the concept of North Country as primarily a place is wrong.

Summertime in the North Country. Nothing beats a cool swim in a North Country summer the following a challenging mountain climb. Charlie Leland and unidentified friend. Fulton Chain, 1920. *Courtesy Leigh Portner, Sr.*

The North Country may be a place or an area, but it is mainly a way of life. It is a return to the essentials, a characteristic to live with, having a very special charisma something like the Twilight Zone!

In order to live the North Country way one must possess certain talents.

It is most helpful if you are in or approaching your middle years. With any luck you will have learned about "making-do." You already know how to substitute a pin, another vegetable, or a sun lamp for a button, a fresh artichoke, or the sun. These substitutions are made with better grace by the middle-aged, who have lived long enough to know what's really important!

If you can master the art of an almost Gallic shoulder movement—not quite a shrug but approaching one—along with a phrase uttered in a patient, resigned-but-never-hopeless, tone of voice, you are almost ready. This philosophical phrase must be as ancient as the rock outcroppings that are so familiar in the area. There are definite times to use it. It certainly isn't applicable to every situation.

When your washing machine breaks down and you discover that the dealer who sold it to you is no longer in business, and then you may say, "Oh, well, that's the North Country." Or when you've carefully chosen a college for your child and you suddenly find out that there's only one bus a day and she must spend two days traveling 300 miles. So, as you begin your four years of chauffeuring, you shrug and say, "Oh, well, that's the North Country."

One thing you must be able to do without is spring. If you are a devotee of that particular time of year and you can't live without forsythia or arbutus, you may be slated for a bad time. And the philosophical phrase and shrug are not applicable here!

Fall is a magnificent season in the North Country, summer is pleasant, and winter is beautiful and to be lived with, but spring is non-existent. Winter slides right into summer. Almost overnight trees that were bare one day are suddenly shade trees the next. This experience is traumatic for the person who learned very young, and always believed in, the myth of four orderly seasons! The true North Countryman is just as startled if he journeys to the outer world in May and sees a tulip tree in blossom!

The North Country is a friendly way of life. A newcomer is warmly welcomed and helped to feel at home. It's almost as though everyone were trying to make up in friendliness for the lack of transportation and buttons and spring and repairmen. And there's an implied "We're all in this together so let's make the best of it." This people-warmth makes up immeasurably for the lack of temperature-warmth.

The kindest advice given the newcomer is that he must invest in an outside thermometer. It is important that this be visible from inside and consulted frequently.

One of the North Country's favorite winter pranks is a beautifully clear, sunny day with diamonds all through the air. Just the kind of day for a long walk with the warm sun on a hatless head. But look before you leap. The joke comes when you look at the thermometer. Your friendly neighbor—the one who advised that thermometer—may have saved you from frostbitten ears.

Many people wonder how long it takes to become a North Countryman. This is a difficult question to answer. There are persons, born in the area, who never really accept the North Country. And there are those who within a very short time make the adjustment.

It is perhaps the basically lazy person who makes the transition most quickly. He doesn't like to rush about all the time. Huge crowds distract his meditations and contemplations. The effort to get a cab or shop in a store with a large selection of merchandise wears him out. Not having to chauffeur his children everywhere pleases him because he'd rather go fishing or play golf. If he leaves his wallet at home, he doesn't have to go back for it, because the gas station attendant knows him and is confident that he'll pay for the gas the next time.

You may wonder how one recognizes the true North Countryman. It is reasonably easy to do. You need not ask how long he's been in the region or any other irrelevant questions. All you need to do is observe with what ease, poise, and calm he unapologetically shrugs his shoulders and utters that deathless phrase, "Oh, well, that's the North Country."

MEMORIES OF AN OLD NORTH COUNTRY FAIR

By Walter B. Gunnison, *North Country Life*, Summer 1959

From the faded grandstand you could scan a Northern New York panorama shimmering under an August sun—the half-mile track like a wide yellow ribbon edged with white fencing; the judges' stand like a squad minaret; horse barns and cattle sheds; the farthest reaches of the fairgrounds, marked off by a weathered wire fence; and the gently rolling country beyond, checkered by cornfields, pastures, and distant woodlots; a horizon jiggled by heat waves.

From the topmost tier you could look down on the roofs of exhibition buildings, grey and dry as dust, their shingles curled by the sun and the years. The only sounds came from the sheds creaking in the wind.

All this was a stage upon which the years unfolded cheerful dramas. Every year had its star piece, the St. Lawrence County Fair, which ran the best part of a week and then became another memory, leaving the grounds strewn with debris, the grass trampled and the buildings once more cavernous and lonely.

The fair was heralded by prize cattle, sheep, and goats herded along the roads to Canton. In the village they squeezed through the streets, brushing against hedges, trees, and front porches.

The fairgrounds, suddenly populated with men and animals, bustled and echoed to hammering and sawing. Trotters, having been assigned to stalls in the barns, exercised on the track with steady hoof-beats.

On a Monday the fair blossomed in a burst of merry-go-round music which filled the breeze and was carried, faint and sweet, to the houses on State Street. From the back windows of those same houses you could catch glimpses of the fair—miniature trotters trailing dust on the track, people scattering about on the field, and part of the Ferris wheel. At that distance the grounds simmered with the lowing of cattle, the tinkle of the starter's bell, snapping sounds from the shooting gallery, the never-stopping calliope.

On Water Street there were little stands on some of the front lawns where lemonade and pink taffy and toy whips were sold under the trees.

The taffy went with the fair, an exciting taste of things to come. Going to the fair, you bought it to calm the excitement in your breast, and on the way home you bought it to ease the pain of departure.

The State Street gate eased you into the excitement. You ran down a little hill and then past the long cattle sheds filled with grunting pigs lying on their sides; cows rolling their eyes and chewing their cuds; sheep staring glassily and jostling each other.

Then you came to a big horse barn opposite the first turn in the track. Men sat silent in the wide doorway, watching the crowds flow past and the blanketed horses being cooled out on a nearby patch of grass. Inside the barn other horses, sleek fellows, looked out over their stall doors. Their names were scrawled in chalk on the outside of each door—Ottway Bird, Little Prince, Direct Alco.

The carnival area was laid out like a gauntlet to distract those on their way to the grandstand. Its noise was a mixture of music, cracking, popping, and yelling, and its odor was a blend of popcorn, hotdogs, hamburgers, sweat, hot canvas, and gasoline engine exhaust.

The merry-go-round revolved with a jolly racket, the glass-eyed steeds bearing wide-eyed children. The tickets were collected by a fat man, waddling from horse to horse and mouthing a cigar stub.

There were canvas booths in which one tried to knock over piles of wooden milk bottles with ten-cent baseballs, and other booths in which one tried to toss small rings over prizes arranged on a rack.

Lounging by the rail at the first turn was a group of horsemen, farmers, and kids watching the trotters and pacers work up steam for the first race.

In the judges' stand the starter worked with a megaphone and a bell. You heard him all afternoon as the trotters and pacers scored for the start of each heat. They circled at the head of the stretch, some rearing, all in a crazy, dusty pattern. As they swept past the stands, the starter yelled through the megaphone, "Watch that pole horse! Watch that pole horse!"

And if they went by without meeting his instructions, he boomed, "No use! No use! Pull up at the curve!" If they continued to ignore him, he yanked the clapper on the bell. This brought them back like naughty boys, and the horses' ears switched back and forth as the starter scolded the drivers.

At last they went by to suit his taste, and he yelled, "Go!" They were off. As they rounded the turn, the ball players stopped to watch, and as they entered the stretch, the noise of the crowd took on a higher pitch. The clamor deepened into a full-throated roar as they neared the finish wire. Whips cracked and the drivers glared at each other as they came on wheel to wheel. Thunder of hoofs, whistle and snap of whips, grunts of horses, flying manes, glistening hides, harnesses white with froth, blurred spokes reflecting the sun on the sulky wheels, a flash under the wire and the race was over.

The winner walked back under restraint to the judges' stand, tossing his head at the cheers and handclapping. Then he was led off the track. Interest returned to the ball game.

The people watched dispassionately the skill of two Negro teams, the Brooklyn Royal Giants and the Cuban Stars. No one cared much who won.

The last day of the fair, the people in the carnival had a distracted air. There was packing up and moving ahead of them.

And then the fair was gone and the kids flocked to the empty grounds to chase ghosts and hunt for money under the grandstand. They poked through empty crates and explored the dark exhibition halls and wandered aimlessly over the carnival grounds. Next week school would open and the high school fellows would be out in the infield for football practice.

RECALLING THE OLD COUNTRY STORE

By Ethel Barnett, *York State Tradition*, Spring 1962

The old country store was not only a business establishment but a social center in the community as well. "In the days when men lived separate and solitary lives," says Gerald Carson in *The Old Country Store*, "it was the country stores that tied the scattered farms into a community. The store was what made a neighborhood and gave it its central nervous system and a conscience. It also put some fun into life."

At the old country store, lighted by kerosene lamps in the evening hours, menfolk, congregated around the traditional pot-bellied stove, passed the time by swapping yarns or discussing politics, playing checkers or whittling, and chewing tobacco and making use of the copper spittoon. Sometimes one would buy a wedge of cheese to eat with the crackers to which he would help himself from the open cracker barrel.

The storekeeper was usually the proprietor. Living quarters were over the store or in the back part of the building. A bell attached to the door would announce the arrival of a customer.

In most cases it was the man of the house who did the "weekly trading." There was very little cash in the era of the country store. The proprietor would take meat products, butter, and eggs from area farmers in trade for merchandise from the store. Later, when farmers had a little more cash, still they often had their purchases "put on the book," with an appointed date for paying the bill. When the bill was paid, the storekeeper would give the customer a bag of assorted candy for the family as a token of his appreciation.

The country store had a line of merchandise that included almost everything that would be needed by any homemaker or farmer in the area. The store shelves were stocked with groceries, canned goods, yard goods and sewing needs, arms and ammunition, patented medicines that were advertised to cure almost all ailments, household utensils, clothing for every member of the family, tobacco products, paint, hardware, farm equipment, horse blankets, horse whips, and veterinary needs. Snuff, opium, and morphine were sold by the ounce. Even tombstones and church pews could be found in many of these early stores. Many food staples came by the barrel, keg, or tub. Some people purchased foods in these quantities, while others would have the clerk weigh out the desired amount and package it.

The glass candy case with its colorful confections is most vivid in the memory of those who had the opportunity to visit a store of yesteryear. In those days one could purchase enough candy for one penny to satisfy the "sweet tooth." There was always a variety for choice, including the red and white stick hard candy striped like a barber's pole, long black licorice sticks, motto hearts, all day suckers, and tiny red cinnamon candies which were measured by a glass mug for the penny's worth. The crystal clear rock candy, strung on a short piece of white twine, was sold by the pound. This candy, immersed in rye whiskey, was used by many adults as a cure for many respiratory ailments.

In the early 1800s the country store, most centrally located, served as the first schoolroom in the community, with the storekeeper's wife as the teacher. This was the case in Crown Point, where, according to the record, five scholars went to school in Elisha Rhodes' store, and Mrs. Rhodes was their teacher. The scholars were seated on the flat side of the pine slab bench in which were stuck pieces of round limbs for legs. That was the extent of the school furniture.

Very often the country store served as the town's post office. This again was true in Crown Point. The proprietor, of course, would be appointed postmaster. These men were very good business managers.

The old country store has vanished from the landscape, but those who knew it recall it now with a feeling akin to affection.

SARANAC LAKE FREE LIBRARY

By G. Glyndon Cole, *North Country Life*, Fall 1956

The beautiful Saranac Lake Free Library has in recent years been acquiring a wide reputation. A glance at the visitors' register reveals names of people from places as far distant as Washington, D.C.

Aside from the beauty of this modest little village library, which is an attraction in itself, its fame has been a-building on its outstanding collection of literature—books, magazines, pamphlets, clippings, photographs, letters—dealing with Northern New York and particularly the Adirondacks.

The foundation of this collection is known as the Donaldson collection. Alfred L. Donaldson was a banker who came to Saranac Lake for his health about 1875. He became interested in the history of the Adirondack area as a hobby. His two-volume *History of the Adirondacks* was the result. All historians recognize this as the basic authoritative source of information on Adirondack history. He collected every printed word he could find, interviewed hundreds of people, and wrote hundreds of letters, the manuscript of his two-volume history, and all the printed material he had been able to gather went to the Saranac Free Library upon his death in 1924, as he had requested in his will.

Donaldson had not been able to acquire quite everything for his collection that he would like to have had. Henry Comstock, a Wall Street lawyer and summer resident of Keene Valley, had some items Donaldson did not possess, and Comstock would not sell them.

Unknown to Donaldson, and Comstock too, was the activity of William C. Munson, a Manhattan druggist who was spending weekends in Saranac Lake visiting his wife, who had come here for her health. He and his wife collected material on the Adirondacks, spending more money on rare books than they perhaps could afford.

Henry Comstock died a few years after Donaldson. Munson then did what Donaldson had been unable to: He bought many of the Comstock items.

In 1929, Munson retired to Saranac Lake. After his death in 1949, his son and widow offered the collection for sale at a price far below its value. They refused to sell separate volumes. In 1951, after an appeal for funds to people interested in Adirondack history, the directors of the Saranac Library were able to buy the Munson collection, consisting of more than 5,000 separate pieces of material pertaining to all phases of life in the Adirondacks from 1837 to 1949.

So now the Donaldson and Munson collections, including items once owned by Comstock, are now together in the Saranac Library. Also some items have been added by the late Kenneth Goldthwaite, once owner of the *Adirondack Enterprise*, the local daily paper.

This collection of Adirondackana is being added to continually. Funds for this purpose were provided by friends of William Morris, New York theatrical agent who lived for many years in Saranac Lake. The fund is known as the William Morris Memorial Fund.

The most notable material obtained through this fund is one of the finest collections of 18th-century maps in existence. Among the 53 maps in the collection are a Dutch map of 1700 showing Northeastern America and a French map of 1755, which shows more detail of the area of Northern New York than was customary on early maps. The most important map is considered to be the map of Lake Champlain produced in London in 1776, long considered the "lost map."

The Adirondack collection in Saranac Lake Free Library is now the best and probably the largest in existence. There is now little or nothing of any importance that has been written on the Adirondacks, from the first magazine article in 1832 to the present day, that is not here. No other library can make this boast—not even the New York State Library in Albany or the Library of Congress. The one unfortunate circumstance in connection with it is the fact that the library does not have adequate space for it. This condition will be relieved, however, through the William C. White Memorial Fund when it has become sufficiently large to construct an addition to the existing building.

WILDERNESS PRISON

By Seneca Ray Stoddard, *York State Tradition*, Summer, 1968

The text of this article, which describes a visit to Clinton Prison well over a century ago, has been excerpted from a lengthy series of articles published in a Glens Falls newspaper in the early 1870s. The photographs [thirteen were featured in his article], which were taken by Stoddard at the time of his visit, are the property of the North Country Historical Research Center, Plattsburgh. —G. Glyndon Cole

The prison is on the mountain side looking out to the south; backward, the mountain rises a little higher in bleak, rocky, rolling ledges; away to the front it slopes down to the river and off toward Lake Champlain.

Enclosing the prison and works, perhaps a mile in circuit, is a fence twenty felt high made of boards set upright. The gate is near the center on the south; along the side runs the road that is also the principal street of the little village that has gathered here, with perhaps two hundred inhabitants, principally the families of the keepers, guards, teamsters who convey the coal and iron to and from the forge, and various others necessary to carry on the work of a large establishment like this.

We drove down the village street and halted at the Clinton House for the night. Across the road the high fence shut off the view, but between the chinks we could see flashing lights and the glow of fires on the chimney tops. We could hear the hiss of steam, the labored breathing of the huge blowers, and the sound of the great trip-hammer descending first on the soft mass of glowing fire that sheds tears of blood and gradually shrinks and hardens until we hear the clear ring of the metals battling with each other.

In the morning, awakened by the prison bell, we were up on top of the hotel in time to see the convicts, accompanied by their keepers, march in to breakfast and out again to their several places of work.

Here, overlooking it, we may glance at the prison and works. Clinton Prison was erected in 1845. It has accommodations for about 550 "guests." It consists of the prison proper, containing 540 cells, a long white building. At its west end is a three-story building with grated windows and doors, containing, on the g round, the kitchen and mess rooms, in the third story, the hospital, while in the middle are the chapel, guard rooms, & c.

In the southeast corner of the enclosure is the forge. Along the side hill toward the west are the various workshops, nail factory, engine room, separator, & c. From the separator, rails are laid on which small dump cars run to the iron mine, the mouth of which is enclosed by an extension of the fence. Just west of the separator is a large three-story building surmounted by a belfry and watchtower combined. It was originally built for a shoe shop but is not used for that purpose at present, as the work is almost exclusively in iron. South of this is the warden's house. Back toward the east is the laundry and tailoring establishment.

Clinton Prison, Dannemora, N.Y. 1890. *Photo S. R. Stoddard. Courtesy Special Collections, Feinberg Library, SUNY College at Plattsburgh*

We apprehended the yawning gate with a feeling such as the celebrated Daniel must have had when entering the lion's den. It was opened by a polite gentleman in smiles and the "loudest" kind of a zebra suit, who welcomed us with expressive silence.

I was surprised to see the freedom enjoyed by the convicts. They were going in all directions and engaged in various employments. Small gangs were unattended by a keeper. Others apparently on the sick list were lolling in the sunshine with all the apparent freedom and enjoyment of first class loafers in a city barroom. Wagons and carts were continually passing out and in through the gate.

At various intervals along the high fence are "posts," the peculiarity of which consists in their design and construction. There are nine of these little houses on stilts overlooking the high fence and having balconies

Main Hall, Clinton Prison. *Photo George C. Baldwin. Courtesy Special Collections, Feinberg Library, SUNY College at Plattsburgh*

all around them. They are reached by stairways through trap doors in the floor. Here men stand all day long from the time the convicts are let out in the morning until they are safely housed for the night. They are armed with repeating rifles, and their duty is to warn convicts away from the fence, enforcing their orders with lead if necessary.

A force of upwards of fifty men is employed, consisting of the warden, principal keeper, sergeant of the guard, with 28 guardsmen and 19 regular keepers, besides the clerk, physician, chaplain, yard keeper, kitchen keeper, two teachers and the foremen of the various departments of the works.

The warden is also agent or superintendent of the works. The present incumbent, General Moffit, is a veteran of the late war, who has earned this position by gallant services.

At 5:30 a.m. the hall waiter goes through the long building containing the cells and rings the inmates up with a small bell; they wash and dress, usually not a very elaborate operation, and at 6 o'clock are ready to go out. Meanwhile the post guards take their stations, the keepers enter the hall, and at a given signal the cell doors are thrown open and the convicts file out, going first to the bucket ground, for each man must take care of his own room, thence to breakfast, and out in squads to the various places where employed. At noon a bell calls them to dinner. With the clamor of the bell comes the sound of many feet, tramp, tramp, tramp, from shop and field and from the dripping mine a thousand feet down under the mountain side. From every side they come, not with the gallant tread of soldiers but with pride less plodding and swaying from side to side in the clumsy rolling gait of the lock-step. The ringed and striped mass, like a huge worm surprised by the sunshine, squirms and twists down the hillside, across the sandy road, along the graveled walk, and around the corner of the stone building. It crawls slowly into the dark hole they call a door and at last pulls its uncanny tail in out of the light of day.

In the mess room the tables are laid for dinner. The ceiling is low, the floor paved with large slabs of stone, wet from a recent scrubbing. On either side of the narrow aisle and running to the side walls are the tables—stationary planks, like old-fashioned desks at school, with boards nailed along one edge and jutting above the top to prevent articles falling off. All sit on stools facing in one direction.

At night the time of entering varies according to season and circumstances, the intention being to have all safe before dark. When the order is given to "fall in," the lines from various directions converge and flow into the long hall, each man receiving as he passes, his supper, which is eaten in his cell. When all are safely locked in and counted through the barred doors, the "all right" bell rings, the keepers pass out, the guards come down from their martin boxes, and the night guards begin their rounds.

Prison band at Clinton Prison. 1890. The Adirondack Museum's exhibit of revolving old photographs is a favorite for many visitors. *Photo S. R. Stoddard. Courtesy Special Collections, Feinberg Library, SUNY College at Plattsburgh*

NORTH POLE, N.Y.

Unknown author, *North Country Life*, Fall 1949

Seventy-five years have elapsed since this story announced the opening of one of the first theme parks to appear in the Adirondack Mountains. Santa's Workshop at the North Pole still continues to attract crowds of visitors to Wilmington, New York. There are now musical revues, a Book Nook where children can listen to stories told by Santa's helpers, a live nativity scene and other attractions. And, for today's technological generation, its upgraded image includes a hip website at http://www.northpoleny.com that is sure to appeal to both children and adults. Santa emails now!

While the North Country was sweltering under a broiling sun, Santa Claus was settling down in a new and permanent home. At the invitation of some enterprising business men of the Ausable Valley, he moved his headquarters last summer from the frigid Arctic to Whiteface Mountain, where an entire village has been constructed to accommodate him and the thousands of visitors who now find it easy to call on him.

The new village has been named North Pole, for, impossible as it may seem, Santa brought the North Pole with him from the Arctic. It is located now near the center of the new village, where you may see it and touch its constant coating of frost.

North Pole, N.Y., is an enchanted children's village, consisting of nine stripped-pine log houses designed with a Mother Goose motif by Arto Monaco, former Walt Disney and MGM artist. Bright Christmas colors predominate. Among the buildings are Santa's home, his workshop, his blacksmith shop, a church, a post office, and several stores.

You may inspect Santa's home inside and out and talk with him as long as you wish. In his workshop you will see his gnome helpers, dressed in medieval costumes, making toys. In the stores you may see their products—hundreds of pre-school age toys along with toys for children of other ages. If you wish, you may purchase these toys or order them for future delivery.

In the blacksmith shop you will see another of Santa's assistants working at the forge. In the post office children may sit down at little desks to write a note to Santa or letters to friends and relatives back home.

A statue of St. Nick looks down from the small chapel and inside, back of the altar, in miniature is the Nativity Scene.

When not working as Santa, Noah John Rondeau lived outside the entrance of the North Pole. His replica log cabin mirrored the actual building he relied on for his survival in the Cold River wilderness. It served as an additional tourist attraction at the theme park.

"I remember having my picture taken with Rondeau. These pictures were taken on a Sunday in late October 1950. My father owned a grocery store in Hudson Falls and only had Sundays off to make the trip to Wilmington. Noah and I had something in common. We were both raised to speak the French language. I spoke only French until I entered school." —Alice Genthner. *Courtesy Alice Genthner*

Harmonizing with the mountain setting are rustic bridges, one of which, beside a huge waterwheel, crosses a little pond for ducks.

Perhaps the biggest attractions for the little folks, next to Santa himself, are the numerous white deer, the goats, and the sheep, freely mingling with visitors, hoping to be petted, and begging you to hand them a biscuit from one of the several dispensers stationed about the grounds. In truth, the deer don't care if you don't hand it to them. If you will just put a nickel in the slot, they will help themselves. And if you ignore the goats, don't be surprised if you get a friendly little butt. Shetland ponies, too, are available for rides.

Except for his trip around the world on Christmas Eve, Santa will be at home here, happy to welcome visitors the year around. The village is located a half mile up the Whiteface Mountain road, which leads off Route 86 at Wilmington. Even for grown-ups it is worth a long drive.

Notable Adirondack hermit, Noah John Rondeau was employed to play the role of Santa Claus throughout the late summer and fall of 1950. "I do not remember much about the occasion except that I did not like Santa. I was young and scared. Mother Hubbard is consoling me." —Alice Genthner. *Courtesy Alice Genthner*

VANISHING AMERICANA

By William J. O'Hern

Iroquois and Algonquin were the first to fish and hunt the Adirondack lands, and warred for centuries up and down the 130-mile Lake Champlain corridor. Beginning in 1609, fur trappers and white explorers followed Native American trails into this wilderness—then a land of mystery, picturesque with the beauties of creation. French, English and colonials all struggled in turn for control of the Lake Champlain-Lake George "gate of the country." Fort ruins and sites along the shores of Lake Champlain and down the Richelieu River to the St. Lawrence tell the story of conflict.

The Adirondack saga has to do in large part with the arrival of settlers from New England, the lower Hudson Valley, and Canada looking for affordable land. Land speculators, who had purchased immense tracts for next to nothing, were subdividing and reselling these sectors at affordable prices to determined men and women bent on taming the powerful waters and inimical forests, and extracting the land's mineral wealth.

The first communities had toe-holds beyond the marshy mouths of such rivers as the Great Chazy, the AuSable, the Saranac, and the Boquet, all on the west side of

PART ONE

Adirondack Memories

Conklingville, N.Y. *Courtesy Marilyn Breakey*

And even now, we can see Walter Aldin and John Wells outside the vertical pole barn, roofed with good hand-split white cedar shingles, the cleared yard in green meadow grass—there is a look of weather-worn pioneer elegance. It is a snapshot reminder that rain and snow and wind and sun and the adjacent forest would be ready at any moment to take back this Adirondack farm clearing. *Courtesy Marilyn Breakey*

Lake Champlain. There flourished sawmills, grist mills, lumber yards, iron forges, tanneries and brick yards, supported by water power that supplied pioneer needs. Pushing further and further up the rivers and into the wilderness, pioneering people followed the lumbermen, cutting jagged trails, surveying turnpike routes, laying plank roads, and building bridges. Transportation everywhere was by boat, foot, ox cart, and horse. What had once been considered a "wasteland" saw the expansion of communities, complete with schools and churches.

In 1891, S. R. Stoddard illustrated the region, naming his detailed drawing the "Map of the Adirondack Wilderness." The rendering showed the range of human development throughout the rough country. The legend listed "Rail roads, Important roads, Ordinary roads, Carries, Trails, and Telegraph offices" linking newly-established frontier-like communities—few of which experienced rapid settlement.

In 1963, Hayden Pearson, a reporter for the Albany *Times-Union*, wistfully wrote "Old Plank Bridges," describing the passage from pastoral days to modern times. Pearson's glimpse backwards appears nostalgic, but I doubt he meant to portray past mountain life as pure pleasure. His article is more of a reflection on life in an earlier northern New York, influenced by echoes of his own country roots.

What he wrote could easily describe the years of movement following Stoddard's rendering of the Adirondack wilderness. Some Adirondack communities rose and slowly expanded, while others faded into ghost towns. Many place names chosen by the settlers are in use today. Their lives and legends are woven into the fabric of Adirondack community history. Twenty-first-century travelers driving through the Adirondack Park would be hard pressed to imagine the land's rich heritage of man-made history and its God-given scenic beauty save for history books and noteworthy personal remembrance. When Glyndon Cole compiled his quarterly, he organized his histories under specific topics, such as the origins of the communities, early industries, early activities and the people who engaged in those activities, transportation, schools, general history, cultures, as well as accounts of the region's natural beauty. The combination of Cole's genius and the expertise of his contributors revealed the color of life in an area that plays such an important part in today's northern New York.

THE FIELDSTONE WALL

I'm just a rambling old stone wall
That parts the forest from the field.
At places I am wide and tall
And farther on a rabbit's shield.

Perchance you've wondered whence I came
And who would bend beneath the sun
To pick and carry to this lane,
Or why was all this labor done.

His name was Smith or Brown or James
And many years ere you here stood,
He came with axe and plough and chain
To wrest a clearing from the wood.

He was a dreamer with a dream
Who plodded slow behind the ox
And wielded saw and axe and scheme
To clear these fields where once were rocks.

His calloused hand placed every stone
And it became his kingdom wall
And all within was his alone
For he was king—however small.

Some quiet churchyard is his berth
Marble bears his name and all.
But no monument of stone or earth
Will tell of him like this old wall.

—George E. Phinney Sr., *North Country Life*, Fall 1954

Each summer Sabbath, work in my grandparents' garden and fields was stopped; stones upturned by the plow sat untouched, the rake and hoe idle; the horses turned up dust curls as they lazily rolled in the dirt. Grandma served cool lemonade and Grandpa relaxed, rocking gently, looking out over his favorite Adirondack hills and talking casually about how things used to be. *Courtesy Marilyn Breakey*

OLD PLANK BRIDGES

By Hayden S. Pearson, *York State Tradition*, Fall 1963

There was a time when boys and girls walked along country roads to the district school. Today, of course, children are carried in buses; otherwise, they would be too tired to take physical exercise in flossy gymnasiums.

Half a century ago, a lad did not have much time for exploring in the morning. With a two-quart lard pail filled with lunch, he pushed steadily along the road to be on time. In those days, discipline and learning were the reasons for schools, and parents backed the teachers instead of arguing with them. Since then, psychologists have discovered children's personalities and have altered school practices.

But in the afternoon, an understanding father appreciated that a boy needed a little extra time. It was fun to explore beneath the old plank bridge. It was a utilitarian structure, laid down long years ago, but it served farm families along the road that led back among the hills.

It was two centuries ago when the first settlers came into the region and began the task of making homes and farms in the wilderness. At first there were rough trails that wound along the valley and up along the slopes and mountain shoulders. On foot and on horseback, bags of grain were carried to the grist mill in the valley settlement.

Then first roads were made, and creaking, lumbering oxcarts followed along the road that wandered from farm to farm. Men and beasts forded the streams, jolting over stones that had been tossed into the stream bed. Time passed, more farms were made, and one day the town's pathmaster announced a bee to build a plank bridge.

Straining oxen pulled great rocks for the abutments; oak or chestnut stringers were laid, and then two-inch hardwood planks were set in place. Sometimes logs were placed at each end of the planks. It was plain construction, but it was honest work, and the plank bridges meant an easier trip.

A twelve-year-old in bare feet edged along the abutment rocks beneath the bridge. The rocks were green with slippery moss. It was a mysterious spot with the water bugs skittering across the shadowed water surface and minnows flashing from side to side.

Most of the old bridges are gone. Cement and steel serve man's needs better in an era of heavy machines. But there are those who remember the old, splintery, weathered, plank bridges and the reverberating roar when a snappy Morgan and a steel-wheeled democrat [wagon] hit the loose planks.

Gone are the horses and gone most of the bridges. But sometimes when the countryman rolls across a modern bridge on rubber tires, he thinks of the days when the plank bridges echoed to a horse's hooves and buggy wheels.

SARANAC LAKE, THE LITTLE CITY IN THE ADIRONDACKS

By G. Glyndon Cole, *North Country Life*, Summer 1956

Nestled deep in the Adirondacks lies the village of Saranac Lake—a name that has been synonymous with "health" for nearly a hundred years.

Being in the Adirondack Park, the village is surrounded by the forest. Only twenty miles away, the highest mountains in the Eastern United States pierce the sky.

The Saranac River flows through town and widens here to form lovely Lake Flower. Upper, Middle and Lower Saranac lakes lie close by. Indeed, within a radius of ten miles are fifty mountain lakes. The village's location here in one of the most beautiful settings of the East, high in the oldest mountains of the world, is accountable for its history, growth, and fame.

Its early fame rested upon the community's "health industry." For many decades this was the most advanced center for the treatment of tuberculosis in the United States, possibly in the world. It was here, in the latter part of the 19th century, that Dr. Edward Trudeau conceived the plan for the treatment of the disease by rest, fresh air, and wholesome food. Here the Trudeau Foundation carried on constant research to find new and better ways of treating the disease. At the height of Saranac Lake's fame as a health center, the village and the surrounding area accommodated as many as 5,000 patients from all over the world.

Many of these patients, through the years, chose to become permanent residents upon being cured—a fact which, combined with the presence of large numbers of physicians, probably accounts for its somewhat cosmopolitan population and a cultural level higher than usual for small

Cinematography advertising was in its infancy when Harry Raymond (far left) was photographed announcing a film being presented at the Pontiac Theatre.
Courtesy Special Collections, Feinberg Library, SUNY College at Plattsburgh

villages, especially in mountain regions. The community's interest in art, music, and the theatre gives it a college town atmosphere.

Because of the success of the campaign against tuberculosis, the community's "health industry" has dropped in importance in recent years. But its healthful climate is still one of its most valuable assets. This and the natural beauty of its location have made its transition to an outstanding year-round vacation resort quite easy and simple.

The community, with its many new and modern motels, cabins, and hotels, is now a mecca for tourists. And since the village has been welcoming visitors throughout most of its history, you can be sure they know how to make you feel at home and to provide opportunities for recreation. Water skiing, swimming carnivals, outboard racing, fishing, golf, horseback riding, and hiking are among the most popular outdoor summer activities. For indoor entertainment, there are a summer theatre, numerous musical concerts, and an annual antique show. There is always something "doing" here.

In winter the community offers a full range of winter sports activities climaxed by an outstanding winter carnival. But Saranac Lake in winter is another story in itself.

"But it is the woods that sooner or later draw most people," wrote the late William C. White, correspondent for the New York *Herald-Tribune*. "In the Adirondack country the woods, miles of them, are the people's...It is the woods that give the land its color, through the greens of spring, the fire reds of autumn when the whole countryside is aflame, and the dark-green of winter."

If you spend some time this summer at Saranac Lake, you are certain to find it rewarding. But one word of warning may not be out of place. Be prepared to be tempted to stay there all the rest of your life. Saranac Lake is full of people who once were visitors—visitors who liked the place so well that they decided to stay and "go native."

INDIAN LAKE

By Gretchen Houghton Fish, *North Country Life*, Winter 1952
Reprinted from New York State *Conversationist*

Indian Lake—if not geographically, then spiritually—is in the heart of the Adirondacks. It is 1,750 feet above sea level. It is surrounded by wooded hills and stretches of big timber with mountains sloping gently back from the shores. It is a famous summer resort and it is also the Matumbla of the Indians, their legendary burying ground.

The township of Indian Lake includes the village and the lake itself, and also Sabael (the hamlet that sits in one of the hollows on the lake), Big Brook, Cedar River, a part of North River and Blue Mountain Lake Village. The lake is three miles south of the village named after it.

The story goes that in the year 1767, a lone Indian left the Province of Quebec and after journeying through the Canadian woods came at last to the shores of Lake Champlain. Here he made a birch bark canoe in which he paddled to the southern end of the lake, then plunged into the deep forests on the New York side. He was looking for big game, especially moose, for his tribe in the north was starving.

One day, breaking through a covert of underbrush, his Indian habit of silence gave way and he uttered an exclamation of delight. Below him was a little lake, gleaming with flashes from the setting sun and reflecting the white birches that hung over the shore. Not a foot of cleared land was to be seen: around stood mighty mountains. The Indian's search was ended, for there was game everywhere.

The lake at this time was tiny, really twin bodies of water about three miles long. At its middle point it was separated almost into two lakes by the narrows formed by sediment brought down by a little mountain brook. This later became known as Squaw Brook.

The Indian, who was destined to play so great a part in the history of the town, was Sabael Benedick, a Banakee. The Mitchell family, whose homes are in the village, are descendants of his. When asked in later years how he knew his age, Sabael informed his listeners that twelve summers had passed over his head when he stood on the hillside above Quebec, while the great battle raged on the Plains of Abraham.

He hunted the territory around his new haven, went back to his homeland and persuaded members of his tribe to join him. He put out trap lines and explored the countryside surrounding his lake. One winter he made friends with an old Dutchman who had settled on Racquette Lake. Sabael evidently was attracted not so much by the Dutchman as by one of his daughters—a red head—and it wasn't long before Sabael brought his bride to his little lake. He built a house on its shores, by Squaw Brook.

The exploits of Sabael are still talked about around Indian Lake. When his wife died, he sewed her mortal remains in birch bark, placed her fork, knife and spoon within the folds of the homemade casket to insure her plenty to eat in the Happy Hunting Grounds, and then buried her on the banks of the little brook, known as Squaw Brook in her memory. This grave was originally on the bank, but since the building of the dam the waters now cover it.

Sabael made his own flint arrows and later bullets from a lead mine, the location of which he never disclosed. Some credit is given him for discovery of the great Tahawus Mines, and it is known that he made a trail through the wilderness to the garnet mines at North River. Many lesser anecdotes are told about him. Late in life he became the first baby sitter, caring for the neighbors' children while they were picking berries or otherwise occupied.

The death of Sabael is shrouded in mystery. Among his grandchildren was one boy who was quarrelsome and disagreeable, and with whom Sabael had many disputes over his secret haunts and sources of supply in the wilderness. All that is known is that when Sabael was 108 years old and still active, he suddenly disappeared, and his body was never found. He was thought to have been killed by his grandson, who disappeared from Indian Lake shortly afterwards.

The first white man to settle near Indian Lake made his appearance in 1840. This was Reuben Rist, a great hunter and trapper, who built a little

Cedar River Bridge and Cedar River House. The Cedar River House was built in 1863. The grassy area on the right is now the Cedar River Golf Course.
Courtesy Bill Zullo, Hamilton County Historian

home down across the Indian River where the Chamberlain road leads off the main highway today. Among the many people he and his wife befriended was a half-frozen boy in his teens who came to the door early one winter morning. The boy had lost his ox team and had been terrified by the cries of the wolves in the deep woods. The boy grew up to become the philanthropist of Glens Falls and one of the great lumbermen of the Adirondacks—Henry Crandall. Down the bank of the Indian River, on the hilltop back of the hotel, there still stands an old monument placed there by Henry Crandall. On it is inscribed "In Memory of Reuben Rist and Wife. First Settlers on Township 15, Where They Lived to a Good Old Age." This is a simple monument in memory of good people.

Lumbering, then as later, was the drawing card that brought settlers into the country. Several families soon came in to join the Rists, scattering throughout the section. There were the Lockes, Pearsons, Websters, Hoxies and Porters, and the first white child born in Indian Lake was W.W. Porter. Among the first to begin lumbering were Webster and Bloomingdale. Hoxie was a jack of all trades, lumbering, building a store down on Indian River, and bringing in supplies for settlers and hunting and trapping. He even cut a trail into Moose Lake so that he might bring out the deer that he killed and twice a week sent out in loads to hotels in Saratoga. Game laws were unknown then—the supply seemed unending.

Wolves were plentiful and panthers were often seen. Trout were also plentiful—so plentiful that when small dams were closed on Beaver Meadow Brook for lumbering purposes, the camp cooks could go out and pick up these prized fish by the panful. Venison was the main source of meat.

Disagreements were bound to occur, even though homes were scattered far and wide in the wilderness. The story goes that one day Mr. Peary's pig got into Mr. Bealie's garden, and it was found that there was no agency to settle the dispute that arose. There were no justices of the peace or other law officials within 25 miles, so the people for the first time saw the need of organizing as a community.

Sabael's lake became Indian Lake and the little settlement on its shores to this day is known as Sabael. His lake is known far and wide for its

The Commercial Hotel was built in the late 1800s and burned in 1917. In the right foreground would have been William Carroll's meat market and undertaking business.
Courtesy Bill Zullo, Hamilton County Historian

great northern pike, its fighting bass and various other fish, while the country around about has its share of deer to test the skill of the hunter.

Sometime in the 50s, the first dam of logs was built on Indian Lake in order to provide a better supply of water to float logs down to the mill. It increased the width of the lake but not its length. Lumbering, which came almost to a standstill during the Civil War, was again upset in 1876, when a raging fire burned all the timber between Beaver Meadow Brook and North River.

Since then, lumber camps have been built, tracts lumbered and relumbered. The lumberjacks would go into the woods in early winter, work long hours and come out in the spring to fling away on a wild carousel their hard-earned wages of months. It was a colorful scene in the spring to see them moving out of the camps, after their logs had been "banked" in readiness for the long drive down the Cedar and the Indian and the Hudson. Horses still in good rig after a hard winter's work, gaily decked with colored rings and ribbons, would pull sleighs full of lumberjacks singing their shanty ditties, and by the river big Milo Daniels, the camp cook, with his stove set up on one of the sleighs and a short length of stovepipe billowing out clouds of smoke in the frosty air, used to flip fried pancakes to the men clustered around him.

Even in the; 70s the village was a part of the wilderness. In 1877, when Oliver St. Marie built his store, the land had to be cleared of trees. This old store still stands in the center of the village, a sturdy landmark.

Until about 1880, lumbering was the chief industry, but already a few city dwellers were coming in to fish and hunt. They were known locally as "sports," and they began a new era. In 1881 the Prospect Hotel at Blue

Kerst's Boat Livery was located near the present Indian Lake Marina on the west side of the lake in Sabael. William B. Kerst, born 1873 at Birdsboro, PA, came to Indian Lake prior to 1900. He was a mechanic. For some years he operated a sawmill near the Indian River Bridge. Later, he and son Leo were boat builders on Lake View Road at Sabael. He was married to Carrie L. Fish, born in 1876 to Elijah Fish, born 1842 at Fort Ann and Martha Emma Porter. Will Kerst died in 1950 and Carrie in 1954.
Courtesy Bill Zullo, Hamilton County Historian

Mountain was built and it was certainly the most elegant of all the Adirondack hotels at the time. It was the first hotel in the world to be lighted throughout with the Edison incandescent light, and Edison personally supervised the job. It also was the first to serve the ice cream sundae on its menu. Its fame grew as a summer resort, and there began the advance into the wilderness of the present tourist trade.

A railroad had found its way into the North Country. The builder's contract was to lay the rails to North River, which was done, but after one load of freight was pulled over the road to fulfill the contract, the rails were pulled up and North Creek became the terminus. Coming to North Creek by train, tourists found waiting for them springy buckboard wagons and four- and six-horse coaches, driven by cable drivers and drawn by dashing carriage horses. Stops for rest were made along the route at hotels and inns, but it was a long day's trip to their destination. Many began staying on at Indian Lake.

Hotels on Indian Lake and Lewey Lake were built and did a big business, with colorful figures such as "Rat" and Martha Farrington, the Lockes, the McCormacks and others who could serve meals and tell tall stories. They kept the "sports" coming back again and again until today their children's children own their own camps and are accepted as natives every summer. They are as proud of their kinship with the wilderness as are the year-around inhabitants.

In 1898, the present State dam was built on Indian Lake to increase the water supply and serve as a reservoir. It lengthened the lake about 14 miles and widened it to about a mile, so that now the "narrows" can be seen only when the water is low. Several times it has been feared that the dam might go out in flood conditions, but the sturdy, hand-cut stone from which it was made has stood up well and is a monument to the workmen of a bygone day. There was a wild time while the dam was being constructed, because many employed were foreigners, ready with a knife to right a grievance.

Fishing in the lake was, in fact, too good in some ways, as so many were caught for the sport and thrown away. Pike, as always, were the most numerous, but in the deep waters, as today, lake trout could be caught by the patient angler. Bass, as well as perch and whitefish, have been planted in its waters and bullheads abound. But today the fisherman must have in his tackle-box so many varieties of bright-colored lures that the spirit of old Sabael must chuckle a good many times.

Standing guard over Indian Lake is Snowy Mountain. Hosea Locke took the first group of tourists up this mountain many years ago, and now a fire warden's trail winds for five miles up to its summit. The path is well-trodden by both natives and summer guests. Below the mountain and for miles along the shores of the lake stretches land owned by the people of New York—a wild summer paradise scarcely touched by the hand of man.

And every summer the population of Indian Lake more than triples as the people of New York come to our town. We cling to our town, but we always welcome the visitor.

Herbert A. Palmatier owned a general store in the middle of town where the small part is now located west of the hardware store. Palmatier's burned in 1921. Herb was married to Olive Kenwell, who was the daughter of Isaac "Ike" Kenwell. Ike was the brother of Wellington Kenwell. *Photo Herbert A. Palmatier. Courtesy Bill Zullo, Hamilton County Historian*

EAST HILL, TWO EXPERIMENTS IN SOCIAL LIVING

By Marjorie L. Porter, *North Country Life*, Fall 1957

East Hill is a buxom country woman—her head resting against Hurricane Mountain, Little Crow and Corliss Point her swelling breasts, upland meadows her ample body, brook bed and highway her sprawling legs and feet. At times a cloud veil lies over her piney tresses. A road necklace, set with scattered buildings, is her habitual ornament. She seems content, looking out across the valley to purple peaks, sky-silhouetted.

But East Hill is more than this. It is the birthplace of fourth and fifth generations of New England pioneers; it is Keene's backbone; it is the essence of mountain living; it is a vacation sanctuary; it is a state of mind!

The Willey House, mushrooming from a dwarfish farmhouse in the 1880s, offered Adirondack hospitality to city folks at a time when Paul Smith was doing likewise up on St. Regis Lake. Now was the heyday of Adirondack hotels and sporting houses, the discovery of the North Woods by followers of W.H.H. Murray, the rush of health seekers to Adirondack resorts, the rash of artists from one end of the region to the other, the to-do at philosophers' camps, and on East Hill, symbol of all freedom, the arrival of Thomas Davidson, forceful protagonist of the "New Fellowship."

Professor Thomas Davidson, a Scotsman born in 1840, arrived at Keene in 1889, purchased a 166-acre farm on East Hill, and established Glenmore. He had organized the Guild of the New Life in London in 1883, headed a branch of the New Fellowship in New York City in 1884, and set up a summer school at Farmington, Connecticut, in 1888. Chiefly by a personality "in which lay the slumbering fires of genius," he led his students into acceptance of a "new attitude of intelligence, feelings, with a desire to lay aside prejudice, to know the absolute truth." A master of languages, a person of wide learning and a student of human problems, this "wandering scholar" made courses in philosophy, literature, sociology, and religion media for presenting his theories.

Glenmore was the outcome of a search for a more suitable location for a summer school and of a gift of money from a boy he had tutored.

The school grew and flourished from 1890, when ten people attended, to 1897, when the main buildings were destroyed by fire. Davidson, then in "reduced circumstances," had to make his writing support him. He authored ten works besides numerous articles, died in 1900, and is buried on East Hill. His property was left to Professor Charles Bakewell of Yale University. The school fell by the wayside, as it were, and today Glenmore is a ghost community with rattling shutters and rotting roofs.

Less than half a mile distant, and overlooking the same majestic Adirondack peaks and valleys, is Summerbrook (originally Summerbrook Farm). Here on property bought in 1895 from the John Deweys, Prestonia Mann conceived the idea of another summer school. This existed in its various phases until the World War I period.

Both schools were based on a large humanitarianism, and both took unto themselves great minds in the fields of philosophy and sociology. In passing, they left their mark both on Keene people and on many in distant circles.

Thomas Davidson was an Olympian giant—a man of physical dignity but volcanic energy, big-chested, broad-browed, with flowing red beard, reddish hair, and bright blue eyes. He was jovial and optimistic and possessed great faculties of thought and action. He was intolerant of pretense, inconsistent in practical things, slightly erratic, and very affable. And on East Hill he wore Scottish kilts!

Prestonia, who became Mrs. John Martin in 1900, was a cousin of Horace Mann. She had been exposed not only to East Hill, but to Davidson, as a child. Her parents, Staten Island residents, had stayed at the Willey House and attended Glenmore lectures.

She determined to foster the more humane aspects of society and to make her school a pattern of the enlarged family—the ideal community. A large woman, friendly, confident, and determined, she gracefully introduced new customs in household management and dress and played Lady Bountiful for miles around. She led her guests in the consideration of social problems and in a daily two-hour labor stint. Nothing but physical labor counted as work with Mrs. Martin, but it was all made a cooperative game in which social reformers of New York and Boston took part—such people as Edwin Markham and his wife, Lillian Wall, Jane Adams, Henry D. Lloyd, Upton Sinclair, and Charlotte Perkins Gilman. Wash day was an occasion for hilarity, with joining of hands and singing, "Glory, glory, and the wash goes marching on!" Flowing summer gowns, brightly decorated blouses, unusual male and female outfits went through the wringer, and popped buttons were lined up for recovery.

At Glenmore, two lectures followed an eight o'clock breakfast. Afternoons were devoted to group reading outdoors, tramps, drives, dips in the brook, or resting. After supper and contemplation of memorable sunsets, evening lectures were given. Both morning and evening sessions were preceded by a few minutes' reading.

At Summerbrook, there were the two hours devoted to labor—cutting wood, tending the grounds, laundry. Each guest signed a labor book at night, telling what he or she had accomplished. There was time for study, for discussions which went on all day and far into the night, for daily reading of favorite passages by Prestonia, and for recreation—climbs on Hurricane Mountain, drives in the pony cart, and long walks. There were no formal lectures at Summerbrook.

Housing arrangements at Glenmore in 1890 were casual. An old farmhouse served as lecture hall, sitting room, dining room, and kitchen. Sleeping quarters were in the barn, where students bedded on balsam boughs. Davidson made his headquarters in a large tent, and a few smaller tents were used by guests. During the next two years several cottages were put up, and in 1893 a lecture hall, with sleeping rooms, was added. There were adjacent cottages owned by John Dewey, professor at Chicago University. Dr. William James of the University of Edinburgh owned property nearby.

Summerbrook proper took care of all its guests. Its spacious living and dining rooms offered, through large windows, a panoramic view of the high peaks.

Perhaps the highlight of Summerbrook's existence came when Maxim Gorky, his son, and his secretary were guests. They came to stay a few days and remained six months.

Prestonia Mann Martin died on Easter Sunday, 1945. A memorial tablet on a gray boulder at Summerbrook carries this inscription: "Prestonia Mann Martin, wife of John Martin, 1862–1945. She created the nearby home and developed the surrounding beauty which her memory and spirit continue to bless."

But there are other memorials—the Keene Public Library, erection of which she promoted and which came into being in 1904, its first books having been given some years before by Thomas Davidson; her home at Winter Park, left to Rollins College; furnishings of a room in the library at Rollins College; and her autobiography, still unpublished.

Few people have ever heard of Davidson or Prestonia Martin. The "New Fellowship" is swallowed up in newer "fellowships." The "social conscience" is buried in governmental socialistic programs. And on East Hill clouds drift above Glenmore and Summerbrook!

FORESTPORT DAYS

By A. L. Byron-Curtiss, *North Country Life*, Spring 1955

I recall with fondness the ten months I spent in Forestport as a young deacon-in-charge of Christ Episcopal Church in 1892 and 1893. There I had my first baptism, my first wedding, and my first funeral. The summer of '93 I spent in getting acquainted with my parishioners, hustling for "prospects," borrowing a horse and buggy and making pastoral calls as far as the timber line on the North Lake road. It was that summer that I coined an expression in my resentment of criticism of my zeal in getting some plain people into the church from the back roads. It was "If there isn't room in the church for the saints and sinners, the saints will have to get out to make room for the sinners; it was for sinners that the Savior founded the church."

Numerous friends paid me visits that summer. Among them were an uncle, William E. Hopkins of Utica, and his daughter, Mrs. C.B.H. White, and his daughter-in-law, Lucy Hopkins, widow of Mr. Hopkins' deceased

Rev. A. L. Byron-Curtiss' Christ Episcopal Church, Forestport, N.Y. before it burned. It's location was in the vicinity of Beechwood cemetery. *Courtesy Dorothy Mooney*

son Fred. Uncle William was treasurer of the Black River Railroad and knew more about people than I did. We all went to the church, a half mile outside the village, and spent an hour there singing hymns. Mrs. White was soloist at Calvary Church, Utica. Mrs. Hopkins was a splendid alto; Uncle William, a good tenor. I rumbled bass in my youthful voice. We had an enjoyable hour oblivious of the neighborhood outside. When we came out, we found a score of people gathered at the door listening to what I suppose was to them a worthwhile sacred concert. I introduced my guests to them with all the smug pride of a callow youth and gloried in the recollections of it for days.

A visit by one of my friends I could never forget because of one incident, which occurred during his five days with me. David B. Matthews, a student of divinity at our little seminary in Syracuse, came for a visit. It occurred to me that a trip to Boonville in a rowboat via the canal feeder would make a grand day's outing. The feeder was nine miles long, winding poetically around the hills from the basin at Forestport to the

Frank O'Connor's store, River Street, Forestport, N.Y. *Courtesy Dorothy Mooney*

basin of the canal proper at Boonville. The feeder had a strong current. I knew it would be easy going down and would require extra power returning against the current. I borrowed an extra pair of oars as well as the boat from the lock houseman.

The trip down was dreamy and hauntingly peaceful. The rower had only to pat the water with the oar blades to steer. We swept along at a good rate and reached Boonville in ample time for a good dinner at the famous Hulbert House. After dinner and a smoke on the upper gallery of the hotel, we took our time and explored this lovely village. We secured the key to the Episcopal Church (which was without a rector then), and said a few prayers in the then rather musty temple.

It was mid-afternoon when we went back to our boat and started on our return trip to Forestport. I took the stroke oar, for Matthews was a strong, athletic fellow and I proposed to set the pace. We speedily got into a rhythmic swing and made fine progress for nearly a half mile of still water on the feeder. But when we struck the strong current, we discovered that we were standing still. When we ceased pulling at the oars to discuss the dismaying fact, the boat drifted back towards Boonville. Matthews, who gloried in his physical prowess, took a single pair of oars to pull while I sat in the stern and tried steering with an oar. But then we lost ground—or water, rather. What to do was a puzzler.

We were in front of the dooryard of a tiny, weather-beaten dwelling on the heel path side of the canal feeder. I espied a clothesline stretched across a corner of the yard and barren of any laundry. I went to the door and rapped. When it was opened by a kindly-faced woman, I doffed my hat and asked if I might buy the weathered clothesline, explaining our need for one. The corners of her mouth twitched in a suppressed smile as she observed that we should have a mule to tow the boat. I acknowledged that but said we would have to turn ourselves into mules to get back to Forestport. The good woman ended her brief banter by taking down the clothesline, looping it up, and giving it to me as she said, "Take it and welcome. Hope you make Forestport before dark." She was going to take nothing, but I thrust a quarter into her hand, expressed my thanks, and hurried down to Matthews, who was holding the boat against the tug of the current.

We paddled across to the towpath, where we fastened the line to the bow oarlock and started off with vim and determination. But alas, the craft would not steer right without a man at the helm. So we took shifts of half an hour each, one sitting in the stern and steering with an oar as a paddle, the other pounding the gravel of the towpath. Forestport was eight miles away.

On a bend, as I was towing, we met a team towing a barge to Boonville. The helmsman of the barge heard us talking but as yet could not see our tiny craft. He bawled out to his driver, "What's coming?"

"A steamboat," yelled back the driver.

Another time, when I was steering and we were passing a barge, the helmsman observed to me, "Cap'n, you've cropped the ears of that jackass you've got towing and it's again the law. I'll report you to the Humane Society."

It was well after dark when we got to the guard lock at Forestport. We returned the borrowed boat and oars with profuse thanks to the lock tender and hustled to the Getman House, where I boarded. "Ma" Getman, who was becoming anxious about us, got us a good hot supper. On bringing it to us in the dining room, she tarried long enough to chide us for our "wild recklessness." But for all of her chiding, "Ma" was a good soul. She came in as we finished supper and told us not to get down to breakfast until nine o'clock, when the dining room closed. She knew we were dead tired.

Dear Matthews is still living (retired like myself) in Randolph, Massachusetts. I haven't seen him in nearly forty years. I know almost the first thing he would say if we were to get together again would be: "Byron, do you remember when we turned ourselves into mules to get back to Forestport from Boonville?"

Editor's Note: Additional material about A. L. Byron-Curtiss can be found in Adirondack Stories of the Black River Country *and* Under an Adirondack Influence.

LONG LAKE

By Roland B. Miller, *North Country Life*, Winter 1954
Reprinted from New York State *Conversationist*

An early preacher-writer, Dr. John Todd, in 1841 noted that the people of Long Lake were neither religious nor ambitious. Their farms were badly neglected, he said, the people preferring to spend their time hunting and fishing without regard to day or season.

Possibly the good doctor was right. But in defense of the people of Long Lake, let it be said that they were subjected to extraordinary temptations, because Long Lake was then, and is now, one of the best places in the State to hunt and fish.

Things change slowly there. Among the settlers who had become established when Dr. Todd took them to task were the Kellers, Kelloggs, Parkers, Austins, Robinsons, Mixes, Sargeants and Burlingames. Descendants of all but the last two are still in the community. Leslie Palmer, well known guide and son of the Si Palmer who with Mitchell Sabattis was a progenitor of the guide-boat, is still living there. And there are still Plumleys in Long Lake, descendants of Joel Plumley, who in 1830 established himself as the first white settler in the town.

1947 fishing party unloading gear at Plumley's Point House dock before the sporting camp and land was acquired from Jim and Carl Plumley by New York State. *Courtesy Albert Smith*

Cartographers place Long Lake in the heart of the Adirondack Mountains; the Biological Survey includes it in the Racquette watershed; the U.S. Geological Survey maps cover it with the Long Lake and Santanoni quadrangles. Both the town and the lake of the same name are in Hamilton County.

A widened, somewhat deepened stretch of the Racquette River, 1,630 feet above sea level, the lake is one of the longest in northern New York, extending from Deerland at the southern extremity 14 miles northeast into the very heart of the wilderness. Altogether, the waters cover 6.14 square miles or 3,929 acres.

An early survey put all but the extreme upper end of the lake in the Totten and Crossfield Purchase, Townships 21 and 22. By 1786 both townships had come into the hands of Theophilus Anthony, probably the first New Yorker to spend his summers in the area and still commemorated by three small ponds named for him west of the lake and back of Buck Mountain.

Lean-tos along Long Lake provide shelter for a variety of outdoor enthusiasts.
Courtesy Albert Smith

By 1844 there were eighteen families and about 100 people in the village of Long Lake, making it the largest town on any lake in the section. Its rapid growth was due largely to glowing accounts circulated by land speculators, who advertised the area as wonderful farm land with a solid understratum of iron ore. Land sold for from one to three dollars an acre. Highways and railroads were promised; the highways came in time (routes 10 and 28 now join there), but the nearest rail stations are at Tupper Lake and North Creek.

The village has grown up on both sides of a narrows in the lake. The two settlements were first connected by a cable-operated ferry, replaced in 1870 by a floating bridge. Later a suspension bridge was built, which was then the longest single span in the State, but this in turn was replaced a few years ago by the present fill and short bridge. The settlements, so connected, made no apologies for their past; besides Dr. Todd's poor opinion of the early inhabitants, there are the descriptive names applied to the two segments of the town by a peddler who had the misfortune to deal with the natives. The part that is now the main village he called "Gougeville," while that on the west bank he termed Kickerville." Walker Road is still proudly called "Kickerville Road" by the townspeople.

The first hotel in the vicinity was the Sagamore, built in 1885, burned in 1889, rebuilt immediately. It was the largest and most modern in its day, and many an expedition into the wilderness began and ended there. A smaller, but still well-known hostel is the Long Lake Hotel, which in the early days furnished guides and stocked all kinds of supplies and provisions for the surrounding territory.

An important link in the Fulton Chain, Long Lake has a special attraction for canoeists, many of whom make the famous trip through the Racquette River to Tupper or Saranac Lake. All along this route are lean-tos and campgrounds operated by this Department and used each year by vacationists from all over the world.

Some prefer the trip up Cold River from the outlet at the north end of the lake. This trip brings one into a region known only by a few hardy hunters and trappers, a region little changed since its shady trails were

Indian highways and its granite cliffs looked down on the British troops pushing a road from Champlain to the Great Lakes. Today the mail boat in summer gives visitors a view of the outer fringe of this wilderness and the big estates that dot the shores. (Whitney Park, comprising 96,000 acres with about 65,000 acres in forest lands, is in the Town of Long Lake.) This wilderness, forest clad, reaches down to the very shores of the lake, and in the background are the State's mountain giants—Marcy, Whiteface, and the Seward Range.

Fishermen find that Long Lake offers a great variety of sport. Natives seem to feel that fishing for great northern pike is the principal attraction, and they spend a good deal of time catching them around the marsh near the middle of the lake. Visitors are inclined to favor the smallmouth bass which congregate near the inlet and outlet. Perch and bullheads are also taken in good quantities, and in addition there are the common and red-bellied sunfish and an occasional trout, whitefish, walleye, or landlocked salmon.

Time was when Long Lake was one of the best in the Adirondacks for native trout. That was before the introduction of pike, perch and smallmouths. But the establishment of these species was not alone responsible for the decline of the trout; lumbering and milling operations at the head of the lake, with the attendant practice of dumping of waste materials into the water, also played a part.

Nor do lake trout thrive here.

Because the lake is a shallow one (the deepest spot found by the Biological Survey was 45 feet), the oxygen content is too low for this species. For reasons best known to themselves, walleyes will not stick around either; they were stocked at one time, but without stopping to ask the way they departed for Tupper Lake.

When it comes to hunting—the other vice with which Dr. Todd said the townspeople were afflicted—Long Lake is still a mecca for sportsmen. More bear were killed in Hamilton County last fall than in any other in the State, and Hamilton is always right up at the top in reported deer take. The small game hunter will find plenty of grouse and rabbits and perhaps an occasional duck, although the lake is not on the main waterfowl flyway. Woodcock, although present in considerable numbers early in the fall, are usually driven south early by a good frost.

Today the Long Lake Improvement Club, a combination chamber of commerce and fish and game club, promulgates the advantages of the lake for vacationers. It boasts of its sandy beaches, tennis courts, bridle paths, golfing, and other diversions calculated to revolve Dr. Todd in his grave. Also of woodland trails and mountains—Mt. Sabattis, overlooking the village and named after the guide; Owlshead to the southwest, 2,780 feet high with a fire tower on top; Kempshall, 3,366 feet, with a fire tower from which you can survey the High Peak Country and also the Green Mountains in Vermont. What with all this altitude and pure air, the Improvement Club claims you don't have to be a sportsman to enjoy Long Lake; you can be just any hay fever sneezer.

What the Club does not mention is what it has not done; it has not spoiled Long Lake. The town's homes and camps and businesses do not stand shoulder to shoulder, and the hand of commercialism rests lightly there. That's one reason why permanent residents believe it's the most beautiful and unspoiled spot in the Adirondacks.

A great many persons other than the permanent residents will concede this.

ABOUT LAKE GEORGE, THE CROWN JEWEL

Developed by Mary L. Thomas, inspired from material that appeared in *North Country Life*, Spring 1948 and *York State Tradition*, Summer 1963

Some two hundred and thirty miles due north of New York City, at the southeast base of the Adirondack Mountains, lies Lake George, a lake which has few serious rivals among American inland waters when it comes to a question of natural beauty, historical association, and legends. An 1880 survey showed it to be about 36 miles long, dotted with 220 islands. Later surveys put the number of islands at 395, the lake's length at 32.2 miles, and its width varying from one to three miles. Depths of 200 feet have been measured.

All along the narrows the shores rise abruptly from the lake level of 322 feet, often with no intervening terraces, to heights of 2,500 feet and more, and on Black Mountain to 2,665 feet. These extensive mountain wildernesses hold scores of smaller lakes and ponds within their lofty, wooded valleys, some of which are seldom explored.

Most of the islands are cloaked with cedar, oak, Norway spruce and white pine, a few blueberry and wild raspberry bushes, and some unusual species of wildflowers. Each spring, the Lake George Association erects hundreds of warning spindles at dangerous shoals. Practically all these shoals and ledges are of solid granite and are disastrous to keels and propellers. Some are barely awash—mere resting places for grey and white gulls to preen and gossip during summer days.

Hotel Champlain at Bluff Point was a rival to the great first Fort William Henry Hotel at the head of Lake George. *Photo S. R. Stoddard. Courtesy Special Collections, Feinberg Library, SUNY College at Plattsburgh*

Hulett's Landing, Lake George. Patron's luggage being moved over a boardwalk. Many clienteles preferred housing in the cottages, which formed a separate resort community in close proximity to the New Hulett House and lake. The resort hotel was located at Bosom Bay. *Courtesy of the Mailtland C. DeSormo Collection*

Lake George was originally called Andia-ta-roc-te by the Iroquois. In 1646, it was christened Lac du Saint Sacrement (Lake of the Blessed Sacrement) by the French priest, Father Isaac Jogues, who claimed it as a French colonial possession. It remained under French control until the autumn of 1755, when British forces led by Sir William Johnson and their Iroquois allies defeated the French and renamed the lake after King George II. In *The Last of the Mohicans*, James Fenimore Cooper referred to it as "Horicon," after a regional native tribe, but the name never stuck. Some early settlers called it "Glimmer Glass."[1] Today, while it is most commonly called Lake George, it also goes by the nickname "Queen of American Waters."

Lake George, which lies on the direct land route between Albany, New York and Montreal, Canada, was an important route in warfare among native tribes long before Europeans arrived. Its key military role continued through the French and Indian War and until the end of the Revolutionary War. Fort William Henry, Fort George, and Fort Gage all stood on its shores. If the rocks could speak, they would tell of much bloodshed.

A Native American Legend. A lot of legends and folklore are associated with Lake George. One native legend relates the story of a lovely maiden taken prisoner in a Mohican raid. The Mohican chief immediately fell in love with her and wanted to marry her. This distressed the women, who had already chosen a Mohican bride for him. The next time he was gone, the women tied the prisoner to a stake, piled wood and brush around her, and lit a fire. Suddenly a flaming figure flew through the camp, rescued the girl, sprang onto a large stone and soared away. The young chief never returned, and each year thereafter one of the tribe's warriors was inexplicably killed by a being that shone like fire and left his victim lying across the same big stone the maiden's rescuer had leapt from. Legend says the footprints of the fiery warrior and the blood stains of the victims can still be seen on the stone.

Diamond Island. In 1777, General Burgoyne used the island as a supply base. Fallen trees had blocked both Wood Creek and the military road that led to Fort Edward, thus cutting off Burgoyne's usual supply route. During the three weeks it took for his army to clear the way to Fort Edward, his supplies came from Fort Ticonderoga across the four-mile portage to the foot of Lake George, then up the lake to Diamond Island. The route continued to the head of Lake George and down Johnson's 1775 military road to the Hudson River at Fort Edward. Burgoyne and his army arrived at Fort Edward on the 30th of July, and the supply route remained until his surrender at Saratoga on October 17, 1777.

Diamond Island Legends. While presumably named "Diamond" for the fine quartz crystals found on it, the island was once home to an enormous population of rattlesnakes. A hog farmer on the western shore of the lake had sold several hogs to a farmer who lived on the eastern shore. He planned to transport the hogs by boat, but near Diamond Island the boat became unbalanced and capsized. The hogs swam to the island, and the farmer back home. He thought the hogs were lost, killed by the rattlesnakes for sure. Later the farmer's son and a friend put on high

Mountain summits surrounding Lake George made scenic destinations for hikers like Mrs. Shaughnessy. *Courtesy George Shaughnessy*

boots and decided to determine the hogs' fate. They were surprised to see only one rattlesnake—and about twenty hogs! When some of the hogs were butchered, there were rattlesnakes in their stomachs. When the hogs were brought home, one of the sows had babies, and each piglet, so the story goes, was born with a set of rattles on its tail!

Another story tells that Friends Point on Diamond Island is so-named because two scouting parties, assuming those they were tracking to be the enemy, realized just before firing on each other that they were in fact friends.

A Sabbath Day Point Story. A settler built a log house on Sabbath Day Point around 1800. He took his corn to Bolton to be ground into cornmeal. One day he ran out of cornmeal, but the lake had frozen over, so he couldn't take his corn by boat. He got out his cutter, but thought it best not to risk the ice supporting a horse. Instead, he loaded a few bags of corn and a jug of whiskey to keep him warm, fashioned a sail for the cutter, and started off across the ice, using a pitchfork as a rudder.

The wind carried him swiftly over the slippery ice. Deciding he wanted a drink, he grabbed the jug and pulled the corncob plug out with his teeth. He had taken his hand off his rudimentary rudder, and, his mind on the drink he was looking forward to, didn't realize he was headed rapidly for one of the islands. He looked up and gulped, nearly choking on the corncob as his cutter slid up on the island and stopped. The man, his sacks of corn, and his jug of whiskey kept going, landing in a snow bank. He had held onto the jug, but it was empty. It's said that the foul language he spouted was so loud it could be clearly heard from shore to shore.

Hunting Stories. As You Were is an island near Tongue Mountain. It's said that a former soldier was out hunting and saw a deer running up ahead of him. Someone had told him a deer would stop in its tracks if he bleated like a deer. The old soldier got confused, and instead he commanded "as you were," military language that means the same as "at ease." Apparently the deer understood because it stopped and the hunter promptly shot it. The island has been called "As You Were" ever since then.

Deer's Leap Mountain is a perpendicular rock cliff on the west shore of Lake George. Over the years, boulders, rocks, and dead trees have fallen from the cliff's surface and they lie at the bottom in a jagged collection. The story of how it got its name comes from a hunting incident. Some men were chasing a deer with their dogs, and the dogs chased the buck over the cliff, where it landed on the pile of jagged rocks and dead trees and died.

Steamboats on the Lake. Steamboat traffic in America—both passenger and freight business—grew rapidly in the decades before the Civil War. So too did both economic and human losses due to accidents. Most steamboats met their end because of boiler explosions and fires.

In the early history of New York, James Caldwell owned most of the land in Caldwell Township (now Lake George village). He is best known for building the first steamboat on the lake, launched in 1817. It had a brick smokestack and was quite slow, but on a good day could chug from one end of the lake to the other. The *Caldwell* operated for four seasons, was once struck by lightning, and caught fire and burned at its dock in 1821.

The *Mountaineer*, completed in 1824, was the next Lake George steamboat. She had a comparatively long life for a steamboat, running until about 1838. The *William Caldwell*, which followed, was deemed unsafe in 1848. Two years later, the *John Jay* was launched, but only ran for six years before a fire destroyed the tiller ropes and caused the ship to wreck on rocks. Reports indicate that five women and one man drowned. The engine and oilers from the *John Jay* were used to build the *Minne-ha-ha* in 1857.

The *Horicon* was a side-wheel steamer, 203 feet long and 52 feet wide. It could carry 1,000 passengers and go twenty miles an hour. Another side-wheel steamer, the *Ticonderoga*, hit the waters of Lake George in 1883. The *Ticonderoga* departed from Baldwin at 7:30 AM, stopped at the main landings and arrived at Caldwell in time for the midday trains that went south. The fare for a trip the length of Lake George was $1.50 and passengers who returned the same day they paid no additional fare.

The *Island Queen* was short-lived, launched in 1890 and destroyed by fire two years later. Other steamboats that ran regular schedules on Lake George were the *Mohican*, the *Sagamore*, the *Mohican II* and the *Horicon II*.

The Sea Serpent. Maps from the Middle Ages showed the locations of sea serpents—areas to be avoided. In 1904, people who lived on Lake George and in the surrounding countryside were awe-struck when they heard about "the monster of Lake George." Several people reported seeing a gigantic and horrific reptilian creature coming up out of Lake George at around dusk. It reportedly had huge jaws and malevolent eyes that looked right at those who sighted it before sinking back down into the water. Sometimes the story came from lovers out for a romantic canoe paddle. Other times people claimed the story came from someone who had had a few too many drinks. There were so many reports, though, that the story took on a life of its own.

When it became a big enough story to be newsworthy, a reporter investigated the waters where the beast had been seen. He was astonished to see the water around his boat and beyond foaming, and even more amazed when the creature towered over him, gnashing its jaws and glaring at him before it submerged. After the reporter caught his breath, he hurried to the nearest telegraph office to report his sighting to his newspaper and to several scientific associations.

Finally, the sightings were explained. It seemed that a president of the National Academy of Design had decided to pull a prank on the residents of Lake George. He and an engineer had created the monster and the apparatus that would raise and lower it. The secret of the sea serpent was revealed, but not before those who were in the know had enjoyed many laughs.

Lumbering. The lumber industry in the Adirondacks, including around Lake George, began after the Revolutionary War ended. It was at this time that settlers began arriving in the Lake George area. Lumber mills were set up, using water to power them. Virgin timber that had stood for hundreds of years came down.

The trees in the Lake George area were transported to the mills using various methods, depending on the time of year. When the ice was thick enough on the lake, the timbers were drawn by teams of oxen or horses to Caldwell and then to the mills in Glens Falls. When the ice was out, logs were rafted north on Lake George, then hauled to Lake Champlain, where they were taken either north or south.

Tourism Begins—and Flourishes. In 1848, a plank road was laid from Glens Falls to Caldwell. That connected the Hudson River, and thousands of people in downstate New York, to Lake George. Trains brought them to Glens Falls, and colorful red stagecoaches met them and brought them to Caldwell, where they stopped at a tavern built in 1759, the

Bathers tent camping in the vicinity of Lake George. *Courtesy Author's collection*

Halfway House. It had been built originally as a stopover for settlers and lumbermen. Over the years it was modernized and expanded, and until 1946, when it was destroyed by fire, it was a favorite place of many famous people who were on their way to or from their summer homes on Lake George.

By 1882 the railroad had built a spur into Caldwell, which became Lake George village in 1903. The region had become one of the greatest vacation spots in America. "Millionaires' Row" was a stretch of Lake Shore Drive on the west side of the lake. Wealthy people built their summer homes here—twenty-bedroom "cottages" on hundreds of acres of wilderness along the lakeshore. Entrepreneurs built grand hotels. The Fort William Henry Hotel, the Sagamore and other hotels became summer destinations for tourists not lucky enough to have friends with a private home on the lake.

As economic woes faced the country in the 1930s and the income tax was introduced, the Millionaires' Row mansions became less sustainable. By the 1950s, Lake George had become extremely attractive, and now affordable, to the middle class.

Of the many islands in the lake, 119 are state-owned and supervised by the Conservation Department. They stretch the length of the lake, each marked by a sign reading "State Land." Many boast lean-to shelters for campers and other facilities including water, tables, benches and fireplaces. In addition there are public campsites at Lake George Battleground, one-quarter mile south of Lake George village, and at Heartstone, on the Bolton Road, which branches off Route 9 just north of the village.

Hotels, resorts, theme parks and other attractions fill the vacation needs of average people, who still marvel at the same lake Thomas Jefferson described as "without comparison, the most beautiful water I ever saw; formed by a contour of mountains into a basin…finely interspersed with islands, its water limpid as crystal, and the mountainsides covered with rich groves."

FOOTNOTE: 1. The author based this comment on the fact that some of the old settlers used to speak of the lake as the "Glimmer Glass."

THIS IS TUPPER

Author unknown, *North Country Life*, Fall 1955

Mr. Tupper, a surveyor whose first name has never been discovered, laid the brass-bound transit with tender care among his other belongings in the middle of the light canoe. He straightened, and looking around once more at the prodigious virgin forest surrounding the lake, he felt a long glow of satisfaction; another parcel of the Macomb Purchase had been surveyed. The famous Macomb Purchase comprised nearly four million acres sold by the state to Alexander Macomb in 1791 for about 16 cents an acre.

Tradition has it that when Tupper surveyed the region, he became lost, and as the story says, nearly left his bones here as well as his name. As Tupper dropped into the canoe and paddled off, he left behind at the stump-pocked clearing one important thing: a name that would come to mean many different things to many different people.

But Tupper was not the first white man to pass through this region. The first one, to use the exact words of Louis Simmons, village historian and editor of the *Tupper Lake Free Press*, "was quite a distinguished individual, but he didn't linger long in these parts. Back in May of 1776, when the American Revolution was just warming up, Sir John Johnson, son of Sir William Johnson, the King's superintendent of Indian Affairs in North America, was suspected of disloyalty by the colonists. Colonel Dayton was dispatched with a force of soldiers to arrest him at Johnstown. Warned by Tory friends, Sir John 'lit out' for Montreal on the double, accompanied by a number of his followers and retainers and a band of Indian warriors. Threading the pathless wilderness via Racquette Lake, Long Lake and down the Racquette River, they paddled through Tupper Lake, finally reaching the St. Lawrence after nineteen days of intense hardship and suffering."

The first settler, Michael Cole, came in 1849, but it was near the end of the century before there were many permanent settlers in the Tupper Lake area. Itinerant hunters, trappers, guides, and loggers knew the region, but it was the completion of wilderness speculator John Hurd's railroad from Moira to Tupper Lake in 1890 that brought an influx of permanent settlers.

To John Hurd, the region meant riches for the taking. He envisioned in Tupper a teeming railway terminal with "sports" coming in and lumber going out. He dreamed of the biggest lumber mill in the state and of a lake choked with logs from the surrounding mountains. His dreams came true at least in part when the first train rolled in July 1, 1890. Overnight, Tupper Lake Village, a tiny tot of the wilderness, was swept violently through a short adolescence to emerge in full manhood, a delinquent bully looking for trouble.

In 1889 the Tupper area had only a few scattered permanent families, but by 1892, when noses were counted for the first time in the town of Altamont, the population was 1,051. "The growth was marvelously rapid for a wilderness town," Seaver notes in his *History of Franklin County*. "Industries were founded stores established, and hotels opened literally overnight."

Seaver also says, "Life was raw and rough at first. The railroad and the lumber interests imported labor, and the varieties were many, without all being attractive." Donaldson, another Adirondack historian, says that the Tupper Lake of 1890 had "all the outward attributes and inner aspects of a western frontier town."

So it went for nine years, with Tupper a place where murder was committed in the stable to save cleaning up the barroom floor. New buildings went up with no more shape than a 'possum, and streets seemed to emulate the irregular shore of the lake—a lake that looks like a multi-legged, humpbacked gargoyle with a choke collar on, caught in mid-air leaping from St. Lawrence to Franklin County, rocky island spines erect down its twisted backbone.

Then one pleasant July evening in 1899 someone (probably) went to sleep with a live stogie, and most of the town burned down. It may have been a blessing, for this time when the streets were laid out, the man who did it was sober and the result was the neat little industrial center of today.

The Village of Tupper Lake nestles around the shore of Racquette Pond thru which the wild and winding Racquette River flows after picking up the waters of Lake Simond and Big Tupper Lake as it continues north, seeking its way eventually to the St. Lawrence. The area is a scenic wonderland, yet unspoiled by man. "Tupper symbolizes everything that's Adirondack and untamed and beautiful," wrote J.D. Bulger in the New York State *Conservationist.*

Tupper's development as a lumber town kept the Racquette River choked with logs for the lumbermen down at Potsdam. Even today Tupper should be "Tummber" to rhyme with lumber, for that's still the main resource. In support of this fact, the wood jacks gather here once a year for a festival called Lumbermen's Field Days, featuring, besides the chopping contests, a parade and an interesting display of the latest tools for timbering.

Excluding this occasion, Tupper has pretty well escaped publicity. Odd, because the climate is akin to that of Saranac or Placid, and geographically Tupper is located at the center pearl of the famous resort

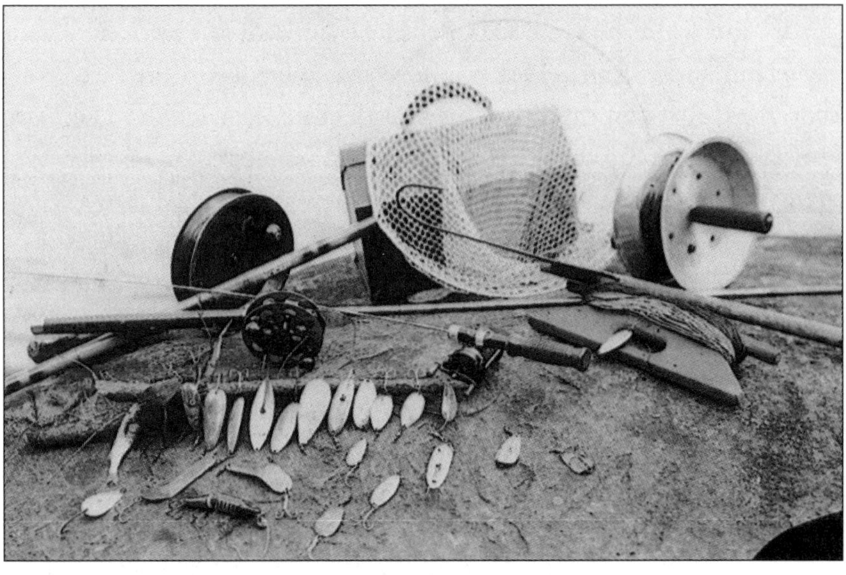

As Adirondack water warms, the bass settle into deeper lodgings, and during July and August—and until the frosts of September chill the water—they stay near spring-holes and tributaries of rivers. *Courtesy Edward Blankman (The Lloyd Blankman Collection)*

string. Maybe the inhabitants, more business-minded than publicity-conscious, like anonymity. Anyway, nobody is going to cram Tupper down your throat; you've got to discover it for yourself.

Today Tupper Lake is a pleasant little village with attractive stores, modern schools and churches, and about 6,000 friendly people. Its inviting stores comprise a lively and up-to-date shopping center for residents of the southwest corner of Franklin County, the southeast corner of St. Lawrence County, and the northern part of Hamilton County.

A unique feature exists in the fact that there are four post offices located in what one usually thinks of as being Tupper Lake village. How one of these came into being comprises an interesting story involving the famous Tupper Lake guide, Mart Moody. Much has been written about Mart Moody, who is famous for his story telling, but we believe this story, which relates how the Moody post office (located on Tupper Lake, two miles from the heart of Tupper Lake village) came into being has never before been recorded.

In 1865 Mart Moody brought his young bride to Tupper Lake and shortly afterwards built a hotel on the lakeshore. About 1887, President Cleveland and Alton B. Parker, afterwards a justice of the New York Supreme Court and candidate for president in 1904 against Theodore Roosevelt, came through by boat from the Saranac region on their way to the Fulton Chain. They stopped with their guides at Moody's hotel, the Mt. Morris House, intending to stay only one night. But President Cleveland's Scotch induced the story telling mood in Uncle Mart, and Cleveland so enjoyed listening to his tales that the party remained three nights. Upon Cleveland's return to Washington, he made Moody's hotel a fourth-class post office and appointed Mart Moody postmaster as a token of his appreciation for Moody's hospitality.

President Cleveland, before leaving Moody, invited him to come to Washington, an invitation which Moody later accepted (accompanied by William Platt Ketcham of New York, who had a camp on the lake and whose widow still spends her summers here). The story is told that when Moody returned from Washington, he was asked to relate the events of his trip.

"What was Mrs. Cleveland like?" was one of the questions put to him.

"Well, you see, it was Monday," Moody answered, "and Mrs. Cleveland was busy washing, so I didn't see her."

In 1914, Parker and his grandson repeated the trip that Parker had made with President Cleveland. He stayed again at the Mt. Morris House. By this time, however, it was no longer Moody's hotel. Moody had sold it to Jabez D. Alexander, who in turn had sold it to his son, Percy H. Alexander. On this occasion the story of the creation of the Moody post office was related by Parker to Mrs. Percy Alexander, who in turn related the story to us. Old Mt. Morris House registers, now in the possession of the Alexanders, show the signatures of Cleveland and Parker, though they are not dated. Parker's signature appears again on the register under the date of August 29, 1914.

You'll discover that Tupper is a sort of vicinity, and "going to Tupper" means a visit to the region that contains Big Tupper Lake, Tupper Lake village, a stretch of the Raquette River, Simon Pond, Raquette Pond, and maybe even Piercefield Flow, which is separated from the rest by a small dam.

Several approaches may be used. A great many still use the best approach that was available to Mr. Tupper; they go by canoe, terminating here the 102-mile journey through the Fulton Chain of Lakes. A lot more come up by N.Y.C.R.R. and still more by Route 3.

Should you run up Route 10 from Blue Mountain way, you'll see that Tupper has really entered the motoring public's eye, judging by the motels and cabins huddled along the east shore. The west shore is something else again; the state owns a sizeable segment of this, and you'll find an excellent tent site at Bridge Brook Bay if you've got a boat to go across.

In a boat rented from a livery or in your own canoe, you can take some really wonderful side trips out of this least-populated large lake in the Adirondacks. One such trip might be up the Racquette River, which, if you're reasonably careful in the rocky channels, is navigable with an outboard for 26 miles up to Racquette Falls. Like most of Tupper's tributaries, the Racquette is good fishing, especially good trolling for Northerns for the first eight miles up to Trombley's. If you prefer trout fishing, you'll find the Bog River a sizeable stream with sizeable brookies. Where this river enters the lake is a good spot for walleyes, and almost anywhere on the rocky shore is a good place for small-mouth bass.

Tupper Lake has never loudly tooted its horn as a summer resort, but vacationers are learning that it has much to offer. The numerous lakes and streams provide excellent fishing, swimming and boating, and Tupper is proud of its 18-hole championship golf course overlooking Big Tupper Lake. To quote from the *Conservationist*: “Camping at this hub means you can boat into a different spoke of the wheel every day. You can hunt here with access to a large block of State land. You have an all-weather place to fish, for when it’s a little rough on the seven mile lake, U.S.G.S. maps will guide you into many miles of still holes, some of which don’t see a plug or spoon from one year to the next. There are several miles of good trails in the vicinity, and a view from the top of Mt. Morris will register with indelible ink in your memory book.”

So this is Tupper Lake, endowed by the Creator with perhaps more than its share of natural beauty—a friendly, pleasant, happy place to spend a day, a week, or a lifetime.

JAY’S 150 YEARS

By Fred Torrance, *North Country Life*, Fall 1948

This year, 1948, marks the 150th anniversary of the formation of the Town of Jay, now one of the eighteen towns of Essex County.

The exact date of its birth was January 26, 1798, when the Legislature of the State of New York brought it into being; but the hardy pioneers of the AuSable Valley had been impregnated with the idea since and before the meeting at what was then called “Mallory’s Bush” on March 12, 1797. At that meeting, the following notice was unanimously adopted:

> *Notice is hereby given that the inhabitants of Mallory’s Bush, in the town of Willsborough, North West district, have called a*

meeting and unanimously agreed to make application to the town of Willsborough to be set off and to be incorporated into a town by themselves, and have chosen John Cochran, Jun. to attend the annual meeting, at Willsborough, to do said business of the application. The boundaries of said Town so to be set off are as follows: Beginning where the military line intercepts the south of Willsborough, then north to the 12 mile tree, then north 45 degrees east to the south line of Peru, then west to the south west corner of said Peru, or west line of Clinton County, then south to the north west corner of Crownpoint, then east to the place of beginning.

Dated at Mallory's Bush the 12th of March 1797.
(Signed) Ely Stone, Clerk; Daniel Hoskins, John W. Southmayd, John Cochran, Jun., Ezekiel Lockwood

At the time of organization, the territory comprising the Town of Jay formed a part of Clinton County. Upon the formation of Essex County in 1799, however, it became one of the four original towns—namely, Crown Point, Willsboro, Jay, and Elizabethtown.

The town was named in honor of John Jay, governor of the state at that time, and the first town meeting was held at the residence of John W. Southmayd about half way between the present hamlets of Jay and Upper Jay on the first Tuesday in April, 1798.

The officers elected at that first meeting were Elisha Bingham, supervisor; Ely Stone, town clerk; Leonard Owen, John W. Southmayd, and Ezekiel Lockwood, commissioners of highway; Zenas Graves, David Clemens, and John Dunlap, assessors. Southmayd and Lockwood also acted as poor masters.

As originally formed, the town comprised not only its present territory but all of the present towns of Wilmington and St. Armand and a part of the towns of Keene, North Elba, Chesterfield, and Elizabethtown in Essex County besides a part of what is now Franklin County.

Just when the first settlers came into the valley of the Great River AuSable in the vicinity of the Town of Jay is presently uncertain, but it is likely that it followed soon after, or perhaps was a continuance or extension of the settlement of the Town of Peru in Clinton County. Peru was organized as a town in 1792.

This assumption is based on the fact that several of the moving spirits—John Cochran, Jr., Ezekiel Lockwood, John Douglas, Levi Arnold, Reverend Solomon Brown, and several others—were former residents of Peru and some of them active in the organization of that town. Furthermore, the Jay Baptist Church was in existence before 1798, when it applied to be set apart from the Peru church. If this is correct, then the first settlers may have arrived shortly after 1790.

In 1794, Zephaniah Platt, after whom Plattsburgh was named, and Platt Rogers received a grant of 3,100 acres of land which included the falls at Jay and much of the arable land along the river south toward Upper Jay. But even before this, settlers had squatted on free unappropriated lands belonging to the state, and in this same year Nathaniel Mallory and 34 of the settlers petitioned the Legislature for the protection of their rights.

Nathaniel Mallory may have been established at the falls in Jay when the Platts arrived. In 1795 he purchased from them land which included the falls. The deed recites that the property is located in "Mallory's Bush," being the property "on which he now liveth." It appears that even then it was recognized and known as "Mallory's Bush."

Mallory erected mills at the falls in Jay, which probably included a sawmill, grist mill, blacksmith shop, tannery, and perhaps a small forge. He was operating mills at this point in 1797, as mentioned in a road survey, and was the first industrialist in the town. Mallory's career, however, as a businessman and manufacturer was of short duration, for in 1804 John Purmort acquired title to the 35 acres on which the mills were located. Mallory was active in civic affairs, however, for a number of years after, acting as Justice of the Peace and at times as one of the assistant justices of the Essex County Court of Common Pleas.

About 1809 Purmort began the manufacture of iron and continued to do an extensive manufacturing and mercantile business in Jay until the freshet of 1856 practically wiped out the whole plant. Business was not resumed except to continue a store and grist mill, which was conducted by members of the family until the early 1860s.

In 1853 and 1854 the business was assessed to James H. Purmort & Co. It included a store, sawmill, grist mill, clothing works, tannery, forge, blacksmith shop, wheelwright shop, and seventeen dwellings.

In 1864 the property was acquired by the J. & J. Rogers Iron Company. New buildings were constructed and the whole plant, except the company store, was relocated on the east side of the river. It included, as time went on, a forge of six fires, grist mill, carpenter shop, blacksmith shop, and brick yard. The store, the blacksmith shop, and the pump house—all made of native brick—are still standing near the old covered bridge.

A thriving business was carried on until about 1892, when a business recession caused the closing of the plant at Jay, and for the first time in its nearly 100 years of existence Jay became, for a time, a deserted village.

The section now known as Upper Jay was settled by some of the Mallory petitioners at about the same time as Jay. The hamlet itself is located

Typical early touring car that brought tourists into the Adirondacks.
Courtesy Bill Zullo, Hamilton County Historian

in Lots 10 and 11 of Mallory's Grant. David Clemens and Larned Lamb were living there before 1795, and William and Russell Jones came shortly after, as did also the Williams and Wells families. Jesse Toby acquired Lot 10 in 1800 and operated a grist mill near the site of the present bridge. The early settlers of this section were largely engaged in producing ashes for the manufacture of potash and pearl ash, which had a ready sale in those days, one of the few pioneer products for which cash could be obtained.

Stickney Bridge-North Jay was another section included in Mallory's Grant which was settled before 1795. A post office called Jayville was established near Stickney Bridge. The first road in the town was laid out by the Town of Willsboro in 1797, extending along the river from a point near the present bridge to the brook in Upper Jay.

AuSable Forks was last to develop. It is possible and probable that some parts of the village were occupied by squatters before the survey of Maul's Patent, in which it lies, in 1800. But if so, there is no evidence of any considerable settlement or activity, although tradition indicates that there was a block house near the forks of the river in early times. Zephaniah Palmer was closely associated with the settlement of the Forks. It is said that he was an eccentric individual spending most of his time exploring the surrounding country. He was one of Mallory's petitioners in 1795, but did not receive title to his land from the state. He was the discoverer and owner of Palmer Hill Ore Mine. He also owned a half-interest in Lot 161 of Maul's Patent, which includes Main Street and the easterly part of AuSable Forks village. This he sold to Burt and Vanderwarker in 1826, excepting and reserving a sawmill. How long Palmer conducted the sawmill before 1826 and the size and nature of the settlement at that time is yet a matter of conjecture.

It is known that Isaac Ferris had a sawmill on the brook at the Forks as early as 1806, but soon afterwards removed to the vicinity of Saranac Hollow and with his sons operated a mill on True Brook.

The real history of AuSable Forks begins with the advent of George M. Burt and Isaac Vanderwarker in 1826, both of whom came from

Northumberland, Saratoga County. Their property, purchased from Palmer, included title to a mill site on the west branch.

They not only were ambitious and industrious, but possessed considerable business ability. They lived in a double house made of logs back of the present George Block and first operated a sawmill. The business grew rapidly. Their assessment in 1827, one year after the purchase, showed 145 acres at $1,800. In 1828 it showed 192 acres valued at $5,000. In 1845 George M. Burt personally was assessed two forges, a grist mill and two houses. The firm of Burt and Vanderwarker was assessed a sawmill and seven houses.

Isaac Vanderwarker was the first postmaster at AuSable Forks, supervisor of the Town of Jay in 1830 and 1831, and a member of the Assembly in 1832.

Burt built the first hotel at the Forks on the site of the present George Block and a bridge across the west branch at Main Street. Ultimately, the property was acquired by the J. & J. Rogers Iron Company.

This firm was comprised principally of James and John Rogers, who came from Warren County about 1832 and engaged in the iron business at Black Brook. Shortly after, about 1836 or 1837, they took over the property of the AuSable Iron Company, consisting chiefly of a rolling mill at AuSable Forks (in which James Rogers was previously interested) and opened business at AuSable Forks, James taking up his residence there and John remaining in Black Brook.

The business grew and prospered. A forge, rolling mill, company store, furnace, nail factory, and necessary shops and outbuildings were added to make a well-integrated and efficiently working plant.

The Burt-Vanderwarker interests were absorbed and all welded into one prosperous business under the able management of the Rogers family. In 1864, as previously stated, the company acquired the Purmort interests at Jay.

Ore from the Palmer Hill mine was used in the forges in all three places—Black Brook, AuSable Forks, and Jay. The separator was located on Palmer Brook in the present town of Black Brook, Clinton County.

In about 1892 the Rogers Company was reorganized, the old iron business was discontinued, and since then it has produced a high grade of pulp and paper in its mills at AuSable Forks.

Space does not permit a recital of the story of the J. & J. Rogers Company from that time to the present, a period of over eighty years, or of the personnel directing it, but suffice to say that for all this time it has occupied a most important place in the economy of the entire valley of AuSable.

CHATEAUGAY—OLDEST TOWN IN FRANKLIN COUNTY

By Glyndon Cole, *North Country Life*, Summer 1949

The oldest town in Franklin County—Chateaugay—passes its 150th milestone in 1949. It was in 1799 that Chateaugay was erected as a town in Clinton County. At first it was made up of four townships of the Old Military Tract. In 1802, however, it included nearly all of what now comprises Franklin County and also the town of St. Armand in Essex County. In subsequent years, as the territory became more populous and other towns were erected, it was whittled down to its present size.

The first settlers were Benjamin Roberts of Vermont and Nathan Beman of Plattsburgh. In 1795 they had assisted in surveying Township No. 7 of the Old Military Tract, had been impressed by the nature of the land, and had decided to make it their home.

In the summer of 1796 Benjamin Roberts set out from Plattsburgh with his family and five hired men. At the time, according to Hough's *History of St. Lawrence and Franklin Counties*, the frontier settlement was Beekmantown, six miles west of Plattsburgh. A mere path had been cut through the dense wilderness to Township No. 7.

Seaver's *Historical Sketches of Franklin County* describes the journey: "A yoke of oxen drawing a sled and a pair of steers were to serve them for transportation, but one of the oxen gave out at Beekmantown, and as much as possible of the party's outfit was then loaded upon the odd ox and the steers, while each of the men 'backed' what he could, and the father toting a child and the mother carrying a babe in her arms, the journey was resumed on foot. The distance remaining to be covered was twenty odd miles, and five and a half days were spent in making it."

During that summer, forty acres were cut and partly cleared a half mile north of the present village of Chateaugay. Nathan Beman made several trips to the new clearing, but did not bring his family until the fall of that year.

Within the first three years a number of other families from Vermont came into the town, purchased land, and made arrangements for making a permanent settlement.

David Mallory, during the second year of the settlement, erected the first grist mill about one and a half miles northwest of the present village. This was built for Nathaniel Platt of Plattsburgh. A sawmill was built the same year near the grist mill.

Indian Point on Upper Chateaugay Lake. Dr. Kellogg discovered important Native American artifacts here in 1894. *Courtesy Special Collections, Feinberg Library, SUNY College at Plattsburgh*

The settlement grew rapidly for several years. During the War of 1812, it was the scene of considerable activity. The inhabitants erected a blockhouse on a commanding elevation on the bank of the Chateaugay River, three miles northwest of the village. It was occupied by troops stationed in the town during the war, and some minor incidents took place along the Canadian border, a few miles to the north. Near the end of the war or soon after, the blockhouse is said to have been burned by someone from Canada.

By the summer of 1949, Chateaugay, a village of about 1800 people, was a trading center for a large surrounding agricultural area. Agriculture in its various forms has always been the backbone of Chateaugay's economic setup. In late years the growing of potatoes had become nearly as great in importance as dairy farming, which has always held the lead.

The two largest industries in the village were based on the dairy farming of the area. The Chateaugay Cooperative Marketing Association, with more than 400 patrons, was one of the largest milk manufacturers and wholesalers in the state. Cheese is one of its chief products [and continues to be in 2014]. Throughout the 1940s the concern grossed an average of $1,500,000 per year.

The Sheffield Farms milk plant, started under the Dawson-Decker Company in 1910, was the home of Sheffield's Evaporated Milk, sold the world over. During 1948-49, the plant commenced the manufacture of a new baby's food known as Formulac.

The New York State Electric and Gas Corporation operated a large plant at a point on the Chateaugay River known as the Chasm, northwest of the village, where electricity for a large portion of northern New York was generated.

The oldest Chateaugay industry was the *Chateaugay Record*, a weekly newspaper published continuously since 1877. The Record Printing and Publishing Company, by 1949, was a co-partnership consisting of William H. Ferrel, Richard J. Peacock, and Russell R. Tolosky.

The village was located on the Rutland Railroad, which ran from Ogdensburg to Boston. Bus service north and south was provided by the

Adirondack Trailways, while the Greyhound Bus Lines furnished east-west service. One of the newest concrete highways in the state, completed in 1948, connected Chateaugay with eastern points.

The creation of a central school district of about forty schools was about to be voted on during the writing of this short history. The erection of a new building to house 1,000 students is contemplated. Maynard Pilling is principal of the present Chateaugay High School, and Dr. John J. Mahoney is president of the Board of Education.

Chateaugay became a mecca for sportsmen since the State Conservation Department began stocking the nearby Chateaugay Lakes and the Chateaugay River with legal size trout. At the end of the 1940s, the pride and joy of Chateaugay, however, was the Chateaugay Ponies, which placed second in 1948 in the Eastern Division of the St. Lawrence Valley Baseball League. The team was sponsored by the Chateaugay Athletic Association.

This brief word-picture of Chateaugay is, of course, incomplete. No attempt was made to record the friendly atmosphere of the town. The neighborly spirit of the people is a part of their heritage from the past. It has no doubt existed...since the days when the town's first settlers found it necessary to cooperate in order to survive.

Editor Cole's Note: North Country Life *is indebted to Richard J. Peacock of the* Chateaugay Record, *for help in preparing this article.*

CHATEAUGAY IN THE 1920s

By Dot Mills, *North Country Life*, Summer 1947

Our town is just a small town, peaceful and quiet; but it has a certain quality of friendliness, a certain charm. It seems unbelievable to the youth of today that at the time they were toddling about, the town was living the most colorful chapter of its history. In the 1920s, prohibition put this small border town on the map. It was a "Bootlegger's Paradise." Money was plentiful and life was good. The only war was the war against liquor.

My actual memories of this era are few. The stories I tell were told to me over and over in later years until the gap between actuality and imagination has overlapped and merged into one. But the atmosphere of the times—that evasive feeling in the air that all was laughter and sunshine and happiness—that feeling was very real to me and gave me a sense of security in my childhood.

This was the decade that hero-worshipped Lindbergh and his "Spirit of St. Louis." Every youngster had his copy of the life of this boy wonder. Planes were scarce in those days, and every time one was lucky enough to see one flying overhead, eyes strained, hoping against hope that he would spot the then-famous identification number, N-X-211, on the wing or tail flap.

This was the "Flapper Era." Over and above political elections, stock market crashes and new advances in the motion picture and in aviation, the "flapper" more than anything or anyone else marked this decade as her own. She is synonymous with short-skirted, waistless dresses, rolled stockings, and sleek shingled hair-do's. She danced herself through endless nights and made famous the "Black Bottom" and the "Charleston." Dancing was an endurance contest. She sang also—gay, catchy tunes like "Mr. Gallagher and Mr. Shean" and "Last Night on the Back Porch." Some of her songs were sweet and sentimental, like "Japanese Sandman" and "Three O'Clock in the Morning," for this flapper was a strange combination of the serious and the light mocking humor.

At this time my father started in business. In 1920 he opened the "People's Cash Market." Every time I enter that store nowadays I think of how it looked twenty years ago.

As you entered the door and to the left, you could always find a huge barrel of Boston soda crackers. To the right, sanitarily protected by isinglass, was an inexhaustible supply of round cheese, a knife conveniently beside it.

I have seen the town's prominent citizens cut a generous slab of cheese, and after supplying themselves with a pocketful of Boston crackers, straddle one of the straight-backed chairs in the rear of the store and settle all civic and national problems in an afternoon.

When one tired of crackers and cheese, the meat block and cleavers were handy, and a slice of cold meat would break the monotony. I was almost grown up before I realized that the cheese and crackers were for sale and that some people actually paid money for them.

Except for one incident, prohibition had little effect on my father's life, but this incident came close to being fatal.

My father kept the store open on Saturday nights until eleven o'clock. Before closing he would stuff his sales money for the day into a little brown hand grip. Carrying that money on a Saturday night in a town of bootleggers and outlaws made my father nervous. He had long since abandoned the sidewalks for the center of the road, where he stated he could "see them coming from both sides."

This particular Saturday night he met a neighbor and, feeling comparatively safe in each other's company, the two men started home, walking as usual in the center of the road. Suddenly the quietness was shattered by the loud rattling of speeding cars and several sharp explosions.

New York State police Troop B about 1925 stopping a car in the Adirondacks.
Courtesy of the Mailtland C. DeSormo Collection

"Backfire?" the neighbor suggested tentatively, moving gingerly out of the way of the approaching vehicles.

But my father rushed past him, shouting excitedly, "Backfire—hell! They're shooting!" And he dashed for the nearest tree.

The neighbor, hesitating only long enough to feel the breeze from a stray bullet, hurriedly found a tree of his own.

For several seconds the two men hugged close to their sanctuaries, but some time later and somewhat shaken, my father arrived home.

After this he discarded his theory that the middle of the road was safer and returned to using the sidewalks, where he said "at least the trees are handy."

It was a mad, gay time—those 1920s. They're gone now, buried by the ever passing years. But still they lived on in memories.

BOOTLEGGERS' PARADISE

By Dorothy LaBelle, *York State Tradition*, Spring 1970

One would be remiss if, in recording a history of the birth and growth of a town, one would neglect a particularly colorful segment of its past.

In the decade following World War I, our country enjoyed unprecedented prosperity. Money was plentiful, and life was good. The only war was the war against liquor.

Bootlegging and hijacking were the rule and not the exception in this border town of Chateaugay. It was the focal point of more than its share of excitement. Thrill-packed midnight rides to deliver a cargo of contrab and liquor from "wet" Canada to the officially "dry" Untied States were commonplace events on the lonely country roads in this territory.

Ingenuity was a prime requisite for the professional bootlegger. It was necessary to route the loaded caravans over back roads and fields to cross Route 11 without detection. From that point on it was comparatively easy to reach a Chateaugay Lake hideaway, where the liquor was picked up by other transportation and carried down state.

In winter the "caravans" consisted of four or five heavy sleighs each drawn by a two-horse team. In the summer it was necessary to switch to large automobiles, usually a heavy Cadillac.

While to an extent traveling was easier by horse and sleigh over snow covered fields and back roads, the load was hard to conceal in the event the Border Patrol caught up with the culprits. The Cadillacs, however, were innocent appearing to the naked eye. Several bottles could be concealed in false roofs and the hollow space between the inside of the car doors and the outer shell.

When hit by a real "Chateaugay Thaw," many North Country roads were made impassable in those days. While some traffickers were discouraged by the weather, others, made of sterner stuff, refused to permit a variable thing like the weather to interfere with their profitable ventures.

One group of smugglers cannot understand to this day how they were trailed to their hideaway. They find it hard to believe that, cagey as they were, a pair of horses outwitted them. The smugglers, carrying heavy

New York State Police Troop B about 1925. *Courtesy of the Mailtland C. DeSormo Collection*

loads on five horse-drawn sleighs, covered their trail carefully after one load had been seized by the Custom Patrol on the Lost Nation Road. Drifting snow helped to obliterate their tracks on the lone journey to a lumber camp hideaway across Upper Chateaugay Lake. The bootleggers had reason to believe that they had successfully eluded their pursuers.

Consequently, they were an amazed and crestfallen group when the Border Patrol rode into camp with the captured team and relieved them of their ill-gotten goods. To this day, the survivors whisper darkly of a stool pigeon in their midst. But the patrolmen insisted that no stool pigeon was responsible. They simply gave the horses their heads and the faithful beasts led them unswervingly to the camp. The only "stool pigeon" was the horses' native homing instinct.

A local native relates another amusing incident. A truck heavily loaded with contraband liquor was backed into a barn east of the village. Several willing hands unloaded the haul. Much to their chagrin, the then weightless truck could not clear the barn door. It took much jockeying and a partial reloading before the truck could finally be freed from its trap.

There was another breed, besides the professional bootlegger, who caused many headaches for the Border Patrol. These were the enterprising individuals who devised unique methods of getting a small haul across the border for their own personal use. One time, an apparently innocent touring car stopped at the border and declared several cartons of eggs purchased in Canada. Quite by accident a patrolman discovered that the eggs were fake and each hollow shell contained pure whiskey.

It is a well-known fact that Prohibition initiated the birth of violence and organized crime. Gangsters flourished, and fortunes were made and lost in a single day. It is little wonder that such powerful mobsters as "Legs Diamond and "Dutch" Schultz were much interested in the lucrative border traffic.

The heyday of the Prohibition Era has been buried for nearly forty years; but memories are still vivid, and the stories have lost none of their dramatic impact. Chateaugay, with its nearness to Canada and its dozens of back roads and wooded area, was indeed a veritable "Bootleggers' Paradise."

CROWN POINT

By Charles E. Hughes, *North Country Life*, Summer 1951

The celebration of the Champlain tercentenary began on July 5, 1909, at Crown Point. Following a sham battle in the morning and the noon interval, a salute from the guns of the United States naval flotilla announced the arrival of the governors of New York and Vermont. Governor Charles E. Hughes that afternoon delivered the first address of that weeklong celebration.

We begin today the ceremonies in commemoration of an event of extraordinary significance. Where in this fair world can be found a place so richly endowed by daring and by exploit and at the same time so favored by Nature? A gateway to a continent, waiting through the silent ages for the approach of the intrepid voyager, soldier, and colonist; an avenue of conflict—a scene of contest in which Algonquin and Iroquois contended for supremacy, of fierce rivalries of Old World powers, seeking to extend the domains of monarchy, of determined struggle for independence, that a new nation might be born and bless humanity with institutions devoted to the maintenance of civil and religious liberty.

Three nations join today in common recognition of the sons who here displayed valor and heroism worthy of the highest standards of each. Without taunt or bitterness, without vain regret for the inevitable, without the suspicions of ill-natured rivalry, we retrace the paths of early strife.

Here Frenchman, Englishman, and American may find their heroes; and in examples of bravery, of high resolve, and of fearless and unselfish devotion, no one of them need yield the palm to others. Champlain and Montcalm, Lord Howe and Amherst, Ethan Allen, Seth Warner, Israel Putnam, Philip Schuyler, and Richard Montgomery forever invest this beautiful valley with the charm of heroic deeds and chivalric loyalty.

It is not for me to recount the tale of discovery and war. It is the privilege of others to tell the romantic story. The spot upon which we stand today is more intimately associated with later events than with the career of the discoverer, whose name we chiefly honor in this week of celebration.

For more than a century after Champlain passed below this point to aid his savage friends in the contest with their hated enemies, the Iroquois, no permanent settlement along the borders of this lake was effected. It was the scene of warlike expedition, but not until 1731 was this strategic point, a key to the control of this great highway of war, fortified. Fort St. Frederic was then established by the French, and within a few years was made a fortress of first importance. Later, in 1759, the English commander Amherst, at whose approach the French evacuated their fort, undertook the construction, at a cost of many millions, of new and extensive fortifications—whose ruins you see—which were to ensure the permanency of the British control.

But these ruins, suggestive as they are of enterprise, of skillful preparation, and of lavish outlay, are in truth the monument of baffled ambition and of disappointed hopes.

The French, destroying their own work, abandoned their fort to the English. Only a few years later, in 1775, the Green Mountain boy, Seth Warner, with his little band, took possession without a blow. The next year, retreating from Canada, the Americans regarded Crown Point as indefensible, and burying here hundreds of their comrades, pushed on in destitution and distress to Ticonderoga. It was from Crown Point, later in the year 1776, that Arnold set forth with his little fleet to check the designs of the English General Carleton, and in defeat in the battle of Valcour Island, won lasting laurels for the American name by his military skill and indomitable courage. Hither, by rare strategy, he succeeded in returning but not to stay; and Crown Point again came into the possession of the British.

The next year arrived Burgoyne, with his great army, spreading terror and confusion, issuing grandiloquent and insolent proclamation, sweeping with resistless force to Fort Edward, holding Crown Point and reducing Ticonderoga, only to meet the appalling disaster at Saratoga, where the success of the American arms destroyed the basis for British hope of dominion over the colonies and assured the final success of the cause of independence.

Upon this vantage point have stood French and English, each in turn bent upon dominating the future of this favored land.

But destiny would have it otherwise, and among these ruins of ambition were laid the foundations of the republic under whose banner we meet today, the friend both of France and England, in whose blessings the children of both the ancient rivals share, whose peaceful progress is a boon to all mankind.

FORT ANNE

By Paul F. Crumley, *North Country Life*, Summer 1954

Reconstruction at Fort Anne, Washington County, of one of the five stockades that occupied the militarily strategic junction of Halfway Brook and Wood Creek in the historic Champlain-Hudson Valley for nearly a century from 1690 to 1780 is well under way, and the Fort Anne Museum of History, being operated by the Fort Anne Restoration Corporation in conjunction therewith, has been open to the public since May 15.

Heading the long-range program designed to bring alive to natives and tourists alike the thrilling pages of Fort Anne's early history are Vincent P. Stanger, head of the science department in the Fort Anne Central School, and Paul F. Crumley, owner and operator of the community's only pharmacy.

Since the time that Stanger and Crumley were pupils in grade school in Fort Anne, each had wondered why so little had been done to recreate the historical lore which obviously was so abundant in the area, but each time the thought came up it was dismissed as too great an undertaking for one or two individuals.

Once, in 1927, a dynamic personality in the form of the late Edna M. Pike, then town historian, spearheaded a gigantic sesquicentennial of the Battle of Fort Anne. On July 7 and 8 of that year, the stirring role of the community in the Struggle for Independence was re-enacted by the townspeople, and then put aside as men, women and children returned to their busy everyday routines.

And, although they did not realize it at the time, Stanger and Crumley, who as schoolboys played minor roles in the big pageant of that year, began unwittingly to prepare for the job that they were to tackle together in the fall of 1953.

Stanger, through association with Harry Smith, a veteran of World War I, who was also destined to play an important part in the restoration of Fort Anne, acquired an early interest in archaeology, which he continued to enjoy through college and into his years as a teacher of science. When a chapter of the New York State Archaeological Association was organized in nearby Glens Falls in 1948, Stanger was chosen as charter president. Through contacts which he made there, he found himself during the summer vacation of 1953 as assistant archaeologist to Stanley Gifford at Lake George, where restoration of Fort William Henry had begun in the spring.

Crumley, meanwhile, after college, had devoted five years to newspaper reporting and editing and then had returned to his native community to go in business with his father in the pharmacy, and since 1939 had been building a business experience which he added to his background in publicity work.

When Stanger returned to Fort Anne after work each evening last summer, he used to drop into the prescription room at the drug store for a little "bull session" with his lifelong hunting and fishing companion. It was during one of these chats along in August that the idea of restoring the fort first began to take shape. After two or three more evenings of discussion, definite plans began to evolve as the two young men moved swiftly to translate their thoughts into deeds.

Their first step was to acquire a two-story brick house built in 1840 on the west side of Route 4, but definitely on part of the original fort site. As soon as they had purchased this property, they approached John N. Pike, husband of the former town historian and owner of the land on the east side of Route 4, which embraced the other portion of the original fort site. After hearing their plans, Mr. Pike, a man past 70, said, "I'll tell you what I'll do. I'll give you a 99-year lease on the land at $1 per year, but I want to give you fair warning here and now that when the lease expires I expect to raise the rent."

As soon as the properties had been secured, Crumley and Stanger applied to New York State for a corporation charter with authorization to issue stock in their enterprise, and on October 28, 1953, the Fort Anne Restoration Corporation became a reality.

As soon as Stanger mentioned the project to his boyhood mentor, Henry Smith, that civic-minded individual placed at the group's disposal a fabulous collection of Indian artifacts and Colonial and Revolutionary relics, which he had acquired locally during his entire life. These form the nucleus for the museum.

Meanwhile, an intensive research program had been launched with lines of inquiry reaching out not only to the archives of this country but also to Canada and England in an attempt to glean every possible shred of information about Fort Anne and its early history.

After studying records and the terrain of the land on the fort site, the boys began excavation last fall, and before cold weather forced a halt, more than 40 stumps of one of the five original stockades to occupy the site, comprising portions of the north and east walls, had been uncovered, together with 79 feet of hollowed-out cedar logs laid end to end and used as a primitive but effective water conduit. Also uncovered were numerous small items such as clay pipe fragments, bits of Revolutionary period pottery and rum bottles, grape shot and hand-forged nails.

During the winter months the boys sold stock in the enterprise to keep the corporation active, remodeled the museum building, and from the fragments of information that kept coming in, pieced together a dramatic story of the history of the Fort Anne area.

Archaeological evidence in the form of numerous artifacts such as projectile points, stone knives and other implements of stone indicate that the Red Man traveled and camped on this area as early as 4,000 years ago in the archaic and early woodland periods.

The forks of Wood Creek and Halfway Brook, where Fort Anne is located, was the northern terminus of the great carry between the Hudson River and Lake Champlain.

In the Indian era it was possible to proceed from the Hudson at Fort Edward by canoe up Fort Edward Creek with a carry from Fort Edward Creek to Wood Creek of only a mile to again find uninterrupted waterway to Lake Champlain. During the historic period, travel by bateau from the north was possible only to Fort Anne on Wood Creek, when a carry of about 14 miles was necessary to reach the Hudson at Fort Edward. For this reason Fort Edward became known as the Great Carrying Place. An alternate route went overland to Lake George with a short carry from the foot of that lake to Lake Champlain at Ticonderoga.

With these facts in mind it becomes evident that the route through Fort Anne was of great strategic importance. It became one of the logical places for fortification, either when invasion from the north was feared or when an offensive against the north was planned.

As early as 1690, the very ground on which the stockade is being built saw occupancy as a military location when Major General Fitz Winthrop camped at the confluence of Wood Creek and Halfway Brook on his first abortive march against Canada as France and England began their struggle for conquest in the New World.

Two years later Winthrop, leading another Canada-bound expedition, again camped here and on that occasion erected the first of a series of forts at the junction of the two streams. This is known as the old stone fort and was simply a rough earthwork.

In 1709 Colonel Nicholson erected another fort here, which was originally named Fort Schuyler, but shortly thereafter the post was renamed Queen's Fort, which in turn was changed to Fort Anne, in honor of the reigning British monarch.

Before he withdrew from the area Nicholson burned the fort, but in 1711, he returned and rebuilt it. During the next few decades this fort fell into disrepair, but shortly after the outbreak of the French and Indian War between 1756 and 1758, a fourth fort was constructed here. During that era such famous men as Putnam, Rodgers and others were intimately associated with the locale.

In 1765 a large tract of land, consisting of most of the present town of Fort Anne, was divided and passed by grant from the king into possession of a group of royal artillery officers. Within a short time a sawmill and blockhouse known as Cheshire's was erected at what is now Kane's Falls, one mile up Halfway Brook from Fort Anne, and in 1776 it is recorded that boards were sawed at this sawmill to be used as planking for the first American fleet a-building at Skenesboro, now Whitehall.

Fort Anne's crowning military glory came in 1777 when Colonel Pierse Long, commanding the 2nd New Hampshire Regiment, halted here as the Colonial forces fled down the Champlain Valley before the invasion of the British Army under Major General John Burgoyne.

The British leader, flushed with his successful conquest of the mighty fortress of Ticonderoga, halted at Skenesboro and ordered Colonel Hill, with the 9th Regiment of Foot, to proceed to Fort Anne. On the night of July 7, 1777, Hill, with about 850 men, reached the narrow defile about one half mile north of the fort. Long, in command at Fort Anne, with a complement of 500 men (mostly sick and wounded) meanwhile had sent for reinforcements and on that same night Colonel Van Rensselaer, with 500 men, reached Fort Anne to swell Long's total to 1,000 men. Learning that they outnumbered the British, Long and Van Rensselaer decided to attack. On the morning of July 8, they marched from the fort and attacked Hill in the defile, where he was awaiting reinforcements form Skenesboro.

There ensued what has been described by numerous British officers participating as one of the "hottest actions" of the entire war, which terminated only when the Americans ran out of ammunition after having encircled Hill and forcing him to withdraw up the steep rocky side of the defile, now known as Battle Hill.

Lacking powder to follow up the advantage they had gained, the Colonials burned the fort and slowly withdrew to Fort Edward after felling hundreds of trees in Wood Creek and the roadway beside it, making passage virtually impossible. Because of the obstacles placed in his path, it took Burgoyne from July 9 to July 29 to reach Fort Edward, twenty miles from Skenesboro. This delay afforded General Schuyler three extra weeks in which to entrench and reinforce his army at Saratoga, where Burgoyne met total defeat only a few weeks later.

An interesting sidelight on this southward trek of Burgoyne from Skenesboro relates that the British general was encamped at Fort Anne when word was brought to him of the brutal massacre of Jane McCrea at Fort Edward on July 23. It was during the July 8 battle, according to Digby, one of Burgoyne's lieutenants, that certain colors of the Americans were captured. Digby described in detail the colors consisting of 13 alternate red-white stripes with a field of blue in which were encircled 13 white stars, the exact design which had been ratified by Congress at Philadelphia on June 14. In addition, the regimental flag of Long's regiment and the New Hampshire flag, which they bore, were captured and taken to England in Colonel Hill's personal luggage. In 1912 they were located in England, and through the efforts of Edward Tuck they were returned and may be seen today at the New Hampshire Historical Society's Museum in Concord. Replicas of these flags are on display at the Fort Anne Museum of History.

After Burgoyne's surrender, the Colonials built a fifth and final fort on the site. This fort, garrisoned by about 75 men under Captain Adiel Sherwood, was surrendered to and burned by Major Christopher Carleton in 1780. The women and children of the garrison were permitted to go to their homes, but Sherwood and his men were taken prisoners. After the war Sherwood operated a tavern in the Pat Smyth House in Fort Edward. In 1953, the Smyth House was restored and it is currently open to the public.

This spring as soon as weather permitted, outside work was resumed. The fort site was leveled and a parking lot constructed preparatory to actual construction of the stockade.

Of special interest is a floating pontoon bridge which extends under a highway bridge on Halfway Brook from the Corporation property on the east side of the road to its property on the west side of the road so that the visitor can tour every section of the grounds without being obliged to cross the heavily traveled Route 4, which almost exactly bisects the project.

Construction of the stockade was begun immediately after opening date, May 15, and the palisades should be completed by mid-August. If the season proves exceptionally successful, work on the blockhouse inside the stockade will be started this fall.

Additional relics are being loaned or donated almost every day, and the organizers hope within a very short time to have one of the most outstanding historical exhibits in the state.

Stanger, who serves as corporation president, directs the museum and historical presentation program, while Crumley, secretary-treasurer, supervises the business and publicity aspects of the enterprise. Their friend, Harry Smith, is corporation vice-president and Dr. Leo A. Thume, the town physician, and Harold W. Haviland, local woodworking manufacturer, are directors.

BLUE MOUNTAIN LAKE

By Roland B. Miller, *North Country Life*, Spring 1955
Reprinted from New York State *Conversationist*

Blue Mountain Lake, Hamilton County, has lifted a shadow cast on it by an historian and now boasts that it is the lake remaining nearest to its natural state of any in New York.

Donaldson, whose pen was merciless, described Blue Mountain as a sister to Racquette Lake in beauty and proximity, and noted that development of the two went together, but with the great difference that Racquette was dominated by the "camp beautiful" idea, whereas Blue succumbed structurally to the "hotel horrible." "The gaunt, ungainly pile of piazzas and windows" that marked Blue's hotels on the outside has been transformed by modernization, and now the inward "refinements in comfort and convenience" they always contained are matched outwardly. Blue's few big camps have always been impressive and attractive; its other buildings have been comparable. The Blue Mountain Lake Association has seen to this and welcomes only structures that fit into the landscape.

Blue Mountain Lake is in the Racquette Watershed, on highway routes 10, 28, 28N, and 365, and is serviced by two bus lines. (It once took a day by rail and steamer via Utica and Racquette Lake or by rail and stage via Saratoga and North Creek to get there.) Blue's maximum depth is 102 feet, its average depth is 45 feet, its level is maintained by a 30-inch dam at the outlet of Utowana Lake, and it covers 1,312 acres. It's dotted by 25 islands, which still have their original growth of timber.

It's a toss-up whether the bass or the lake trout is the main game fish. Excellent catches of brook trout also have been reported. Frost fish were once abundant, but now are rare or extinct; there's no report of rainbows. Lake trout fishing improved after whitefish were stocked, but fell off after the introduction of bass. Brook trout fishing is good in the spring at the mouth of Minnow Pond outlet, and whitefish are moderately abundant, a few being taken at buoys.

Blue's chemistry is interesting. From a depth of 98 feet (or practically on the bottom) all the way up through its waters dissolved oxygen was found comparatively high; the lowest reading at 80 feet was 5.6 parts per million, well within the tolerable limit for fish life. Periodically and culminating last year there was some local desire to stock the lake with smelt, but there is little evidence to indicate that fishing would be improved by such a program.

Test seining has brought up lake trout, bass, perch, brook trout, sculpin, two kinds of whitefish, two kinds of sunfish, and suckers. The Indian Lake/Blue Mountain Fish and Game Association co-operates in stocking Blue with thousands of lake and brook trout annually.

Blue is not altogether for the rocking chair brigade and game fishers; local hunters will find some grouse, a few pheasants, rabbits, hares and squirrels, bears now and then—and plenty of deer in the woods. The vacationer will find Blue Mountain with its elevation of 3,759 feet spectacular if they climb the trail to the fire observation tower. On a clear day, six or seven other fire towers and a panorama that's breath-taking can be viewed. The hike to Terrell Pond, locale of an early Irish immigrant settlement, is fun; if it's camping you want, there are the sites at Lake Eaton and Golden Beach at Racquette or, closer still, the new campsite at Lake Durant.

Blue Mountain Lake and its environs also has much to offer in the way of antiquity, much of which is to be collected and displayed in the Adirondack Museum at Blue Mountain Lake village. Among the memorabilia will be the Adirondack pack basket, the Adirondack guide boat, relics of the resort era symbolized by the old Prospect House (first hotel in the world to be lighted by electricity) and relics also of the three-quarter mile rail carry from Racquette to the Marion River and the steamship lane through the Marion and Utowana and Eagle lakes into Blue Mountain Lake, abandoned in 1929 after a half century of operation.

Utowana, Eagle and Blue once were called the Eckford Chain after Henry Eckford, noted engineer and shipbuilder who made a state survey in 1811. Later Professor Emmons, during his geological survey,

Prospect House porch, Blue Mountain Lake. *Photo S. R. Stoddard. Courtesy Special Collections, Feinberg library, SUNY College at Plattsburgh*

named them beginning with the largest—Lake Janet, Lake Catherine and Lake Marion.

Emmons' names were so early that there was no one to perpetuate them and for a long time the chain of waters was called the Tallow Lakes. (A greedy old Indian overloaded his canoe with venison tallow and was overtaken on Blue Mountain Lake by a storm which upset his cargo of grease. The scene of the tragedy was referred to as Tallow Lake. This was hardly acceptable on letterheads when John G. Holland built the first hotel on the lake in 1874, so the proprietor renamed the lake after the adjacent mountain which the guides referred to as often being conspicuously tinged with blue.)

Holland's Blue Mountain Lake Hotel burned in 1886, was rebuilt, but burned again in 1896 and never rose again. Holland found two permanent residents on the lake when he began to investigate the hotel possibilities there—Chauncey Hathorn, who was living a secluded life, and Tyler M. Merwin. The success of Holland's venture inspired Merwin to turn his cabin on the plateau into a hotel, still standing and known as the Blue Mountain House.

When Frederick C. Durant built the Prospect House in 1881 (it was razed in 1914), it was the largest and most luxurious in the woods. Its erection thirty miles from a railway was held a remarkable achievement. It had no outward beauty but contained 300 rooms, many baths and open fireplaces, a steam elevator, electric bells, bowling alley, shooting gallery, a billiard room and a telegraph office, and each bedroom had an Edison electric light.

The large hotels on this lake have remained its most conspicuous man-made feature, yet even they are almost swallowed up by the natural beauty of the surroundings. Blue Mountain Lake is certainly one of the most beautiful, perhaps the most beautiful, of Adirondack waters.

EARLY VACATION DAYS IN THE TOWN OF CHESTER

By Caroline H. Fish, *York State Tradition*, Spring 1969

A century ago, William ("Adirondack") Murray made the Adirondacks leap into public attention with the publication of his *Adventures in the Wilderness* (Boston, 1869).

In a few short years, all the Adirondacks and particularly northern Warren County had become a tourist mecca. North Creek had been characterized by one writer as "a good place to depart from," meaning for adventures in the Adirondack wilderness.

C. F. Taylor and Son, proprietors of Taylors-on-Schroon in the town of Chester, were shortly to issue a brochure entitled, "Mountain, Lake and Brook," from which the following is quoted.

"A very few years ago the Adirondacks were known only to the hunter, the fisherman, and the woodsman. It was almost an unexplored wilderness. It is, in one sense, a wilderness still, a great portion of it unsurveyed by chain and rod, its labyrinths of mountain, forest, lake, river and brook scarcely touched by the devastating hand of unromantic man. Its virgin fastness has not yet been made to yield to the demands of settlement. The iron-horse [Adirondack Railroad, later Delaware and Hudson] has

It is during July and August that most folks set out upon their annual vacation trips, and for this purpose there's no more rewarding place to enjoy the summer season than in the Adirondacks. —Mortimer Norton. *Photo Otto Grolinger [sic]. Courtesy Edward Blankman (The Lloyd Blankman Collection)*

only penetrated to its boundaries and stopped, apparently loath to break the silence of its rock-bound forests with his noisy tread or pollute its pure atmosphere with his grimy touch."

The lover of Nature (always personified by our Victorian ancestors with a capital) was able by a round-about method to come from the metropolitan areas to the stronghold of Nature in the town of Chester. The Adirondack Railroad brought the traveler to the Riverside depot. From here, Waddell and Emerson coaches took the passengers and their luggage, which usually contained the famous Saratoga trunk, to the steamboat landing at the foot of Schroon Lake in Pottersville.

Daily, three trips were made up the full length of Schroon Lake to Schroon Lake village. The first leg of the trip was diagonally across the lake to Mill Brook (Adirondack). Then the steamer went directly across to Taylors-on-Schroon.

Whether the boat was the *Effingham*, owned by Mrs. P.S. Russell of Schroon Lake village, or the excursion steamer Gypsie, which she also owned; the *Wilhelmina*, owned by Wilhelm Pichardt; the Ellen, owned by E. A. Bush; or the *Evelyn*, owned by the Emersons, the route continued through the Narrows to Grove Point, past Isola Bella (Word of Life Island) to the village of Schroon Lake.

As a child I used to sit enthralled and listen to my father tell of a trip to Mount Marcy he took as a young man. Starting from Chestertown, the party, which consisted of my father, Frank E. Haskell, Gregory Paine of the Chestertown High School, the Rev. Harvey Dunham, the dominie of the Chestertown Presbyterian Church, and their guide, "Klondike" Charley Fish, hiked to the steamboat landing. Here they took a boat and went to Schroon Lake village. From here they continued on foot to their goal, Mount Marcy.

How they were trapped for three days in a late snowstorm on the peak is another story. The point is that in the early 1900s the best and most regular transportation was up Schroon Lake by boat.

With the coming of the horseless carriage, new roads became necessary. The first water-bound highway in the state was built about 1917–18 from Chestertown to the suspension bridge near the Riverside depot. Later new macadam on the state road from Loon Lake followed the lake to Pottersville and Schroon Lake village.

A vehicle, known simply as "The Auto," now carried passengers from the depot to the steamboat landing. The *Evelyn*, built in 1897 and named for Mrs. Emerson, was still twenty-two summers later carrying passengers and freight twice a day up the nearly ten miles of the lake.

In the spring the *Evelyn*, fueled by a coal boiler, rafted logs from the inlet of the lake to the other end. From Pottersville they were taken down the Schroon River to the Hudson feeder. But it was the passenger business that interested the native as well as the summer visitor. The *Evelyn* functioned for Sunday School picnics, family parties, and just plain "joy riding."

Schroon Lake, soon to be called the Lake Como of the Adirondacks, could be viewed from her decks, and I have it on family authority that nothing could equal the view of the mountains as seen from her double decks.

For many years Capt. Freeman Sanders steered the boat. His crew consisted of a boiler man, an engineer, a purser to take the fares, and men to handle the ropes at the four stops—the Wells House, Taylors-on-Schroon, Grove Point, and the village of Schroon Lake. The Evelyn stopped carrying passengers in 1919, and several years later stopped rafting.

Can't you see the women in long dresses covered by dusters, large picture hats tightly veiled to anchor them against a mountain breeze, standing at the steamboat landing in Pottersville with their parasols to protect their complexions against the bright sunlight?

OUR TOWN—WILLSBORO

By Arthur Hall, *North Country Life*, Summer 1960

The area in and around Willsboro is one of historical interest primarily since it is on that great artery of trade and of war and peace—Lake Champlain. During the many battles of the French and Indian Wars, the War of 1812, and the Revolutionary War, this area changed hands so many times that it is almost surprising that we in this village are Americans and not French or Canadian.

With all the changes, names changed, too—sometimes not for the better. In Anglicizing the beautiful names in this Adirondack Green Mountain area we did mankind no service! Listen to the pretty bells in "Carillon," now called Ticonderoga, or the ominousness of "Couchant de Lion" (crouching lion), now called Camel's Hump Mountain, or "Isle de Quatre Vents" (Island of the Four Winds), now called the "Four Brothers." Willsboro Bay has been variously called Corlear's Bay, Bay de Perue, Soney Bay, Sabousin Bay, Picteau Bay, and Willsborough Bay.

Willsboro in particular, now the home of wollastonite and a paper industry, was settled in 1765 by William Gilliland, who, calling it Milltown, built the first house within fifty miles in either direction. During the Revolutionary War, Milltown was exterminated, but sprang back as Willsborough.

In the 1810–1835 period, we were known for the old grist mill (still standing), two stores, two sawmills, a Congregational church, and four taverns. We even built a distillery, which supplied our army with whiskey until 1812. Itinerant shoemakers lived with each family until all members were shod. We are famous for the local blue limestone, which supplied the foundations for our capitol in Albany and the anchors for the New York and Brooklyn bridges. In 1881 a pulp mill was built, and it is still running—24 hours a day.

Flat tires were common in the early days of Adirondack auto-touring. *Courtesy Leigh Portner, Sr.*

Local residents Captain Hagglund and Payson Hatch have had wondrous experiences in the past twenty years while locating, raising, salvaging, restoring, and displaying boats and warships which had been sunk during the many wars of yesteryear. Among these were the gunboat *Philadelphia* of the fleet of Benedict Arnold and the steamboat *Vermont* (the second steamboat in the world), which sank in 1815 as the result of a thrown connecting rod.

In 1952, John Kiehl, a local resident, surprised us all when he badgered Willsboro into giving a county record quantity of blood to the Red Cross, beating towns five times our size. This, however, is evidently nothing new according to an old quote: "Every town in Essex County gave generously of its blood during the dark struggle of the Civil War, and Willsborough's record will compare favorably with them all."

Ausable Chasm, ten miles north of Willsboro, is a 100-foot-deep, 20-foot-wide, mile-and-a-half long gorge of rushing water and high, jagged walls. It was used in the early movie days for "Grand Canyon" shots. If you ever saw a cowboy being swept to his death in the rushing waters, it may easily have been our own Koert Burnham, who at the age of 17 swam down the Chasm twice for *Pathe-News*.

Back in 1875, a Professor Holden went back and forth on a rope eighty feet above the water, sitting and lying on the rope and, for good measure, drinking lemonade and watching the fireworks.

One legend of the Chasm has to do with a village ne'er-do-well. It was suggested that his morals might be improved by suspending him from the eighty-foot-high bridge by his heels. No sooner said than done—the successful outcome being that he lost his wits permanently and became a very offensive idiot!

Suicides, lovers' leaps, dives by riders and horses, all have been part of the Chasm's history.

Today in Willsboro we're proud of many nearby things, including the Plattsburgh Air Base, the new Whiteface Ski Center, and the Olympic Bobsled Run. And naturally we are proud of Willsboro and Cabot wollastonite.

PART ONE

Adirondack Memories

Ice harvesting was an important Adirondack industry. Great stacks of block ice survived in the aftermath of a fire that leveled the entire ice warehouse owned by the George C. Wood Company at White Lake in the 1920s. *Courtesy Fred Worden*

A BOY'S MEMORY

By William J. O'Hern

As I write this, I am reflecting back to a younger age, a time when I daydreamed about putting a few personal things in a small cloth bundle, tying the corners on a stick and starting off on foot to some place, I knew not where.

Reading Lindon Riggs' note to Glyndon Cole is what got me thinking in this direction. Riggs lived in St. Lawrence County. While he was visiting friends, he noticed an old clock on the shelf. "They told me it was a much-prized heirloom, although it had not told time for many years," he told Cole. "They asked me if I could repair it, and I consented to take it home and examine it. I discovered several cogs of the wooden wheels to be missing, and the striking system needed some fine adjustment. When these faults had been corrected, the old clock was once more tick-tocking away."

Mr. Riggs was not only a skilled handyman. He was also interested in the record of the timeworn clock. He said as he watched the hands move and listened to the spring windings he "became aware of a small voice. Listening closely, I heard the voice say, 'Would you like to know how old I am, where I came from, where I have lived, and how I happened to be with your friends?'"

Lindon E. Riggs was also an antique dealer and a student of old relics. He said he, "answered in the affirmative," to the imaginary clock voice and went on to enlighten Cole that he learned the clock was manufactured in Farmington, Connecticut by George Marsh & Co. and named THE IMPROVED CLOCK "in about 1772." He said he had to rely on a chain of events to establish that date and went on to tell about that sequence. Then, based on clues he found inside the workings of the clock, he went on to explain much more about the various people who had owned the timepiece and the repairs and modifications that had been made by them, right up to the owner whose homestead was sold in 1913.

The clock had grown "old and rheumatic" by then. "Edna Crane, a retired teacher who had purchased a home in Winthrop" liked the look of the old clock, which she saw in an estate sale. Prizing the clock, although "it was silent," she purchased the vintage piece and placed it on a mantle among "her most cherished possessions."

1921 Maple Sugar camp near Old Forge. In the remote Adirondack communities, any caller was welcome, and the peddlers with their "packs" were doubly welcome. They brought bits of the outside world, and often supplied much needed thread or other commodities to the secluded housewife. *Courtesy Marilyn Breaky*

Glyndon Cole saw a story in the repairman's tale and got him to tell it in "The Story of the Old Clock," that appeared in the Fall 1958 issue of *North Country Life*.

The clock repairman's tale made me think of a foreign-sounding merchant who worked on cuckoo clocks—at least I always thought he was foreign because he hadn't mastered English. He knew his clocks. He was kind, yet never refrained from saying a timepiece brought in for repairs was *cheap* in his opinion.

That line of thinking led me to other tinkers and tradesmen who would show up in our community from time to time—my grandmother called them "peddlers." I saw them as footloose and fancy-free, wandering to see the world, and they pricked my interest in doing the same thing. These pack peddlers used horses and wagons to follow a circuit from one community to another—door-to-door salesmen you might call them today. I remember Mattie. He collected rags. In trade, he sharpened anything that needed an edge. Mattie was the first to come to mind when I read about the clock tradesman. There were others too. A seed salesman; the bread man; the milkman and the ice man. I still have the metal tongs used to carry blocks from his wagon to the house. I understand the large, heavy blocks of crystal clear ice were cut from White Lake, then transported by train to nearby cities. I never had any intention of setting off on foot to see the world, but I often took my "wanderlust" to near-by places. Those were my earliest days of escaping to something I found exciting and interesting. It's an uneasy disease I admit I still harbor.

Nobody reading this today would probably consider the appearance of an itinerant salesmen fascinating—not with the attractions of today's array of electronic toys and games. But back then their arrival changed a boy's ordinary daily routine. I thought these peddlers had cut themselves loose from all of life's complications and accountabilities, and I envied their freedom to travel throughout the Adirondacks in what I imagined was a search for adventure, never thinking that they were simply working for a living.

Today I travel the trails, bushwhack mountainous terrain and paddle big and small bodies of water, sometimes in spite of hunger and cold, for pure recreation, happiness, and the occasional unexpected adventure. I hope those peddlers found these things as well. An appreciation of the beautiful country they traveled and the mountain characters they met would have made all the difference in the lives of these gentlemen of the road.

THE LURE OF THE NORTH

Somehow I love the Northland with
its fresh and balmy air;
For fragrant woods and meadowlands
I have a special flair;
The mountains, lakes attract me
and its places of retreat;
Then there's the friendly populace
whom I am pleased to meet.

I love the Northland in the spring when fields are lush and green,
When all about me everywhere new, budding life is seen;
I love it in the summer when the herds in pasture graze,
Then hither come vacationists to spend some restful days.

I'm enchanted by the autumn when the woodlands are aflame
With colors that the artists scan with welcome-acclaim;
Nor do I shun it winters when the sturdy north winds blow
For then I'm thrilled by hardy sports when fields are white with snow.

Its wild life strongly calls to me from woods and air and stream,
And if I'm far away from there, I sit me down and dream
Of fishing in the summer and of hunting in the fall—
The lure is so enticing that I need to second call.

—Willis N. Bugbee, Syracuse, N.Y, *North Country Life,* Summer 1955

ABOVE: Late autumn's second call. Bette O'Hern at Calkins Brook lean-to #2. *Author's photo*

BLUEBERRIES, A"GRAPES OF WRATH" INDUSTRY IN EARLY CLINTON COUNTY

By Marjorie L. Porter, *North Country Life*, Summer 1952

Whortleberries—huckleberries, blueberries—'twas all the same to great-great grandma who pioneered in Northern New York! Spread out on the ledges of Clinton, Essex and Franklin counties is a summer crop that has vied in economic importance with outcroppings of iron ore found from one end of the Adirondacks to the other since the days of earliest settlement. Probably great-great-grandpa found the blueberries before he did the iron ore!

Consider the fact that from the Flat Rock section in the towns of Altona and Chazy, (there are other "Flat Rock" areas) as many as 25,000 bushels of blue beauties were picked or "scooped" in a good year from low, massed bushes on an exposed tract of about 2,000 acres! Here was a two months employment for over 100 entire families (every member a picker) and a July–August sojourn that yielded cash, recreation and longed-for social pleasures. And less Canadians take over the prerogatives of Clinton county folks, along in 1890 W.C. Casey of Altona leased Flat Rock at a meeting of the Land Commissioners of the State of New York, proposing to exclude "foreigners"! A sort of "Grapes of Wrath" setup, since pickers moved on to the Malone section in Franklin County to pick hops. The Flat Rock crop in 1882 was valued at $5,000.

Associated with this North Country industry, which in the town of Altona centered about "Cold Spring" and Robinson Brook, were the Trembley brothers, Feinberg, Murray, Charlie Chamberlain, Bert Wakeman and John Wakeman, and others who occasionally leased the property on Flat Rock from the Trembleys.

Log camps became the temporary homes of the itinerant berry pickers and in some cases one cabin housed four or five families. Forty or fifty camps grouped around in a store and dancing pavilion, for among the French Canadians there was always a fiddler or two who provided music. Here was a picturesque, barefoot, carefree life, one that contrasted

The Blueberry Girls. Nora Courtney, left, and Mary Hubbard.
Photo by Grotus Reising. Courtesy Edward Blankman (The Lloyd Blankman Collection)

sharply with winter existence in a semi-barren, up-h'isted part of New York State.

Less than fifty years ago, over 600 persons found employment on the Altona Flat Rock, while many others picked blueberries on the plains north of the Saranac River above Morrisonville, where there was a store and warehouse on the north bank adjacent to Kent's Falls, or on the plains between the valleys of the Little Ausable and the Great Ausable rivers, and hundreds of Americans and Canadians took this crop from the Rock on Covey Hill, as they do today, picnicking in family groups near the "Gulf" northwest of Mooers.

Contracting for the berry output were such men as Henry Guibord of Plattsburgh, Pat Casey, Dubray, Stratton and Atwood, and others. In earlier years, pickers received only two or three cents a quart, carrying them off the Rock to sell to Pat Casey at the railroad station at Altona—twenty five cents for a ten-quart pailful!

The blueberries were shipped to commission houses in Boston, Albany and Troy, as many as 100 crates a day leaving the depot. At one time Casey and Dubray engaged in a blueberry war. Eight or ten buyers were at the Casey camp, getting one cent a quart commission on the crop. The price of the berries was juggled up to 10 or 12 cents a quart. The berries were measured in wooden measures at the camps. They were poured into a square box with sides sloping toward a hole under which was another box into which the berries dropped. Buyers would handle these boxes instead of letting the pickers do it, thus managing a bit of "chiseling."

In spite of these sharp practices, it was not unusual for a family to go away at the end of the season with eight or nine hundred dollars, a fine tan, and some pleasant recollections of summer evenings, as dancing frequently continued throughout the night. Overindulgence in the use of spirituous drinks was not customary.

About 1910 pickers were receiving six or seven cents a quart. They disposed of their berries each night, those at the north end of the tract being collected at the Altona station and those at the south end, at the

Chazy station, although some years all were shipped from Altona. Only a small percentage of the crop was used locally.

Ambitious, fast pickers could harvest 150 quarts a day, but 40 or 50 quarts was considered average. In off years the price per quart was raised a few cents to encourage workers. In earlier years the south end of the tract yielded the biggest output; then the crop appeared to be heaviest in the north end.

Difference in output in the two areas was due in part to fires which burned underbrush that throttled the growth of berry bushes. One picker boasted that he and his wife gathered six and a half bushels of the fruit in about three hours, scooping them with a dipper or basin that held three pints and that was filled with each scoop.

Decrease in the Altona crop of blueberries followed erection of the W. H. Miner dam, 2,300 feet long and 38 feet high, which flooded about 350 acres at the headwaters of the Little Chazy River on the Rock. The increased use of jalopies and trucks by people who are berry pickers has made it possible for them to stay at home in summer, traveling to these tracts with baskets and crates each day, and nowadays they can sell berries for 45 to 50 cents a quart before the peak of the season.

The camps, stores, and pavilions that made up communities on the Flat Rock remain only as ghost towns in the memories of old timers, but the crop of berries still spreads a blue carpet on gray ledges each July, and underneath the pines in September the bushes, scarlet-leaved and hob-nobbing with goldenrod and asters, are not the least among the lavish offerings of autumn!

TANNING: SCHROON LAKE'S FIRST INDUSTRY

By Brenda Rawlins, *North Country Life*, Winter 1960

The hemlock, loveliest of trees, dotted the countryside when the first settlers set foot here in the Adirondacks. Surely, Mountain Phelps considered the shimmering beauty often as he gazed across his "heaven up-h'isted" country.

The hemlock grows to a considerable size with bark rich in tannin. The needles are flat and thick, dark green above the silver underneath. The slightest wind sways the branches gently, turning the tree from green to silver and back to green again. The cones, which resemble little brown roses, dangle from their tops. Thus was the magnificent beauty of our hemlock. The hemlock also played an important, useful part in an early profitable industry—the tanneries.

The tanneries, the first industry of Schroon Lake, were in full swing by the middle of the 19th century. Twenty to thirty men were generally needed in the actual operation of a tannery. Large additional numbers were employed both summer and winter in lumbering, peeling and transporting bark, and drawing logs by sleigh to the Schroon River, an important tributary of the Hudson, by which they were floated to Glens Falls to be manufactured into lumber for the southern market. The tannery relied on many important middlemen vital to the increasing growth and survival of Schroon Lake and the surrounding area.

Resembling a long shed in size and shape, the tanneries contained cast iron stoves which provided warmth needed for working during the long, cold winter months, for tanning was a year-round industry.

Leland House, Schroon Lake. Guests would enjoy sitting out on the front porch drinking iced tea and lemonade as they tasted the Adirondack sweetness, its summer afternoon-cooling breeze and refreshing balsam air. *Photo S. R. Stoddard. Courtesy Special Collections, Feinberg Library, SUNY College at Plattsburgh*

Every tannery, even the smallest, needed several vats. Each was about six feet square and four feet deep, built of plank and sunk into the ground so that the tops were only a little above the floor, with only a narrow passage between them. We have been told that life was one long nightmare for the mothers of the tanners' children because of the haunting fear that the children would fall into a vat and drown. In one of our chats with a prominent woman in Schroon Lake, we learned that once a man fell into a boiling vat in a Schroon Lake tannery. The man died instantly.

The actual tanning process was a long, tedious task. Lime was used first to remove the hair from the hides, an important step in securing soft, durable leather. After being scraped free of hair, the hides were removed to another vat, where they were put to soak in a "witch's brew" known as *late*, which was composed of hen dung, salt, and water. This strange brew was a tradition among old tanners. After a period in this vat, the hides were very thoroughly scrubbed and rinsed in pure water.

Then the soft, plump hides were ready for the long immersion into the tanning liquor. Here is where the hemlock's bark appears on the scene. The hemlock bark was ground up into many small chunks about the size of your fingertip. A layer of the ground bark was then spread over the bottom of the vat and covered with a hide. On top of this would be spread two or three shovels of bark and then another hide and so on until the vat was filled. Water was poured over the hides and bark to fill up the vat.

After coming out of the hemlock solution, the hides were rolled and pressed to even them up. Next, black oil was added to color the hides black. Of course, many were left their natural color. We have been told the hides commonly lay six months in the tan vat and it was often a year from the time a hide was brought to the tanner until the finished leather was ready for delivery.

The first tannery was started by Simeon Rawson about one half mile above Schroon Lake. Because of a lack of waterpower, Mr. Rawson soon moved his tannery into the middle of Schroon.

(The writer here comments on other early tanneries in the Schroon Lake area; namely, Burham's, Hall's, Wickham's, and Hoffman's.)

All of the tanneries mentioned were run by waterpower. The power of the water wheel was used for grinding the bark, pumping, heating the liquor, and peeling the bark.

The hemlock was peeled during the months of May, June, and July. A tool called a spud was used for the peeling. It is said that a good man could peel and average of fifty trees a day. The peeled hemlock logs were then poled down the river to Glens Falls. There was very little waste in the tanning industry.

The tannery buildings in the Schroon Lake area have fallen into ruin, burned to the ground, or merely left to decay. Little is left of the tanning industry, which was the beginning of the thriving village of Schroon Lake.

MR. HAMMOND'S IRON TOWERS

By E. Eugene Barker, *North Country Life*, Spring 1957

Charles Franklin Hammond was in high spirits as he drove down the dusty village street to the dock one fine morning in the autumn of 1844. His affairs were making progress, and today would mark the beginning of a new epoch in his fortunes, he felt, and in the business of Crown Point.

The steamboat was already in sight in the distance. Her paddle-wheels were churning a rough furrow in the tranquil surface of Lake Champlain, shattering its reflection of mountain shores, colored forests and cloudless sky. Her walking-beam threw off glints of sunlight as it rose and plunged.

When she finally reached the dock, her great hempen hawsers were thrown over her side and their looped ends quickly secured around the snubbing-posts. The gang-planks were now a-bustle with freight and passengers coming ashore.

"Hello, Mr. Tower!" called Hammond, as a well-set efficient-looking man dressed in "city" clothes walked down the gangplank. "How are you this fine morning? Put your carpetbag in here under the seat of my buckboard."

As they swung into the main road behind Hammond's team of bay mares, he resumed, "We are going to make a day of it. We'll pick up my brother-in-law, Allen Penfield, when we get to Irondale. The place Penfield and I are going to show you—where we think the furnace might well be built—is only three miles beyond Penfield's. The mines, if we have time to see them, are a mile or two farther."

A remark on Tower's lips was cut short as the bays brought the buckboard around a sharp curve and swung into a straight-away at a clip that closed his mouth with a snap and caused him to clutch at his tall beaver hat.

"This Morgan breed of horses from Vermont," Hammond remarked, "is the finest horseflesh that America has yet produced. There will never be a better breed for speed and endurance. As for looks and spirit, have you ever seen finer ones anywhere? That mare on the off side was sired by Blackhawk. Her name is Fanny Baker, and the nigh mare's name is Fanny Essler. They're a perfect match. It will take the city kinks out of you to ride behind them."

Whether or not Tower was interested, that ironmaster had to listen to pedigrees of Justin's Morgan, Blackhawk, Ethan Allen (the horse, not the patriot), and other famous sires and dams of the Morgan breed.

Nearly a mile of the smoothly graveled road had now slid under the swift wheels of the buckboard.

"I want to show you one place I have in mind," said Hammond. "It combines several advantages. It is about one mile this side of the mine and there is a downgrade haul for the ore all the way. I have bought a likely-looking ledge of lime rock about a mile in the other direction. It looks to be pure crystalline limestone, and I'm told there is enough of it there to supply flux to all the furnaces likely to be built in Essex County. It seems to me the logical place for our furnace is midway between the mine and the quarry. This would provide a downgrade haul for both the ore and the limestone. It would not be a difficult lift to draw the pig iron up out of the hollow. From there to the Lake is nine miles, all downhill."

The first two or three miles of comparatively level ground had been covered, and now they were beginning to meet the hills. They paused to give the horses a moment's rest.

"Jonas, how many tons of ore will it take to make one ton of pig iron?" Hammond asked.

"About two tons of ore to one ton of pig iron, depending on the richness of the ore," answered Tower, unbuttoning his gay plaid waistcoat and relaxing for the first time against the back of the seat.

"Then half of the haulage will be saved the closer the furnace can be located to the mine," continued Hammond, "and bars of pig iron are easier to handle than chunks of ore. How much charcoal will it take to feed her?"

"It usually takes about 300 to 330 bushels of charcoal to make one ton of iron, and I reckon a furnace with the capacity you intend to build will require 650,000 bushels of charcoal a year to keep going at full blast," replied the ironmaster.

"Goodness, gracious! Think of that!" exclaimed Hammond. "I can't imagine it all in one big pile. It will take thousands of acres of forest to supply wood to make that amount of charcoal. Well, there's little but trees on our lands—enough of them to feed our furnace and ten like it, I guess. White pine grows on some of our best land for farming. It's well to have it cleared off and free the land for use."

By this time the road was following the wooded gorge of Putnam's Creek, a small stream, but swift, and falling steeply over numerous rapids and waterfalls. In answer to a question by Tower about water power, Hammond replied, "There are a dozen good sites to the mile for mills and factories, but hardly one in ten is now utilized. One day soon there will be every kind of mill along this stream, not just grist mills and sawmills. There will be tanneries, cabinet shops, wood-working factories, yes, woolen and carding factories, like the one my father owned when I was a boy at Pittsford, Vermont."

"Here at the left," he pointed with his whip, "do you see where the creek drops out of sight over the ledge there? About twenty years ago my wife's uncle, John Renne, built a forge there and turned out the first manufactured iron in Crown Point. At first he got all his ore from the old Cheever bed in Moriah that was worked before the Revolutionary War. That mine is only eight or nine miles away, but the ore had to come by boat to the Crown Point dock, and then it was hauled four miles upgrade to this water power site. In 1823 he used ore from the Saxe bed, which is only a mile away, but after Penfield opened his mine, he used Penfield ore."

"How long has iron been mined here in Crown Point?" asked Tower.

"Well," answered Hammond, "the Saxe ore bed was discovered in 1818 and was opened two years later. That was the first. Lots of ore was taken out of it and shipped to a furnace that Mr. Saxe owned on the Salmon River in Clinton County.

"My own ore bed was discovered in 1821 by a man who was hunting for a bee tree. He saw what he thought was iron ore and brought some specimens home in his pocket. Later, he took several friends into his secret and they helped him to get out eight or ten hundred pounds of the ore. They carried this on their backs more than a mile to a road where a wagon could be used to haul it to Ticonderoga. There it was tried out in a forge. These friends played him false and cheated him out of the value of his discovery."

"Doubtless there are many rich ledges of ore still concealed by the forest," commented Tower.

"Yes," continued Hammond. "Penfield's ore bed was discovered by Cram's young boy, Reuel. He was hunting partridges one day up on the mountain. As he climbed a steep ledge, he took hold of a bush to pull himself up, and the whole mass, roots and all, came loose from the rock. There lay the shining blue-black iron where nature had concealed her treasure. He took samples of the ore to his father, who owned the land. His father opened the bed, and its promise was so good that later Penfield and Taft bought it. All the ore that is used in the Irondale works is taken from that mine. It is only one half mile from ours. The ore of the two mines is almost identical in chemical and physical characteristics. It is black magnetite without a trace of sulfur and with only a slight trace of phosphorous. There's none equal to it from Canada to Georgia."

Hammond's enthusiasm was boundless. "I have had my ore analyzed," he continued, "and I've had it worked in a forge. Some of the bar iron I had made at Penfield's and some at forges at Vergennes, Vermont. I've had the iron rolled into round and band iron and also made into nails by the Peru Company at Clintonville. The foreman and his workmen there said they never before had seen iron that would roll into thin 4d plates and 4d nails without cracks or fractures at the edges. Their Peru iron had been called the best, they said, but it could not stand the test for strength and toughness beside mine."

"Has your ore ever been run in a furnace?" asked the ironmaster.

"Yes," answered Hammond, "I got out about twenty tons of the ore. It cost me a plenty, too. What a time we had getting it out to a road! We used oxen and hauled it on a wood-shod sled over bare ground to the Wooster place. From there I had it hauled in a wagon to the wharf. I shipped it by boat to Greenbush (now Rensselaer) on the Hudson across from Albany and from there by rail to Stockbridge, Mass. It was worked there in a small charcoal furnace and yielded a very fine quality of pig iron. I have sent samples of my iron to the U. S. Navy Department and I've a letter from the Commandant of the arsenal there in which he testifies in highest terms to its qualities of toughness and ductility. I tell you, Jonas, there's a fortune in this iron business for us and for our children, and it will bring great prosperity to the town."

Tower asked questions about funds to finance the proposed new enterprise. "I've worked this out all alone so far and at my own expense entirely," said Hammond. "I have tried to get my brother John to go into it, but he showed no interest until it had been tested and promised to be worth his attention and investment. He's as canny as a Scot—or a Connecticut Yankee. He never said a word against my project, but he didn't do a thing to encourage me. Now that it promises to be a very good thing, he is coming in with us, money and all. There isn't a shrewder business man nor a gentleman of finer character than my brother John anywhere in the country."

By this time they had made the top of the last long hill and were approaching Penfield & Harwood's Iron Works. In contrast to the loveliness of the landscapes they had been passing, here was evidence of devastation to nature such as seems too often to be the outcome of man's enterprise when he exploits the earth's resources. In the vicinity of the works everything bore a black, sooty look. The surrounding hills had been stripped of timber far up towards their summits, and at the margin of the forest smoke of the charcoal kilns could be seen. Above the works and on a higher level was the village street lined with neat cottages, a church, parsonage, and schoolhouse and the two big houses of the proprietors.

The Penfield house stood four-square in a corner of the crossroad behind its post-and-board fence. As the two visitors approached the house, its door opened and Allen Penfield appeared under the fanlight. A moment later his wife followed him out to greet them.

"She's my sister," Hammond explained to Tower. "And Penfield's partner, Harwood, has married their daughter Ann. You see, it's quite a family affair, our iron business here."

As they approached the Penfields, he greeted his sister heartily, and to Penfield he said, "Here's Mr. Tower, Allen. I've brought him right off the morning's steamboat. We're fortunate to get him. There isn't a man in the country who knows as much as he does about building and running iron furnaces. I tell you, Allen, Crown Point is going to boom when Tower builds this 'tower' for us. He is going to be our 'Tower of Strength.'"

Little time was lost in these greetings. Penfield climbed into the buckboard, and the three rode away toward the mountains to decide on a good location for the iron furnace they were planning to build.

The road emerged from the forest into a spacious valley that lay midway between the mines and the limestone bed. Steep cliffs of gneiss and rugged mountainsides surrounded it. A little brook of clear water, the outlet of a mountain pond, flowed through it. Already a cleared space of several acres was in cultivation. It seemed to Hammond that here was a choice place for the hamlet that would cluster about "the works."

"Charles and I," said Penfield, "have considered every possible site, and we have come to the conclusion that this place affords an almost ideal combination of suitable conditions."

"Yes," agreed Tower, "it seems you two have fixed it all pretty well. The only thing you have failed to do is to bring the Lake alongside. That oversight is not too great a drawback, however. Your iron can be hauled to the Lake. I think you have used very good judgment."

So, with the sense that they were performing a rite, Hammond took his axe out of the buckboard and with the manner and air of a high priest, he ceremoniously felled a log across the place they had selected.

As a result of this decision by Hammond, Tower, and Penfield on that autumn day in 1844, preparations were made, and the furnace was built during the next spring and summer under the expert supervision of Jonas Tower.

It was forty feet high and nine feet across the base inside. It was built close to a steep hillside so that wagons loaded with ore, limestone or charcoal could drive to the rear at a high level and deliver their loads across a wooden trestle to the top of the stack.

The ruins of this tower, built of rough, native stones, can still be found in the forest that has grown up around it. Stones from the upper portion have fallen about its base, and young trees, rooted in crannies between the stones, are continuing nature's slow work of demolition.

The first iron was run out on January 1, 1846. Tower remained in charge six years. Then he sold his interest and left. The iron produced was of the highest quality. The first steel made in America under the Bessemer patents was made from this iron in the steel works at Troy. As was well known, the armor plates which protected the Union warship "Monitor" in its historic battle with the Confederate ram "Merrimac" were made from this iron.

Hammond's confidence that the forests were inexhaustible was ill-founded, for in 1861, after only sixteen years of operation, wood for fuel became so scarce that the furnace could be run only about three-fourths of the time. In 1865 it was destroyed by fire and immediately rebuilt. In

1872, however, its fire was allowed to go out forever on account of the scarcity of food for fuel and because it was now outmoded by newer types of furnace and improved methods of operation.

Furnaces were now being fueled with anthracite coal. Already those situated along Lake Champlain were using this fuel, which could be shipped in by water. The business acumen and readiness to grasp opportunities that had characterized Charles Franklin Hammond during his youth and earlier manhood kept him abreast of the profound changes that followed the Civil War. His brother, John Cross Hammond, Tower, Penfield, and other former business associates had now passed out of the scene, but two sons, John and Thomas, who had grown up in the business, were well trained to carry on.

In 1872 his company was reorganized with greatly increased capital. A narrow-gauge railroad was built from the lake to the mines, and two large, up-to-date blast furnaces were erected at the shore with facilities for shipping both ore and pig iron by water and by rail.

The Company's holding in the 1880s comprised more than 20,000 acres of improved and forest lands, the two blast furnaces, a large machine shop and other buildings close to Lake Champlain, a forge for the manufacture of bloom iron with separator and foundry at Irondale, and the mines with their shops, smithies, dwellings, store, offices, and the railroad.

In the vicinity of the mines all ledges of outcropping rock that might yield ore were explored until more than fifty pits were opened. At one time 750 men were on the payroll.

This intensive working of the mines brought about depletion of the ore, and one after another the mines had to be abandoned. The reserves in the ground were nearly exhausted when in the early 1890s a grave industrial depression prostrated business throughout the country. The demand for iron and steel fell off. The Crown Point iron was expensive to produce. The company could not continue to operate in competition with mines recently opened in Michigan and Minnesota, where vast deposits of excellent ore could be inexpensively mined and shipped thru the Great Lakes to coal regions. Under this combination of adverse circumstances, the Crown Point Iron Company became insolvent in 1893. A few years later, its whole plant was sold and dismantled.

Charles Hammond's vision and enterprise brought not only fortune to himself but prosperity to his town. He lived to see the primitive iron industry of his early years expanded on a scale undreamed of by any man before the middle of the 19th century, and his own role in this drama was an important one.

The great blast furnace plant on Lake Champlain has vanished. The course of the railroad can be traced by extensive fills and deep cuts. At Irondale a few vestiges remain which can be identified by only those few persons who have memories of the busy past. The stone tower of the charcoal furnace still remains.

At the site of Hammondville, the mining village, not a single structure remains. However, the mines—fearsome yawning chasms, bottomless shafts, and dark, mysterious pits—even though nature has concealed them with forests, will remain forever to afford evidence of that large and important enterprise that developed and flourished here because of the vision and labors of men of staunch integrity and business ability.

REDFORD GLASS

By Marjorie L. Porter, *North Country Life*, Spring 1953

Ever hear of Redford glass? More than a century ago it was being made at Redford on the Saranac River, about twenty miles from Plattsburgh. Pieces of Redford glass are in much demand by collectors of old glassware, who are constantly on the watch for the ornamental "witch" balls, for the Bo Peep canes, for the bull's eye panes of crown glass, and for a variety of bowls, tumblers, pitchers, etc. Even a double flask has appeared.

The men who were concerned with glass making on the storied Adirondack River didn't intend to manufacture it at Redford. It was just that community's good luck to be made famous. Actually it didn't exist before the establishment of the glass works, and the origin of the name is a matter of conjecture. It may have been for an early settler.

The site originally selected for the factory was much farther up the river in the vicinity of Bloomingdale. Some of the required ingredients for the glass, however, were not available there, so a spot not far below the forks of the river, where the North Branch joins the parent stream, was decided upon, since the fine sandstone deposits lay not far distant.

In 1830 Charles Corning (Elias W. Corning, according to the New York State *Gazetteer*) and Gershom Cook, both residents of Troy, purchased a tract of land one mile square. The hamlet of Redford was located on this tract.

In March, 1831 they erected a sawmill and a grist mill under an agreement that the latter was to be kept running "forever." Work on the stone buildings of the glass works was also started, hundreds of men and teams being employed during the summer. In October, 1831 the first lot of crown glass was turned out. The factory cost a minimum of $50,000 and probably considerably more than that.

White Potsdam sandstone of exceptionally fine quality was utilized in the glass manufacture, together with other ingredients which included fine potash or pearl ash, some of which is said to have come from Franklin County.

The formula for Redford glass was kept secret, of course. According to Daniel Trombley of Redford, grandson of Peter Trombley, early settler and iron maker at Redford, valuable papers such as those on which the glass formula was written were kept in a secret room on the second floor of the residence known as the "company house." This pretentious house burned some years ago.

The expensive melting pots, made of Stourbridge clay, were imported from England. Most of the glass makers were also English. Mr. Trombley has an old account book in which their names are preserved. He has also an oil painting of the company house, the flag that flew over the glass works, the clock used by the company, and the bell that hung on the stone factory.

The factory building had space for two furnaces so that no interruption in manufacture might occur. The mixing room adjoined this factory, and beyond was a room in which the sandstone for the glass was crushed. The stone was roasted in a kiln.

Another building housed a cutting room, packing room, and pot room. Close by was the dry house, where wood for the furnaces was made ready in ovens on a 24-hour schedule in two 12-hour shifts. The wood was split into slender sticks called shiders.

When it was desired to use a furnace, about three weeks were allowed for heating it preparatory to a melt. It was not allowed to cool off until it was no longer fit for use, the whole works operating on a seven-days-a-week basis.

Two melts were made every week, the pots of Stourbridge clay being filled with the various ingredients according to the directions of the melt master, whose judgment was depended upon to produce glass of desired quality. As these materials were reduced to a molten mass, more materials were added in two successive fillings, and finally broken glass, called cullet, was put in. Firing of the furnace stopped when the melt master decided the molten glass was ready for blowing. All openings were closed for several hours so that impurities might rise to the top of the mixture and be skimmed off.

When the time arrived for blowing the glass, a call boy appeared at the home of each of the approximately 20 blowers, notifying them to come to the factory.

The establishment was conducted by Mr. Corning and Mr. Cook until 1836, when Matthew Lane became a partner and the firm name became Cook, Lane and Corning.

In 1843, manufacture of glass was discontinued for three years. There had been a disagreement between the owners and the superintendent, John Samuel Foster, who asked for higher wages and, being refused, went into Jefferson County and set up an establishment where he manufactured "Redwood?" glass.

At Redford, some of the finest crown glass ever made, glass famous for its color and brilliance, was sold for nearly twenty years, the hamlet humming with industrial activity. Today Redford, with a population of only a few hundred persons, chiefly French Canadians, has no industry. The stone factory buildings, abandoned in 1852, have been torn down. Only the site remains to be pointed out by Dan Trombley on a tour of the place.

Many pieces of Redford glass are in the form of bottles, bowls, tumblers, maps, hats, and a variety of other objects. Some pieces exist on which there are decorations. There are known to be a goblet with bands of white and several pieces of the pond lily pattern. Paperweights have also been found, several having initials inside. Panes of the bull's-eye crown glass remain in a number of buildings in the area, such as the Federated Church at Peru and the Lapham homestead at the Quaker Union. Nearly 200 of these panes were in use at the Redford home of the Trombley family when it was destroyed by fire. After the fire, about six dozen of them were sold. A "table" of the glass, about three feet across, in the gable window of the Banker house four miles west of Plattsburgh, was sold in recent years. Legend has it that Elisabeth and Elihu Briggs, pioneer settlers in 1796 in the town of Chesterfield, Essex County, journeyed to Redford to purchase glass when they built their pretentious farm home. The home still stands near the site of their original log cabin, and window glass in another residence not far distant is believed to be Redford glass.

Collections of the glass include those owned by the granddaughter of Matthew Lane, the late Mrs. Bentley of Plattsburgh; by the late Warner McLaughlin of Port Henry; by the Dupont family of New Jersey; by Mrs. Boire of Mooers; and smaller collections owned by other persons in the North Country. It is believed there may not be more than 250 pieces in existence, although the search continues.

Redford on the Saranac is almost a ghost town now, but there are those who remember the days of its glory and the men who helped make crown glass in the Adirondack wilderness.

PIT BURNING CHARCOAL

By David B. Carl and Roland B. Miller, *North Country Life*, Winter of 1959
Reprinted from the New York State *Conservationist*, August–September 1952

Charcoal, to most of us, is a lustrous, lightweight, brittle black solid that comes in quarter bushel paper bags, makes a clean, hot fire on which to roast picnic hamburgers and hot dogs. At today's prices it is strictly a luxury product and often unprocurable because of the erratic supply.

Yet only a century ago, charcoal was the basic industrial fuel and the only one that could be used for smelting iron ore. As a result, the woodlands within reach of the early iron furnaces were cut clear for charcoal wood, leaving vast areas of stump land—to the consternation of many an early conservationist.

This apprehension can be better understood when we note that in the 1880's, the Chateaugay Ore & Iron Co. was consuming the virgin forests of Clinton and Franklin counties at a rate of more than 2,000 acres annually. A bit farther south, the J. & J. Rogers Iron Co. at Ausable Forks was skinning another 1,000 acres a year. Our early center of iron production extended from the lower Hudson Valley north to the Canadian border and around the northern Adirondacks as far as St. Lawrence County. Each furnace drew its charcoal supply from the nearby woods, in an ever—widening circle, and the effects of their wood procurement operations can still be seen in square mile after square mile of even-aged hardwood forest that replaced the original uneven-aged, mixed timber.

The making of charcoal is a very ancient art, stemming back to the very beginning of civilization. Fundamentally it consists of heating wood under some sort of cover, in the presence of just enough air to burn the gases, which are driven off, leaving behind almost pure carbon. This was first done in a pit dug into the ground. Presently, the pit was abandoned and a covered heap built on top of the ground for better draft control and greater ease in handling the coal. However, the old names stick; in eastern New York at least, the heap is still called a "coal pit" and the product "pit burned charcoal."

With the coming of coke for blast furnace fuel, iron production in New York declined and the charcoal business faded. The great bulk market, where a charcoal burner could always be sure of selling his coal, disappeared and with it the race of woodchoppers with it the race of woodchoppers who made a living at a laborious and dusty trade. Gone from the mountain roads are the high-racked charcoal wagons. Gone from the mountain air is the pungent smell of coal pit smoke. Gone are the charcoal burners—almost.

The hills east of the Hudson River, in Columbia and Rensselaer counties, were for long a center of charcoal burning. Soon after settlement, charcoal became an important "cash crop," for it was light enough and valuable enough to stand considerable transportation even over the rough

This is a scene at The Narrows on Chateaugay Lake about 1885. The charcoal produced by the kilns on the farther shore was hauled to the iron forges on Lower Chateaugay Lake. In the foreground is a hand ferry used in crossing the lake at this point. *Photograph by Seneca Ray Stoddard. Courtesy of the Maitland C. DeSormo Collection. This S. R. Stoddard photograph is now part of Special Collections, Feinberg Library, SUNY College at Plattsburgh*

roads of those early days. Some of it went west to the more populous areas along the River, but most of it was hauled south. At Ancram, Robert Livingston, a grandson of the first Lord of the Manor, had established an iron works in 1748, based on local charcoal and iron ore brought in from nearby Salisbury, Conn. A century later the Copake Iron Works started up just a few miles to the north. At peak production the latter consumed nearly half a million bushels of charcoal a year—quite a drain on the local forest resource.

In the charcoal business, Ancram and Copake are only names now, the sites of their once busy iron works marked by slag heaps, waste ore and the cold and silent masonry of their abandoned furnaces. Scattered over the hills are still to be found the old coal pit floors, little patches of carefully leveled ground cover with a layer of carbon chips and surrounded by little rings of earth—feeble but enduring monuments to the once numerous clan of colliers.

But, on the hills back of Troy, there are still a few men who burn charcoal in the ancient, time-honored way. One of these is Joe Timber, who lives (See editor's note at end of article) on the road between Taborton and the Dutch Church, right on top of the mountain. Joe was born 79 years ago on the place north of where he now lives, and he has always lived and worked on the mountain. He was been burning coal pits more than 50 years.

The first essential for making charcoal is a good floor. This is a carefully leveled area, say 30 feet across, from which all sod and woody material has been removed (such stuff burns) and all the rocks grubbed out (they explode when they get hot). The soil must be porous enough to drain well without letting to much air up through. And it must be so situated that surface water and rainfall drain away. Old floors are best, for they have been thoroughly burned out and the soil pores pretty well filled with charcoal dust.

The denser hardwoods—beech, birch, maple and oak—made the heaviest and best charcoal. The softer hardwoods, like aspen, produced a coal that was clean but light. Softwoods were seldom used; pine and spruce gave off too much tar, while hemlock snapped and crackled too much. Besides, the yield from softwoods was unsatisfactory.

Wood for coaling was air-dried; green wood took extra fuel and extra time to cook the water and the resulting steam, if pocketed, might cause an explosion and blow a hole in the covering. The wood was cut four feet long. Sticks over 6 or 7 inches were split so as to insure charring all the way through. But there was no minimum size and the men who cut charcoal wood took everything except the softwoods and used everything except the smallest branch wood.

The sticks were piled on end to form a hemispherical mound, usually about 10 feet high and 25 feet in diameter. This was covered with a layer of hay or ferns and then with a mixture of sod, earth and charcoal dust, to form an airtight but flexible cover. The pit was fired from the top thru a hole down into the pile. When the fire got going good, the pit was capped and a ring of holes poked in the covering just below the top. Cooking proceeded from the top downward. As the steam and gases were driven off or burned off, the pit shrank and the cover had to be patched and pounded down to keep it tight. For a ten-cord pit, burning took about two weeks, after which another week was required to cool it down.

When the fire was all out and the pit cooled, the covering was removed, the charcoal broken up, screened and sacked for market.

Good hardwood was rated to yield 32 bushels of coal to the cord, poorer wood somewhat less. That means that a ten-cord pit made about 1,300 quarter-bushel sacks. At today's prices, that is real money. But burning coal is a tedious, time-consuming job, with a 24-hour day rain or shine and nothing extra for overtime. While a burning pit does not require much actual labor, it has to be watched all the time. One small explosion of steam or a sudden settling can break the cover; it must be patched immediately or the pit will burst into flame and work and wood all go up in one big blaze. And no dirtier job was ever found than screening coal, for the charcoal dust flies all over and gets into everything.

Editor's Note: Since this article was originally published nearly seven years ago, statements regarding Joe Timber may not now be accurate.

PART ONE

Adirondack Memories

COLLECTION ONE
Adirondack Places

COLLECTION TWO
Adirondack Communities

COLLECTION THREE
Trades and Industries

COLLECTION FOUR
Exploring Nooks and Crannies

The sun would soon set, the adventurers' footsteps would remain on the sandy shore of the landing for only a short time. Campfires would be started and supper eaten, followed by time for sitting on log and stump benches to listen and talk.
Courtesy Lake Placid-North Elba Historical Society

COLLECTION FIVE
Adirondack Thrillers

BORN IN MY HEART

By William J. O'Hern

Sometimes I like to think back to the days I spent at my grandparents' camp, when I was a young boy, and recall the seemingly carefree life in the neighborhood along the riverfront. "Shuggie" was a steady presence in my life as I grew from childhood to adolescence. He was married to Viola, and they were my grandparents' neighbors. The two would have made wonderful parents, but I assumed they couldn't have children of their own. So they doted on their nephews, nieces and neighboring children—like me.

The Shuggs lived about a hundred yards from Camp Oasis. Our doors were connected with a well-matted grass path. I would visit them almost every time I went to camp. I remember watching out the picture window for their red canvas canoe, and was one time surprised at how fast they paddled in unison. They were the first people I ever saw motoring along with double paddles in almost precise form and in almost exact unison.

Sometime around 1959 "Vy" and "Shuggie" announced they were moving to Indian Lake. They believed the shores of the lake were probably one of the first sections of the "Dismal Wilderness," a translation of the

The breeze freshened as we sat lakeside, idle at last. The yellow pond lilies, blue Iris, Jack in the Pulpit, Indian cucumbers, wood sorrel, and partridge vines are in bloom. The setting is noiseless; the water has the crystal-like sparkle of an engagement ring's diamond.
Courtesy of the Mailtland C. DeSormo Collection

Native American term for the Adirondacks, to be settled by white men.

I knew the locations of Old Forge, Inlet, Raquette Lake and Blue Mountain Lake, but beyond that my orientation became fuzzy.

It wasn't long after they moved that we drove over to visit their new digs. Later, a float plane flight from Fourth Lake proved Indian Lake country was one of the most beautiful stretches of inland waters in the Adirondacks. An immense dam across the Indian River at the foot of the lake was built in 1898 for water storage, and has created a glistening expanse of water fourteen miles long and one and a quarter miles wide at its widest point.

Shuggie liked to explore, fish and hunt. His new home was once one of the haunts of the Iroquois on their hunting expeditions before colonization drove out the Six Nations Confederacy.

Indian Lake country has an attention-grabbing appeal. Rising above the west side of the lake is Snowy Mountain. Its expansive summit at 3,903 feet above sea level was once home to a fire observation tower and fire warden's cabin.

Looking east, across Indian Lake is Blue Ridge Mountain, 3,865 feet high, another lofty peak of the central cluster of ridges which form the backbone of the ancient Adirondacks.

I have climbed to the summits and enjoyed views of surpassing grandeur.

Farther east are the summits of Chimney Mountain and Bullhead Mountain. They are not as high as Snowy or Blue Ridge, but each is also a great peak in the central mountain chain. Exploring Chimney Mountain's nooks and crannies is a worthwhile adventure. There are twin shafts at its summit which Shuggie said are believed to be of volcanic origin. At the mountain's base is Chimney Mountain Cave, a cool nook under the rock where snow and ice can be found throughout the summer months.

Shuggie worked as a part-time caretaker maintaining a nearby state campground, but still had plenty of time to explore and learn the history of his new mountain homeland. It was visiting the Shuggs' new Adirondack home that first acquainted me with the beauties of the wilds surrounding Indian Lake. Its beauty has come to be appreciated by city people outside the mountains. Today the Indian Lake country is one of the best known and most-frequented of the summering sections of the Adirondacks. It might not seem as "wild" as it did in my younger days, but I never tire of re-exploring its many nooks and crannies.

DRIFTWOOD

Tossed about by angry waves,
Dashed against the rocks,
Washed upon the sands,
A twisted mass am I.
Like a piece of driftwood,
Blanched and gnarled with open wounds.
Yet like the driftwood.
Found was I.
Taken home and polished up,
Though the gnarls still show,
The changes wrought by loving hands,
Turned a piece of driftwood
Into a thing of usefulness.

—Louella Waterman, *North Country Life*, Summer 1958

Driftwood found floating on the water or cast ashore along Adirondack waterways is often adapted for use in rustic interiors and hand-crafted furniture. *S. R. Stoddard postcard image. Courtesy of the Mailtland C. DeSormo Collection*

Atop the bank, beyond the dock, Camp Cheerio stood among shading trees, its weathered, cedar shingle siding greying in cool shadows of root-beer-colored tannic water, where reflections from the bleached stumps and driftwood poke above the river's backwater.
Courtesy Leigh Portner Sr.

COLD RIVER VALLEY—BY CANOE

By Frances Boone Seaman, *North Country Life*, Summer 1947

It was the morning of August 12. I was home on vacation, and this was the day of a long-planned canoe trip with my sister Ethel into "hermit land." The morning sun had barely risen over Kempshall Mountain when we embarked on the three-day trip that would take us down Long Lake and into the Raquette, then up Cold River and finally by foot through the giant solitudes of Cold River valley, where lived Noah John Rondeau, the well-known Adirondack hermit.

That first day, under a sweltering sun, we paddled eleven miles, most of it on Long Lake, where on either side the forested mountains rolled ever onward, ridge beyond ridge, till in the distance they seemed to merge with the blue waters. Over this lovely panorama and directly ahead of us over the foot of the lake hung the brooding and little-known peaks of the Seward Range, and before long, massive Santanoni appeared to the right, blocking off the other side of Cold River valley. Between these mountain monarchs, some fifteen miles away, lived Rondeau.

At one o'clock we floated, in less than a foot of water, over the big sand bar where the lake once again becomes the Raquette River. There was little need to paddle here, for the current was quite swift. We enjoyed ourselves and took a few pictures. Soon we reached the Big Rock and here left the Raquette, turned right and floated like a leaf around several swift bends. They were so swift, in fact, that on one we lost control of the canoe and found ourselves riding backwards for an instant, narrowly missing a partly submerged tree trunk before we could get whirled around in the right direction again. There were some misgivings that Cold River was something of a demon, till we struck the main stream, where the river was sufficiently cowed to permit normal paddling again.

It wasn't long before we had taken the wrong turn and ended up in the middle of nowhere when the stream we were following suddenly dried up at a beaver dam. For the first time, we dug out our one and only map, a topographical one of the Cold River section, printed in 1914.

Little did we know then that that map would be nearly worn out before another day was over.

Around every bend we expected to see the "rocks" which, we had been told, would probably retard our progress to the point of having to cache our canoe and proceed on foot. That didn't faze us; a little walking would be welcome after so much sitting.

Calkins Creek lean-to was picturesquely located on a high sandy knoll overlooking a bend in the river. We might have tarried for a swim, but our objective was to camp as far upriver as possible before nightfall.

The sun was very hot and clear, making the shallow riverbed easy to navigate and giving me a frightful sunburn on arms and face. Nobody would have recognized me, I'm sure, for I had an old straw hat pulled as far down over my face as possible and my face was so greasy from olive oil that it shone as bright as the water that day.

Finally we spotted the "rocks" just ahead and, to our amazement, found them to be a continuous gravel bar across the stream. The first riffle wasn't bad. We waded and dragged the canoe over the small stones, got in and proceeded to the next about a hundred feet upstream. With ice water (felt like it, anyway) rushing over my feet and those stones beginning to feel like nails, I was sure I couldn't last on many more of these riffles. Ethel was carrying the packs near shore, where the riverbed was dry but the stones just as hard to walk on.

When finally our progress was halted by real rocks, black, jagged ones in swift water, it was nearly four o'clock, and ahead of us on a high pine knoll was a perfect campsite. No shelter except the pines, but someone had left a fine fireplace of stones and that we soon put to use. That evening a thorough search upstream on both sides failed to show any sign of a lean-to or what was worse, any trails.

This wasn't the first time Ethel and I had slept out under the stars on balsam beds, and we feared nothing but the mosquitoes. They were soon thwarted when we placed over us a large piece of mosquito netting which had been covered with a mixture of several kinds of fly dope. The pack-basket and knapsack had been hung in a tree nearby and, of course, we hoped there wouldn't be any nocturnal visitors. Just to make sure, we had brought along a bottle of "Dogzoff," a well known repellent. This we sprinkled liberally around the campsite, for we felt that it would keep raccoons and porcupines away just as well. It was not until morning, when the wind changed, that we wished we had left the stuff at home.

Upon our awakening, the sun was shining and I was annoyed to find my watch had stopped. While eating breakfast, we speculated on how much farther we would go until we discovered a trail, for the old map showed that one crossed the stream somewhere in our present vicinity. If we could only find the ranger's cabin in Shattuck Clearing, we'd be all right. Everything was wet with dew, but we set out hopefully, taking along only a knapsack with lunches and five pounds of new potatoes as a present for the hermit.

The undergrowth along the river was terrible. Vines, bushes and bracken grew waist-high, and after pushing through them for a quarter of a mile, we were ready to turn back. However, by walking farther back

Francis Boone knew the whereabouts of hermit Noah John Rondeau's huts.
Courtesy Edward Kornmeyer

from the river, we found the woods were at least passable. The sun shone hot, and when we came to open clearings, our thirst was acute. Nowhere could we find the trail marked on the map, nor had we met anyone yet on Cold River.

The "topo" map was consulted again amid much anxiety and consternation, for the terrain seemed identical with that of the map except for the trail, which we couldn't find. Was it possible that everyone bushwhacked up Cold River?

The sun cast a sultry heat, deer flies bothered us continuously, our thirst became greater and the sole on one of my hiking boots had come apart and flapped with every step. Then came a bend in the river. The map showed it and the terrain ahead seemed to indicate it. The phantom trail on the map showed a short-cut over the hill; we decided to cut off, too, and then if a stream came in on the next bend, we'd know where we were. Our hopes were justified, for there was running water under the alders and we knelt and scooped it up by the handfuls.

The Burning. The Seward Range rises in the distance beyond Cold River. Taken from Shattuck Clearing in November 1921. *Courtesy C.V. Latimer, Jr. M.D.*

So this was hermit-land? No, not quite, though we were entering the great valley between Seward and Santanoni. This was Shattuck Clearing, once scourged by fire—the land of small hardwoods and brush. We imagined Noah Rondeau's home was in the deep, quiet solitudes of a heavily wooded glade where here and there a sunbeam managed to dart through the towering hemlocks to dance a fleeting moment on some gurgling little brook among the mosses. Nothing would meet his ears but the sounds of the forest and the voice of an occasional guest, who was always welcome in his "city." His nearest neighbor was probably the ranger stationed here in Shattuck Clearing.

It couldn't be much farther now. After again studying the map, we headed up-river through what seemed impenetrable masses of brush. Here near the top of the hill we knew the trail from Plumley's Camp, back on Long Lake, connected with the ranger's camp not far away, but where was it? In disgust we finally turned around and started for home.

We hadn't gone a hundred yards when I happened to look back. I could hardly believe my eyes! There on the farther end of the hill we had just traversed was the roof of a dwelling, and smoke lazily drifting from the chimney, and the American flag flying. To think that we had come so close to missing our first objective!

Back we went, knowing a cool drink and a friendly welcome awaited us at the ranger's cabin. He looked at us in surprise as we came up the trail from the river. We certainly looked bedraggled, and we were so hungry that we scarcely waited for an invitation. We sat down under a tree and started eating.

Our greatest disappointment was hearing that Noah John Rondeau lived six miles farther up Cold River—a twelve mile round trip—and since it was then noon, we decided it was unwise to go farther, for our rations were getting low. Our long-planned hike to Big Dam had to be canceled!

There were more disappointments for us. It was hoped that our friend could tell us a better trail back down the river but no; we must traverse the jungle again. It was little comfort even to know that we had done something few others had attempted. We had followed a trail that hadn't been mowed in twelve years—the old riverman's trail. Now we knew why it showed only on the old map!

Late in the afternoon of the next day, as we paddled leisurely up Long Lake, homeward bound, rifle shots rang out and hung in the air toward town. Probably the fellows at the rifle range, we thought. All the way home we hadn't been able to console ourselves for the failure of our trip; for by this time we should have seen all the wonders of Cold River "city."

Suddenly our thoughts were disturbed by the ringing of church bells. They swelled louder on the still air and in our hearts we knew that something had happened. Every bell in town seemed to be ringing. Would they never stop? The joyous peals were punctuated by more rifle shots, and we were paddling like mad.

A Chris-Craft came roaring down the lake toward us. We hailed them and as they swung past in low swells, someone shouted, "THE WAR IS OVER—JAPAN HAS SURRENDERED!"

"He's kidding," we said. But no—those bells were telling the truth. "Thank God," we breathed, and then we thought of Cold River. Suddenly we realized it had all been for the best. We might not have heard this wonderful news for days.

EXCURSION TO SPRUCE LAKE

By Helen Ireland Hays, *York State Tradition*, Spring 1971

My father's words, "If you are exempt from your examinations this June, you and I will go to Spruce Lake for a week's trout fishing," are as clear to me today as when I heard them at the age of nine.

That is just what happened, and we went.

Mother packed us up and drove us to Piseco Lake, where we met our guide, Bill Courtney. When we learned that his two sons had gone ahead with most of the supplies, Father said, "Let's get started."

Father and Mr. Courtney placed their packbaskets on Mr. Courtney's porch. Then, turning their backs to the baskets, they slipped their arms through the straps, gave a slight jounce to adjust the packs comfortably, and straightened up. Father helped me arrange my knapsack. I picked up my Teddy bear, and we started through the woods on the twelve-mile walk to Spruce Lake.

"You notice this is a good trail, but always watch the blazes," Father cautioned. "An animal runway can cross a trail and mislead you. You can depend on the blazes to show the right way to go."

"I've been reading a book about blazes," I replied. "A large blaze means the trail bears right—"

"Bears blaze trails, too," Mr. Courtney told me. "Their blazes aren't solid like a blaze from a hatchet. They rip the bark off in streaks with their claws. Mebbe I can show you some. Mebbe some of these will tell that the trail turns. We'll see if we can find one."

Of course, we all watched for the bears' markings. Presently Mr. Courtney led us aside where the bears, reaching high as they stood on their hind legs, had clawed the bark. On one trunk there actually was a small mark beside the large blaze.

Lean-tos offer ready-made shelter. *Courtesy Meredith Flerlage*

"Here," Mr. Courtney said, "This is a good one. I'll just see if I can get that blaze off, so you can take it home and show your friends how the bears up to Spruce Lake mark their trails."

And he did!

Every three miles we crossed a stream. The water ran swiftly, so we could drink from each one. Just before we came to the Jessups River, a long V-shaped trough made of weathered boards snaked its way down the mountain.

"Some of us come in here to make maple syrup," Mr. Courtney explained. "We pour the sap into the trough and it flows over there, down the slope a little, to where we have a sugar house. Yes, it takes a lotta sap. Easier than carrying so many pails though."

I was sure Mr. Courtney was right, but it did seem like a wasteful way of gathering sap.

Late in the afternoon, an opening in the trees, an increase in light, and a shallow stony beach told us we had reached Spruce Lake.

"My place is up to the right," Mr. Courtney said. "Tim Crowley's place was over there to the left. The state just took it down. Poor location anyway. Pretty low."

As soon as I could speak to Father privately, I asked why the state took down Mr. Crowley's camp, and who was Mr. Crowley?

"Mr. Crowley is another guide. There may be some rivalry between him and Mr. Courtney," Father replied. "This is all state land. No one is allowed to put up a permanent building. The guides build cabins, and the state, after a time, takes them down. Then the guides build again."

Mr. Courtney's log cabin stood on a hemlock knoll. The door, made of vertical boards painted green, was ornamented with the white outline of a large fish.

"That was the biggest lake trout ever caught here," Mr. Courtney told us. "Tim Crowley claims a party of his got a bigger one but 'tisn't so, and they never made a picture, so ours stands."

Mr. Courtney's two sons joined us. The older son, Floyd, was a fine-looking young man. George, the younger, was near enough my age to play with me and teach me to climb up the sides of the log cabin. We had wonderful games of "Follow the Leader." Scrambling after George, with Teddy tucked under my arm, was exciting for me. As I look back, I think George set a pace that was beyond me but not impossible. His lead was a constant challenge.

One night George and Floyd said they were going out to get a deer. On being invited, Father and I accepted. Whether I understood what was afoot I can't remember, nor do I understand why Father let me go.

Together we walked down to the beach, and all four got into the canoe. George paddled stern; Father and I sat side by side on the bottom, and Floyd paddled bow. The light from our reflector lantern moved along the stony shore as we slipped silently through the darkness.

"By that log!" George whispered.

Three mink played up and down the beach. As we approached, they paused, looked straight at us as our light "jacked," or blinded, them. Without a ripple, we passed, and they were lost again in the darkness.

Presently the stony shoreline changed to a small meadow of swale grass, where a stream emptied into the lake. Cautiously we approached the marsh. The tin reflector behind our kerosene lantern sent the light far ahead. Suddenly, a deer, framed in the circle of light, lifted its head and stood blinded before us. Without a sound Floyd lifted something to his right shoulder—To my horror, I knew!

"Don't shoot!"

My words were in time.

Neither Floyd or the others admonished me. We continued around the margin of the lake, and about midnight returned to the cabin. I was sleepy, but also happy that the number of wild creatures along the shore was undiminished.

The next day, as we prepared for an expedition to the beaver dam, I noticed that Mr. Courtney was putting rocks in his pack basket.

"Why do you put rocks in your pack, Mr. Courtney?" I asked.

"Well, you see, a guide is supposed to carry sixty pounds. There isn't much to carry today. I don't want to get out of practice."

The walk through the woods that morning was especially beautiful. Pink moccasin flowers grew under the tall evergreens. There weren't a great many, but more than I had ever seen before.

In his usual helpful way, Mr. Courtney offered to dig some for me to take home. Mother had taught me the names of a number of flowers and had taught me also that wild plants should be left where they grew. It wasn't hard for me to decline Mr. Courtney's offer. However, we appreciated his concern for our pleasure, and he was grateful for our interest in his woods.

Standing on the beaver dam, we caught enough speckled trout for supper. The men put all the fish in my basket and let me carry them.

"Plenty more if you want them," Mr. Courtney told Father.

"These will make a good meal," Father replied.

When we returned to the lake, late that afternoon, while the men tied the boat, George and I ran up the slope toward the cabin.

The old couple was sitting on their front porch when I came upon them after padding through a narrow channel. The old man slithered to the edge of his chair, bent forward, shaded his eyes from the bright sun with his hand and called for me to come up to the cabin as the woman continued to knit. They were dear and gentle mountain folks who told wonderful stories of places I might enjoy investigating. *Courtesy John Chamberlain*

George grabbed my arm, "Stop!" he breathed. "Stand still!"

Ahead of us a mother bear was cuffing her cub up a tree. A second cub played near. The mother swayed slowly, backed up a little. The cub came down. To our immeasurable relief, after a few minutes, all three ambled away into the dimness of the forest.

The men, coming up from the lake, received us and our outpourings with quiet interest.

"Must have been a land breeze," Mr. Courtney observed.

That night, sitting around the comfort of the wood stove, Mr. Courtney told us stories of his experiences in the woods. To me, the most dramatic one was "—that time Floyd and me was here all alone. I'm not clumsy as a rule, but somehow I managed to get my right foot down between the rocks and I broke my leg. Well, of course, I couldn't walk and there wasn't no doctor in here, so Floyd, he put me on his shoulders and he carried me clean out to Piseco. Every stream, I thought we'd never make it, but we did. Yessir, he carried me all the way."

Then, quickly, to change the subject, he turned to me.

"Tomorrow you and Teddy and your Daddy goes out the same twelve miles. If your teacher lets you off from your examinations next year an' you come in here, I'll have more moccasin flowers and more trails the bears have blazed to show you."

DESTINATION: BROWN'S TRACT

By Robert Anderson, *York State Tradition*, Winter 1963

In the register of guests of Lawrence's Hotel at Moose River under the heading *Destination*, the most frequent entry was Brown's Tract. Brown's Tract included, among other places, the Fulton Chain and Big Moose Lake.

Almost anybody in the Boonville and Port Leyden area in the 1860s and '70s could tell you the story of John Brown, the Providence, Rhode Island, merchant who had purchased the land and tried to develop it. A polite listener might hear also of his son-in-law, Charles F. Herreshoff, who lost his fortune trying to develop the tract by mining, forging and agriculture. The story of the 210,000 intractable acres that did not respond to agricultural efforts and were too remote for an economically successful iron mining and smelting business, with the intriguing details of the Manor House and the forge near First Lake, and how the bankrupt Herreshoff shot himself would gradually be explained.

But this was all in the past by the time Abner Wood Lawrance built his hotel. According to his daughter, Mrs. Loua M. Thomas of Chadwicks, New York, the young Abner on a trip to the woods saw a spot he liked, and peeling a sapling as a landmark, he announced he would come in and build a hotel there. He did, and opened it in 1859, when he was thirty years old, and ran it until 1878. He was not unequipped for the business, having run a hotel in Lee in 1854–55, and apparently succeeded in his new venture almost at once. At least, he had a large number of patrons. Practically all the adult men and many of the women and children of nearby places, such as Boonville, seem to have signed the register. In all, there are about 6,600 signatures. Many of these are duplications from recurrent visits of the same persons, but still they represent about 3,000 different individuals.

Brown's Tract at this time was, at last, ready for exploitation, but not as Brown and Herreshoff had envisioned it. Local people had hunted, fished and wandered around there for years. But now they had been joined by outsiders seeking sport and recreation. In addition, the lumbermen and tannery interests had their attention directed to the area. The tract even had a few permanent settlers, or squatters. The chief of these was Otis Arnold and his large family, who had discovered tourists as a source of income.

The favored way to go into Brown's Tract was by the road from Boonville. This was probably the same general route surveyed by Stephen Smith of Russia in 1817. The description given of it in 1848 probably still held in 1859:

Exploring Adirondack nooks and crannies by motor car. The scent of balsam, the scenery and the singing birds were often the instigators of a particular exploration filled with laughter and banter as they rode along. *Courtesy George Shaughnessy*

"The route now taken to approach it from this direction is to leave the northern turnpike at Boonville, Oneida County. Taking a northeasterly direction, you pass the last improvement some eight miles from Boonville, beyond which the road is impassable for carriages. Pack-horses or what we call drays are used for carrying our provisions, etc. in our hunting and fishing excursions; last September (1848) I went in with a dray.

"On reaching Moose River, about five miles from the last settlement, we have to scow our luggage over; and frequently to swim our horses." (From *Trappers of New York*, by Jeptha R. Simms. Albany, J. Munsell, 1871. p. 191–92).

Lawrance built his hotel at this crossing. From there, there were miles to Arnold's and then two and a half miles further to the old forge. Many of the summer visitors pressed on to the relatively insect-free Fourth Lake.

Adirondack dirt roads were filled with lively bumps. After going over a teeth-jarring thump, Mabel Quackenbush and her siblings would giggle and call out, "Thank-you-mom."
Courtesy Leigh Portner

We get many hints about the travelers along this road when we read, with the imagination that sees between the lines, the two old registers of Lawrance's Hotel, dated from May 15, 1862, through October, 1878. There are the local names giving home addresses of various camps, mills and tanneries and nearby settlements such as Port Leyden and Boonville. Going to and from home, they stopped for a drink or a meal, occasionally to spend the night. They serve the sports as guides and teamsters, or have woods jobs as teamsters, mill employees and owners, lumberjacks, timber scouts, etc. They may be in search of recreation, hunting, fishing, dining out, going to parties or just woodsing and visiting. To and from Arnold's, Shepard's, Forge House or wherever a sportsman needed a guide; to and from Anderson's Mills, Shed Mills, Gang Mills, the Pulp Mill and Welch's Moose River Tannery, their movements are recorded. On these travels G. H. P. Gould and George P. Noble and Napoleon Gagnier may all have had the same destination.

The drivers advertised for business by signing their profession after their names: "Chas Phelps, Leyden, N. Western Teamster; Wm. McDonal, Teamster; J. T. Jones, Port Leyden, Livery Stable; James Brownlee, Hosilier; Chas Kent, Teamster; B. Baker, Stage Proper.; Thomas Carlon, Boonville, Livery Proprietor," and others signed the book.

The guides also advertised in this way, and sometimes their clients endorsed them. The famous guides, the professional guides and the part-time and obscure are listed there. Otis Arnold, Otis Arnold Jr., Ed Arnold, Jack Sheppard, Samuel Dunnakin, William Dart, Augustus Syphert, A. W. Halliday, Alonzo Wood, Paul and Richard Crego, George C. Balland and Jack Van Valkenburgh were some of the names. Their clients wrote: "P.A. Robbins is one of the best and most intelligent guides in the wilderness," and "Should any party going to John Brown tract want guides we can recommend to them Reuben Howard & Joseph J. Joslin as guides who understand their business—are attentive, efficient and trustworthy." But the endorsement of another man was written over, citing him as being, on better acquaintance, tricky and dishonest.

There are hints also of other business activities, as the notation under destination, "Mineral Bed." Another says, "The Corner Stone Laid for the Tannery in the year of our lord Sept. 6th/78," while G.H.P. Gould notated, "Commence the Drive Apr. 13, 1877."

Characters added spice. The uninhibited Brownlees must have kept things stirred up. Certainly they were given to self-advertising. Joseph appears first in a simple entry as a log peeler, then as "dead beet." Then there is a quiet statement, "This is my birthday." Then this startling notation appears: "Joseph Brownlee conquered Victor with Shialia along-side the ear. Mar. 17, 1877. b. good boy Joseph."

James Brownlee next put in an appearance: "James Brownlee landed in Moose River Apr. 27, 1877." Later he signed out: "James Brownlee leaves for to go to Canada, Province Quebec." And Joseph tamely followed: "Joseph Brownlee Bound for Canada."

But Joseph Gagnier represented an opposite extreme: "Joseph Gagnier, came back to Moose River the 10 of May in 1877 he only stayed a year and a month away from Moose River."

The hotel of that time also fulfilled the function of the dance hall, and this was true even in the backwoods. A long list of names on March 21, 1886, after the destination, given as A. W. Lawrances, has the notation, "All with the intintion off having a Dam good Dance."

Death is kindly absent from the register, but taxes and other aspects of government appear. Walter Johnson, collector, made it in on January 16, 1874, and "Wm. H. Mealus, Town Collector," made even better time, reaching Lawrances, appearing on January 4, 1877. Some value received was given for the taxes, however, for C. L. Phelps, R. O. Paul and Edward Fallon, commissioners of the town of Wilmurt, came on a survey of Brown's Tract road on October 3, 1876. They returned, with J. T. Comstock and Peter Clancy replacing R. O. Paul, on December 17, 1876, as the Herkimer County commissioners. The notation says, "Came in to accept Road and Bridge." This probably establishes the time when the Brown's Tract road became a charge on public funds. The tract itself had been parceled out in 1866. On September 13, 1866, Ansel Foster, J. H. Wetmore, and D. A.

Clay with guides stopped at Lawrances, their business being described as, "Come for Partition of Brown's Tract." This we can use as a dating of the start of the modern development of the area.

And what did the Civil War soldier do on leave? Right. He came to Brown's Tract. Outsiders came, like Colonel, later General, H. A. Dowe of Ithaca and General Rufus Daggett of Utica, although the latter commanded the 117th Regiment of the New York Volunteers, in which the local visitors, the Boonville boys, Lieutenant H. Dwight Grant and Sergeant C. S. Sperry served.

More and more outsiders came in. Many were from upstate New York and in hunting and fishing parties. But there were far off addresses, too, like St. Louis and Baltimore. Some were just passing through Brown's Tract on their way to or from another part of the Adirondacks. S. H. Babcock, R. U. Owens and N. Saltus of Utica left the note, "Members of the Walton Club. From 'Grants'—homeward bound. Went in via Lake George. May 16, 1864." They arrived at Lawrances on May 27th, which

The Moose Head Inn [Herkimer County] was located along the Moose River Road. Parts of the original complex are still standing. *Courtesy Town of Webb Historical Association*

was, it would seem, very good time. And when Theodore Roosevelt signed in September 1875, he was probably on his way from Paul Smiths.

Others had more serious business. Officials came. The Adirondack Survey showed up on February 27, 1877, headed by Verplanck Colvin of Albany with the local men, E. L. Sheppard and Alva Dunning. Wood industries were represented by timber scouts, buyers, investors, lumberjacks and mill employees from places like Ulster County, Bradley, Old Town and Bangor, Maine. There were peddlers, buyers and jobbers who advertised themselves after their signatures: James Friary Pedler "Just goin out to the States;" Pat O'Brien Tea Pedler; Reuben Sparrott and Asa Forbes, jobbers; Wm. A. Anthony, vegetable dealer; C. A. Smith, barbering; and even on December 11, 1872, a sewing machine agent. With these last, civilization would seem to have arrived at Lawrances.

Seventh Lake Landing, Brown's Tract country. July 21, 1920. "We packed our lunches, boarded the launch and started over Fourth Lake about noon. Walked from Fifth to Sixth Lake. Traveled by motor boat through 6th and 7th lakes. Walked about a mile from 7th to 8th Lake. Saw an eagle's nest in the top of a tall pine tree and saw the eagle and her young. Saw the tallest and largest trees in the Adirondacks, also beaver dams and houses. Returned to Camp Fulton at 5 PM." —From the 1913–1929 diary of LeNora Mae Quackenbush Portner.
Courtesy Leigh Portner

Whether the appropriately named "Dr. Swan, Vet. Sur., Watson, N.Y." was bound on business or pleasure is hard to tell. But even in the great group of persons headed for recreation, self-advertisement was not lacking. Ministers, lawyers and doctors, such as C.E. Swift, M.D., a yearly visitor from Auburn, New York, appeared. Hotel men recorded their establishments.

In addition to the St. Louis Stickneys, Richard P. Johnson, proprietor, Dudley House, Utica, and Mr. Blair, proprietor, American Hotel, Boonville, were hosts who felt that they might attract trade to their establishments. Neither were newspaper men shy. The list included Frank N. Merrill, Watertown, Lines Printing Office; S.N.D. North, *Utica Herald*; R. J. Briggs, Cortland, *Standard & Journal*; and Wallace Kelly, Marathon, editor of the *Independent*.

There were a host of other outsiders, many identifiable in large measure by the readers' knowledge of their relative prominence. Mention probably ought to be made of Ned Buntline, the novelist, of Eagle's Nest, and R. U. Sherman of New Hartford, father of the Vice-President and a moving spirit in the Walton Club.

Many of these people, locals and outsiders, wrote their comments in the register on such topics as the state of the road, the weather, fish and deer, food and drink and each other. Some are serious and some are meant for humor.

There is an element of tragedy in such entries as "lost overcoat," "Fell in river, March 15, 1878," "compas lent," "hungry," "homesick," and the simple notation, "lost."

Or consider this entry: "On our arrival here, Doct. Merett & Wm. Hall, having walked here in 4 hours, took courage and thanked God. Doct. Merett offered up a prayer for the two poor Brothers who were in the wilderness up Moose River." Another wrote: "Don't see riding a horse bare back, isn't good for the bones. Oh Ye Gods preserve one from these horrid roads." And there were others: "Never to be seen in here again By god," and "To full for utterance & half the day. Played out at half past two. Single beds."

But on the other hand, there is a happy note in this entry: "Tower and his party of the 11th went in in a shower and come out in a rain, but all in good spirits."

Hints on the state of the road and modes of travel as well as traveling prowess are the themes of a number of entries: "through the mud to the woods," "July 21, 1865, E. Arnold arrived at this place at 12 o'clock from Brown's Tract with a wagon," "James Carlon left Boonville 1 o'clock he arrived in Browns tract 55 minutes past 8 in the morning, Bait that if you can (August 1865)" "started for Grants at 5 a.m. and arrived at Lawrances at ½ past 7a.m.," "made the trip from Arnolds to this River July 22 in 2 hrs & 40 minutes from Arnolds, 1 packhorse and 1 riding horse," "walked from Hellgate today in 4 hrs," "from the Forge House through with a sled and no whiskey, but two deer," "footed it from Forge House with heavy pack. 45 lbs. Rainy. Time 7 hours," "left Jack Sheppards Camp 6 a.m., arrival here 4 p.m. with 60# speckled trout taken yesterday from Big Moose."

Fishing and hunting entries are plentiful. Like the above, some recorded the amount of fish caught: "9 ¼ lbs speckled brook trout caught on Twin Sisters creek in half an hour," "19 ¾ lbs Salmon Trout caught J.W. Husted May 27(1878) in Raquette Lake," "on the way out with 20 lbs trout, one weighing 2 lbs," "no fish, on account of not having any whisky with us."

Often drinking notations appear in the standard forms of "drunk," "drunk as usual," "awfully weary," "sober and drinking," "sober," and variations, as "happy going home," "half seas over," "drunk all day," "drunk as a piper," "half drunk," "expect to get sober," and "drunk and broke." Forms of two old standard longer statements also appeared: "The hardest case in town," and "Thomas Rafe is the biggest drunkard in Moose River and a liar and don't you forget it."

Weather comments are frequent. On December 7, 1871: "Snow four feet on the level, good prospect for four more." On December 23, 1877: "Regular thaw out but Ed Arnold predicts a foot of snow within 24 hours—sic!" But the most notable weather information, from the modern winter sport's viewpoint, was contained in this entry: "July 7, 1871, Snow fell so that we snowballed in the yard."

The sports had names for each other in what passed for humor. At the same time, they give us mental pictures of the people. We see labels such as Shorty, Sweet Bands, Long Bill, Happy Jack, State Engineer, Bummer, Rough & Ready, Never Weaken, Old Doc, Peanuts, Guide, Dog Tender, Potato Buyer, and the Old Hunter. They also gave themselves group names like Wanderer & Co., Jolly Jokers, Stove-ins, the Excelsior Fishing Club, and Modac Club. Humor allegedly resided in fanciful destinations such as "going to a wedding," "going to a funeral," "to the devil," and "on a whaling voyage."

But the more serious business of politics occupied some travelers. Notable are the entries "Going to Election," "Strait Republican," and "South Democrat."

There are new and better roads now to Brown's Tract. The lumbermen and the tannery are gone. But recreation is a booming industry and we still stop for refreshment along the way. Unfortunately there is no register to sign and so we will not leave the record of our passage. There will be no record to show that our reactions are much the same as those of the visitors who recorded their names here at Lawrance's Hotel nearly a hundred years ago.

WEST CANADA CREEK TREASURE

By Theobald Clark, *North Country Life*, Summer 1950

Glyndon Cole said: "Legends of mines and treasures constitute one phase of the priceless heritage of the folklore of the North Country. An attempt should be made to preserve them—the purpose of this department ["Treasure Roundup"]. Any of our readers who know any such stories are invited to submit them for possible publication." Readers who had information for this department were to communicate it directly to Theobold

Clark. This article and the two that follow resulted from that effort to gather information on Adirondack treasure.

Away over on West Canada Creek there is a treasure, which I heard about by consorting with the natives of the region.

It seems that when Captain Walter Butler and his Tory Rangers descended upon the peaceful but ill-fated village of Cherry Valley, they over-played their hand by their blood-curling deeds of murder, rape, and torture, not to mention looting. An outraged militia under command of Marinus Willett pursued them all day through a desolate country to the banks of West Canada Creek near the town of Ohio. In the oncoming twilight a blinding snowstorm swept down as the two forces locked in deadly engagement at the ford in the creek. Butler and his men were all but wiped out. A few managed to escape to perish in the howling wilderness, then in the first grip of a northern winter. The wolves fed well that week.

The legend came to me in a strange manner, although the preceding paragraph is information taken from books, which I delved into after

Picnics came with exploring. *Courtesy George Shaughnessy*

Adirondack beaver were nearly extinct by 1894. In 1901, a campaign to restore the animals began. State-protected beaver lodges and dams were typical destinations for exploring tourists. This stick-and-mud lodge, photographed in 1917, was located near Eighth Lake outlet. *Photo LeNora Mae Quackenbush Portner. Courtesy Leigh Portner*

hearing the treasure legend from local persons. One evening I stopped at a small roadhouse between Piseco and Lake Pleasant. The owner, a woman of about fifty-five, took a keen interest in the metal locator, which I brought into the hotel from the automobile. Let me here explain that this hotel was a very tough place, catering to the wants of a horde of lumberjacks in that section. These wants were along both the bibulous and the amatory lines although I did not know this at the time I stopped. The woman somehow managed to keep everything in order and down to a modest tempo while I was there, and it was only the following evening that decorum finally burst its bounds and I became aware of the true character of the place. However, the madam told me that night that she knew where there was a buried treasure, and if I would go with her the following day, she would take me to the spot where she was certain my instrument would locate the cache. I was quick to accept.

The next day found us in the vicinity of a certain ford on West Canada Creek. The woman told me that in her younger days she had gone to a fortune teller or seer who told her that when she (the hotel owner) was a little girl, she had played often beside a certain rock near the ford. This was true. The seer explained that a large amount of gold coin was buried near that very rock. This part the woman had often heard, too, but never before had a fortune teller told her. Consequently, this is why she took me to the spot on her childhood farm where the rock was located. There were many rocks there. At the base of all of them on the west side was a large hole, which had the appearance of being very old. All I could detect with my instrument was an old stove top.

All this took place in 1939. Since then I have become acquainted with a family who are direct descendants of the Marinus Willett who commanded the pursuing militia. I know now why I couldn't find the gold. It is buried near a rock all right, but it is some paces out and at the foot of a very large elm tree. Perhaps the elm is gone. I don't know the habit of elms—whether they would last that long. What I'd like to find is Walter Butler's gold-laced hat, which fell into the creek and sank by its own weight when an avenging bullet tore into him. It would make a good hunting hat.

SILVER NEAR THE HUDSON RIVER HEADWATERS

By Theobald Clark, *North Country Life*, Winter 1951

In the Spring 1950 issue of North Country Life, *Cole said: "Legends of mines and treasures constitute one phase of the priceless heritage of the folklore of the North Country. An attempt should be made to preserve them—the purpose of this department [Treasure Roundup]. Any of our readers who know any such stories are invited to submit them for possible publication." Readers who had information for this department were to communicate it directly to Theobold Clark. This article and the two that follow resulted from that effort to gather information on Adirondack treasure.*

A letter from Adirondack enthusiast F. Gordon Hay of Jenkintown, Pennsylvania, starts the ball rolling with this information:

> *On one occasion I learned of a silver deposit somewhere near the headwaters of the Hudson River in Essex County. The silver was being used by either the Indians or French soldiers to mold bullets. The exact details are vague from available information but should make interesting reading for some subscribers including myself.*

Congratulations, Gordon, for being the first to answer our previous request for treasure rumors (Spring, 1950 issue). Lately we've had to scratch around at the very bottom of the "treasure barrel," which is now just about empty, in hopes of finding suitable material for this issue as it refers to a tale we ran across some years ago.

Back in 1929 I was attending Silver Bay School on Lake George and struck up a friendship with an old gentleman whose boyhood days were spent around Brant and Schroon lakes near the town of Adirondack on the wild, eastern shore of the latter lake. Bob Johnson was his name, and a finer Christian gentleman would be hard to find anywhere. Of the veracity of his accounts there exists not the slightest doubt, and what he related to me in honest simplicity I now give you as nearly verbatim as the passage of twenty years will allow me:

> *I'm not a bit surprised to hear you're interested in that mythical silver mine. You're not the only one by any means. It's up in near Pharaoh Mountain somewhere, and that's an awful country I'll tell you—all cut up with swamps and ledges and hogback ridges where many a deer hunter got lost and your compass won't work half the time on account of the iron ore pockets.*

'Twas around 1900, I remember, when two Englishmen came to Adirondack and hired old Patrick Sheely to guide them in. After it was all over, I talked with Pat. It's no wonder they didn't find it, though, in that tangle up there.

Pat said they were looking for blazing on trees which was made by the men who found the silver years before that. They found the blazes all right, but couldn't locate the ledge with the ore. One of the other markers was a tree with a heavy log chain around the trunk, and they found that, too. But they were not sure how far from the chain the ledge was, and after two weeks of rainy weather they got disgusted and quit, and so far as I know just where to tell you to look for those markers. Like as not the lumbering in there has destroyed them and old Pat died around 1920. I sure wish I'd followed it up more, but then I'd just got married and was too busy raising my family to chase off after something those rich fellows spent so much time and money on and couldn't find. But I'll tell you, my brother Hollis over to Adirondack might give you some information. He lives all alone over there on the farm and would be glad to have you visit him.

You know there was a tannery at Adirondack some years back and one fall one of the fellows who worked there went deer hunting up the lake (Schroon) about a mile from the village. He left the lakeshore and began working up along Sucker Brook 'til he was well up into the highlands and headed toward Pharaoh Mountain. You've been back in there and know just how thick it is. Well, somewhere up on one of the slopes rising from the creek this fellow got tired and sat down to rest behind the roots of a big upturned tree. He happened to look down in the bare dirt and saw a queer looking blue rock, which he picked up and 'hefted'. It was so heavy and odd looking he put it in the pocket of his hunting coat and forgot all about it until a long time after when he had occasion to use the coat again.

Fun under the Adirondack sun, as this climber enjoys the freedom of woods and mountains. With a pair of wool socks, and medium-height hiking shoes, she's good for miles of trail-hiking. *Courtesy George H. Longstaff*

Mabel and Marion Quackenbush. Adirondack Mountain boot explorers. 1923.
Courtesy Leigh Portner

He knew it was some kind of ore; lead probably, so he sent it to Albany to be tested. Well, sir, the report came back that it was lead all right but that it had a very high percentage of silver in it. The fellow rushed out to Sucker Brook valley and tried to find the tree roots he had sheltered behind when he picked the rock up, but you know, he never could find the right spot again although he hunted for it about five years. Then the tannery went out of business and this fellow moved away. I've hunted for that spot myself, but I guess it's like the silver mine; I just didn't get the right bearings on it.

Now when I was a kid I used to hear Daddy talking about the silver bullets the early settlers used to find now and then after a rain had dusted down the plowed fields. Nobody knew where they came from but Grandad used to say it was the Indians who made them to shoot in their old flintlock muskets. They were pure silver, different looking from the regular old lead musket ball. These silver ones would take a high polish if you'd rub 'em on your sleeve. There was quite a few found in the vicinity of Adirondack and Brant Lake. Seems as though they must have come from the silver lodge the Englishmen were hunting for.

Another thing I used to hear them tell when I was a kid was about how the Indians used to trade lead ore with the settlers for flour and salt and such like. Back in those days about the only one living on the south end of the lake (Schroon) was a trapper and farmer who had his cabin on the west shore about opposite Adirondack. Pat Sheely knew his name but I don't remember. Anyway, this trapper would go in his canoe with two Indians who always came to the cabin at night. They would blindfold him and tell him to sit in the middle between them. Then they would paddle out into the darkness and cross the lake. They would land on the opposite shore and while one Indian stayed to see that the man did not remove the blindfold, the other Indian would go into the woods for about ten minutes and then return carrying an armload of lead ore. The blindfold would not be removed until the canoe reached the western shore again. Now this settler used to go and hunt for this lead vein after the Indians had gone because he knew where they had beached the canoe on the eastern shore. How did he know? Well, that was easy, for every time the canoe went up on the shore to let the Indian out, the trapper could hear the bottom hissing over fine sand and he knew that there was only one sand beach on the eastern shore of Schroon Lake within that time and distance from his dock on the other side. That was Sucker Brook!

In addition to these tales told by Bob Johnson about the Pharaoh Mountain region, there is another significant one, which I came upon only recently. It is related that a man by the name of Adolphus Lavigne, while cutting wood for charcoal kilns northeast of Pharaoh Mountain, discovered a man-made shaft in a mountain side and within it a pile of bar silver. He did not mark the spot well enough and, as usual, could not return to it again. They

A comfortable headquarters camp was often established to explore out from.
Courtesy Meredith Flerlage

say he became insane during his subsequent years of searching for the treasure. There is also the story of an old Indian who used to bring chunks of silver out of that region whenever he needed supplies.

Old Jim Leach, who passed away not too many years ago, used to relate to me an incident of his youth in Minerva, a village not far from and west of Adirondack. An old Indian who lived in the woods nearby told him that somewhere east of Schroon Lake was a mountain honeycombed with caves and in one large cave was much pure silver. Jim, like everyone else, paid scant attention to this revelation of great wealth and did not press the aged Indian to definitely pin-point the cavernous mountain.

Now as the years creep slowly past, the few isolated old timers who know these tales from `way back are fading away and one by one leave us and with them go their tales—unless gathered and properly recorded. That is why Treasure Roundup asks you to write in if you know of any such accounts. Let us preserve this folklore, what little left there is.

Can we believe these legends? When so many stories crop up in one specific locality, it seems that there must be some manner of truth behind it all. To sum the whole thing up I quote a paragraph from a letter recently received from no less a person than the New York State Geologist, John G. Broughton:

> *Silver has been produced in the state only as a by-product in some of the zinc mines, although every county has its legend of a "lost Indian silver mine."*

THE SEARCH FOR THE INDIAN LEAD MINE ON LYON MOUNTAIN

Compiled by William J. O'Hern from *North Country Life*, Fall 1951, & "Chateaugay Iron," *North Country Life*, Spring, 1953

> *Ralph Bellows read the story about the Indian lead mine which was supposed to have been located in the vicinity of Upper Chateaugay Lake. The story interested him because his grand-*

father was born in 1813, and in 1820, the family settled on the lower lake. His great-grandfather, grandfather and father knew all the stories about the lead mine.

Ralph told Glyndon Cole a story about Indian lead just as his father told it to him.

"Back in the 1820s and 1830s the Indians were still coming to Chateaugay Lake in the summer to camp on the sand bar and Indian Point. One time in the fall, when they were returning home, they stopped at my grandfather's place on the lower lake. One of the Indians showed my grandfather a chunk of pure lead and wanted to sell it to him. This Indian told him he got it in the woods west of Indian Point. My grandfather recognized it at once as an ordinary bar of lead that you could buy in most any store in those days, only it was battered and hacked with a hatchet. This Indian probably showed it to some other people who believed him or wanted to. As my father said, this was probably the source of all the stories about the Indian lead mine.

"My father knew Nat Collins for over 40 years, and I often heard him speak about him. Nat was born in 1829 and died in 1906."

★ ★ ★

Legend has it that a lead mine, once known only to Indians, exists in the Lyon Mountain area of the Adirondacks. The story of two white men's attempts to discover the location of this treasure was told years ago by Captain E. E. Thomas of Chateaugay Lake. He claimed to have secured his information from descendants of the white men who were in contact with the Indian users of the lead from this mine. His account, which is here condensed, appeared in the Chateaugay record in May and June, 1950.

After the Chateaugay Ore and Iron Company sold out to the Delaware and Hudson Railroad Company, I was hired by the latter to go through their holdings and estimate the amount of standing timber. I was also to find the old lines and watch for lumbermen who, having no respect for boundary lines, kept chopping in the direction in which they could see the best timber. This work took me into all the logging camps of the area and into the homes of the oldest inhabitants. When the business talks were over, I would frequently be entertained by stories of bygone days.

In one of these I became greatly interested. It concerned an Indian lead mine, and lest I should forget the details, I wrote the story down, as it was told to me, on the back of my report blanks.

Nathaniel Collins was one of the first white hunters or trappers to paddle a canoe on the Chateaugay Lakes or to roam the surrounding woods. His camp was located on what is now called Baker Point.

One day while fishing in South Inlet, he heard an unusual noise on the shore below him. He paddled toward the spot and caught a glimpse of someone walking on the shore. Suddenly a pretty Indian girl, attired in a buckskin suit, stepped out on the beach almost in from of his canoe. To his salutation of "Good morning," she replied in unbroken English.

She told him that her father and mother were with her and that they were on a hunting and fishing trip. They were going to build a canoe to use while they were there and also a bark wigwam to protect them from the rain.

Before she had finished, the old squaw appeared, and then the girl's father. The father said very little but looked at the white stranger with a frown.

In a few minutes the girl turned and began to converse again with Nat. He told her that they need not build a canoe, that they were welcome to the use of his, and he also invited them to his camp for as long as they wished to stay. When the girl told this to her parents, the frown left her father's face, and a smile revealed their appreciation. Their scant belongings were carried to Nat's cabin, and at the first meal they devoured nearly all the food Nat had.

Before sunset that evening Nat took the Indian girl out on the lake to hunt for game. The girl demonstrated her expert marksmanship. During their stay she went hunting with him three times, fired four shots and killed three deer. The Indians helped jerk this venison, and this with the fish they caught comprised most of their living.

One day Nat and the girl went out fishing. She, feeling quite free with him by this time, told him the real reason why they were there.

"My father is getting old," she began. "There is but one chief over him. He has been here many times, but he says he will come only once more. We are here to get lead for bullets for his rifle."

"Where is the lead mine?" asked Nat.

"I will tell you," she replied, "what no other white man ever knew. Go up this brook about one hour. On the side of the brook on which the sun rises there is a pointed rock about three feet high. This rock is held in position by two smaller ones. Go about fifteen minutes and you will come to a spruce log lying directly across the stream. Now you are half way between the pointed rock and a hemlock tree, which is blown over and has several pegs driven into it. When you find this, go straight towards the sun about twenty minutes and you will come to the lead mine."

"But," said Nat, "if I go in the morning, the sun will be in the east, and if I go in the afternoon, it will be in the west. What time of day shall I go?"

"Ah, ha!" laughed the girl. "That I can't tell you. As much as my father loves me, he would shoot me if he knew I have told you what I have, for he says no white man shall ever see this mine."

One day the girl told Nat that she and her father and mother were going to the mine and cautioned him against following, "For if you do," she said, "Father will shoot you."

It was near three o'clock when they started out, the old chief in the lead, his squaw following, and the girl bringing up the rear. The girl suspected that Nat would follow in spite of her warning. They were not quite out of sight when the girl turned and motioned to Nat to go back. But Nat was not afraid of a bullet at such a long distance as he meant to follow. He started slowly on behind and was careful not to gain too much on them. As dusk set in, Nat knew it was useless to go any nearer. It was obvious that they were waiting for darkness.

Then an idea struck him. Across the big inlet there was a high elevation from which he could get a good view of Lyon Mountain. By going to this elevation, he could surely locate their campfire.

As there was a bright moon, he made good time down the brook and up to the highest point on the ridge. There he waited and watched for the fire that would help locate the mine. He watched throughout the night, but no campfire appeared.

Breakfast was of little importance to him next morning. He swallowed a bite, and cramming some venison into his pocket, he went to the hemlock log where he had last seen the Indians. Their footprints were plain until he reached this spot. Then where did they go? Nat searched, but not one footprint did he find to give him the slightest clue to the direction in which they had gone.

All that day he hunted, traveling in ever-widening circles around the old hemlock. As the sun went down, he went back to camp, ate a hearty supper, and started out again. This time he went to a place where he could get a different view of Lyon Mountain, but the results were the same. For the next five days he hunted for smoke by day and fire by night, but neither did he see.

On the eighth day, the Indians returned with all the lead they could carry. Most of it was in long strips with much charcoal in it. This revealed to Nat that they had got the lead out by building a fire on or beside it and as the lead melted, scraped it out with sticks.

After that they stayed but one more night with Nat. The girl told him as they left that they would be back in a few days for more lead.

They were barely out of sight when Nat again started out on the hunt for treasure. He thought that the old chief would have been unable to wipe out the tracks they would have made with the heavy load on their backs. But his search was in vain, and he returned to his cabin with much respect for the Indian's crafty ways.

Shortly after this, the Indians returned for their final trip to the mountain of precious minerals. This time Nat did not try to follow them but awaited their return, which was on the third day.

That night the girl asked Nat for a kettle and bullet mold. When the lead was hot, they ran a large supply of bullets and gave them to Nat. (At the time I was gathering this information, Collins' daughter,

Mrs. William Shaw, who lived at Lower Chateaugay Lake, had three of these bullets.)

The Indians never returned for more lead. Nat persistently continued the search, but with no success.

At Chazy Lake, about five miles from Upper Chateaugay Lake, Mose Sangimore had settled about the same time that Nat Collins came to Chateaugay Lake.

One day Mose went hunting on Lyon Mountain, but whenever he went in this direction, it was not for the game to be found there. He had heard about the Indians' lead mine, and it was this that pulled him like a magnet towards the top of the mountain.

As he advanced, he smelled smoke, yet none could be seen in any direction and there was very little wind to carry the odor very far. Putting a finger in his mouth, he let it remain until it was blood warm. Then taking it out, he held it above his head. The side on which he felt the cool air told him in which direction to go to locate the source of the unusual smell.

Advancing carefully, he was soon standing beside an opening from which smoke was issuing. "I have found the lead mine!" he said to himself.

But Nat Collins had told him of the Indian girl's threat, so very cautiously he explored the opening. On two sides there were solid ledges, and leading down into the depths, he could see stones which were used as stairs. He ventured down for about eight feet. Overhead he could see logs laid side-by-side and reaching far back into the blackness of the cavern. No sound came from the depths, but there was a strong smell of smoke.

He climbed out of the cavern, made a mental note of the nearby trees and bushes, and slowly walked down the ridge, looking back to familiarize himself with the surroundings. When he was about 200 yards away, he climbed a yellow birch tree, and taking his overalls off, hung them in the very top. Then he climbed down and proceeded toward home. Every bush that came within his reach he broke until he was sure that he could return by this well-marked trail.

The next morning, with his rifle on his shoulder and four neighbors accompanying him, he began to climb to the opening he had seen the day before. The trail was easily followed, and at last they reached the yellow birch tree.

"This is the tree," he said, "on which I hung my overalls, but they are not here. Yet I am sure this is the ridge."

They searched the area but no trace could they find of the mine. They finally returned to their homes, no wiser and no richer than they had been in the morning.

It is my belief that the Indians were in the mine getting lead when Mose Sangimore discovered it. Anyone familiar with Indians knows that they would have seen his broken bushes and found his overalls in the tree. Undoubtedly they erased his trail marks by cutting all the brush and then breaking other bushes on a similar ridge to mislead the white man.

Now time has worked many changes, and death has sealed the knowledge of what little the white men were permitted to learn. The location of the Indian lead mine remains to this day a mystery.

IN SEARCH OF THE REAL AMERICAN TRAGEDY

By Richard G. Case, *York State Tradition*, Summer 1969

The death of a farm girl named Grace Brown more than 60 years ago on Big Moose Lake still has the power of deep personal sorrow. A few years ago I talked with an elderly woman, also a Brown, who was living hard by the old Brown farm at South Otselic. We sat in her front yard. It was the same sort of summer day on which the news of the murder reached the hamlet. Pastures were filled with new daisies; locusts hummed. My informant's memory wandered over the hill and years to 1906.

The night before Grace left on the fatal "wedding trip" to Utica and the Adirondacks she stopped by this neighbor's house to return a spool of thread. They talked of "sociable" things. Grace's family had picked some apples that day, and they were drying beef for storage. It seemed to my informant that Grace mentioned she was going on vacation the next day.

"At first the neighbors didn't believe Grace was dead. Then her father phoned back that it was true. I helped tend the Brown babies the day of the funeral. Afterwards, one of Grace's brothers took me home. He said, 'Oh, he didn't have to kill her. He didn't want her...we would have taken care of her.'"

Her voice faded. She choked on a sob. "I never wanted to read the book or see the movie. I lived through it."

My search for the real "American Tragedy" has taken me into many sorrowful recollections—many yards, living rooms, cemeteries, newspaper files, official and court records, and scrapbooks during the past ten years. It has been an unconcentrated, now-and-again investigation, when time was available and an opportunity presented itself. I have tried to collect memories while memories were alive in the people they happened to—before the colors fade.

I have gone beyond the story as it has been told again and again. It is familiar to us Yorkers. Grace Brown, the pretty girl from Otselic, goes to Cortland and a job in the skirt factory. She meets Chester Gillette, a foreman. They are lovers; she is pregnant. Then the death at Big Moose. His trial and execution. The aftermaths. The books. The legends.

The principal vehicle for carrying forward the sad facts of this rather conventional homicide has been Theodore Dreiser's book, *An American Tragedy*, originally published in two volumes in 1925. Dreiser built his novel around the case.

One frequently hears that Dreiser himself covered the trial at Herkimer in 1906. My research has yielded nothing to support this. The author apparently got most of his information from New York City newspapers.

Dreiser's most recent biographer, W. A. Swanberg, said the author studied a dozen cases before he selected Gillette-Brown. Another biographer, Robert Elias of Cornell University, said Dreiser decided that Gillette's actions, "both in their details and typicalness, had been misunderstood." In the author's view, Gillette was the victim of circumstances over which he had no control.

Dreiser made a trip into upstate New York to absorb atmosphere in 1923. He motored with his wife to Herkimer, Cortland, South Otselic and the Adirondacks. The trip included a row onto the waters of Big Moose, during which "Teddie," as his wife called him, seemed quite moved. Mrs. Dreiser later recalled that "the sensation and mood of this moment never left me and never will."

Obviously, Dreiser used the case as a framework on which to hang his own imaginings and prejudices. Emil Greenberg, who did a study of Dreiser's crutches in the novel, concluded that he had lifted about 30 pages verbatim from newspaper accounts and liberally expanded on equal amounts of material. Some of the pathetic letters from Grace to Chester were read at the trial. Dreiser used smatterings from these, but adapted them to his own orchestration.

There are many paths available to the researcher in search of the real "American Tragedy." They are both short and long, straight and curved. Bypaths abound.

Chester Gillette obtained a boat and rowed trustful and naive Grace Brown on an outwardly romantic boat ride in the central Adirondacks. *Courtesy Jane Ritz*

There is, for example, the music of the case. My research yielded a piece of sheet music dedicated to Grace Brown in 1907 by Maud E. Gould, a semi-professional musician who lived in Ilion. Almost everyone has forgotten Mrs. Gould's song, "Entreating." It may be just as well.

A more interesting chase is after the ballad that still is on the lips of the few Yorkers who learned it about the time it first was sung in 1907. I have collected half dozen variants of the basic words and music of "The Ballad of Big Moose Lake," or "Gillette and Grace Brown." Most of my informants learned the ballad as youngsters in northern New York. At this moment I am unsure of its origin. One of the people who supplied me with the verses from memory believes it was written by a Lee Cramer of Wells. Another possibility is that the song originated in a lumber camp. None of my informants knew of a printed version.

One may also attempt to flesh out each of the interesting characters associated with the People vs. Gillette. They range from minor to major. There was the Herkimer deputy sheriff, who was supposed to have fetched a bouquet of water lilies from Big Moose Lake to Chester's cell. The young girl who offered to take his place in the electric chair. The strange little man named Edwin F. Davis, the state "electrician" who executed Gillette at Auburn. The prisoner's mother and father, two wanderers fresh from the ranks of the Salvation Army, and "Elijah" Dowie's colony at Zion City, Illinois. Edith Cornwall, the "sob sister" reporter from Syracuse who gained a news beat on her male colleagues during the trial when District Attorney George Washington Ward read to the jury Grace's letters to Chester.

Miss Cornwall, in private life Mrs. Mary Lennox Parsons, supplied her Central New York readers with vivid, although sometimes inaccurate, accounts of the murder and trial. She favored large, flowered hats and florid details that did not necessarily jibe with the facts. Perhaps because she was an Upstate, Miss Cornwall did not receive the scorn of the people of the Mohawk Valley which they had for the visiting press from metropolitan New York.

One finds a number of accounts of how wrong the New Yorkers were in their reports. "The modern Munchausens," the Utica *Saturday Globe* called the visitors in a snarling post-trial essay. Herkimer Historical Society had an account in its files of the "confession" of a New York photographer whose office was pressing him for a picture of Grace Brown. When none was found, he simply posed a Herkimer girl and forwarded the picture to New York.

A fascinating sidelight to the locals' distrust of their guests was the "arrest" of W.B. "Bat" Masterson and two of his editors on charges of criminal contempt after the trial. "Bat" had left the West and his legend behind him and was writing a "sports" column for a New York newspaper, the *Telegraph*. He didn't get to Herkimer until the trial was over, but some of his comments on Herkimer County justice (mention was made of the "Herkimer bushmen") aroused George Ward sufficiently to swear out a warrant. The matter was settled in a way that seemed to allow Herkimerians to feel they had taken some revenge for what they felt were the libels of the New York press corps.

There are, of course, many souvenirs of the case. I have seen the tennis racquet which Ward alleged was a murder weapon. It rests with a family near Herkimer. Grace's letters, carefully saved since 1906, are not far away, in the keeping of another family connected with the trial. Another souvenir may or may not exist. The boat in which Chester and Grace rowed out into Big Moose—a St. Lawrence skiff—was brought to Herkimer as a trial exhibit. Sometime later (immediately or several years, the versions vary), the boat disappeared from the courthouse. Several people I have talked to swear it still exists, bogged down in a little lake somewhere in the heart of the Adirondacks.

Yet, with all these sad relics, one reconstructs the case with some difficulty at this distance. Over the years, obviously, some of the truth has been lost, never to be recovered. Some never was public knowledge; it belonged, and still belongs, to personal memory. "There are some things that will never be known," I was told twice at South Otselic. Why not? And of all of the elements of the case, it is the human element—the feel of a pulse—that one misses most in 1969. Even as this is written, John Denio, described as the "last surviving witness" at the trial, has died (on May 31).

The Browns are among us in New York, still silent, for the most part, and still in sorrow. The Gillettes have vanished into the West. I have thrown out several inquiries about them, but these, to date, have returned little information. Chester's parents were in Denver after the execution; then they moved to Texas, where his father died in 1915. With the family yet today may be an interesting document. This is Chester's "story" of the case, which was alluded to in newspapers at the time of the execution. "Let it be read when I am gone," he is supposed to have told his minister, the Rev. Henry McIlravy of Little Falls. If such an account did, in fact, exist, the family does not seem to have followed their son's wishes that it be published. One account has it that it was entrusted to McIlravy, who vanished from the Mohawk Valley shortly after the execution. Or, it may have been the "pocketbook" carried in Auburn prison records as having been turned over to Frank Gillette after his son's death. Wherever it is, such a document would certainly fill in a large gap in what we know of the case.

THE LION COUCHANT

By Marion S. Fresn, *North Country Life*, Winter 1954

As French voyageurs sailed down through the northern part of Lake Champlain 300 or more years ago, a glance to the westward rested upon a land form of considerable impressiveness. To them it suggested the familiar classic form of a "lion couchant." It seems appropriate that the figure of the king of beasts should lie as guard on the western side of a valley, which has proved a strategic path of invasion through the centuries.

But the only real comfort the Lion can give is an aesthetic one. Lyon Mountain, for those of us who live our days in view of it, is always an inspiring sight. Its snow-capped top may, in winter, be clearly etched against the western sky by the new rays of the morning sun; it may loom darkly against the rosy horizon of evening; or its familiar shape may appear but vaguely in the distance against a murky sky; always it is there.

It has been there for a very long time. The geologists' estimate is 60,000,000 years—more or less! Like the rest of the Adirondacks, it is of pre-Cambrian formation, and was probably shaped by magmatic pressure, that is, the action of molten rock under the cooled crust of the earth. The geologist does not find Marcy or Whiteface anorthosite in the make-up of the mountain. Neither does he find Lyon Mountain granite, companion of the magnetite ore deposit which lies north of the mountain and which has resulted in the considerable mining development of the same name. The substance of the mountain is a coarser-grained granite, containing no ore, and known as Hawkeye granite.

Perhaps the most interesting thing that happened to our mountain during the passage of its millions of years was the Great Glacier. There is no evidence that the ice sheet altered the shape or size of the mountain mass, or indeed that of any of the Adirondacks. But it accomplished curious things. The course of the glacier in the area was toward the southwest. About six miles northeast of the mountain is the highest and

Trail parties did not always charge along. *Courtesy Jane Ritz*

Early 20th century trail attire. *Courtesy Jane Ritz*

nearest outcropping of Potsdam sandstone. Fragments of this rock and at least one sizeable boulder can be found on top of the mountain, proving not only that the glacier rode over the summit but that it carried large stones more than 2,000 feet uphill in the space of a few miles.

One can easily find ripple stones among the rocks along the trail up the mountain. They, too, are of Potsdam sandstone, very ancient and with a history of their own. Their presence on the mountain, like that of the larger fragments, is more evidence of the presence of the great ice sheet.

The Lyon Mountain mass is roughly six miles long by four and a half miles wide. Its drainage is northeastward into Lake Champlain through the Chateaugay River to the St. Lawrence. The mountain itself rises steeply from the southwestern shore of Chazy Lake for 2,300 feet to an elevation above sea level of 3,830 feet. Its second peak, Averill, is 20 feet lower.

Although our subject appears to have been known originally as the Lion, during the past century it acquired, by odd coincidence, a change of spelling and meaning. It attracted into its shadow one of our more intrepid pioneers. In the winter of 1803–04 Nathaniel Lyon moved from Vermont to Plattsburgh. Here he did not pause long but traveled up the Saranac River on the ice by ox-cart. He remained for a few years near what is now Saranac village. But the mountain must have drawn him for he again moved his family and his stock five and a half miles westward, well up on the side of the Lion.

At this place he cleared a large farm. With other stock he kept sheep, and at night it was necessary to herd the sheep into a high-sided pen to protect them from the wolves that roamed the area. To a daughter of Nathaniel we owe the story of one of these wolves. This was a large one, one of a pack, who ran up to the pen and placed his forepaws on the log siding of the sheep corral, in order to climb over and help himself to some prime mutton. But at this juncture Mrs. Lyon ran out and clubbed the hungry wolf away.

Nathaniel is known to have lived at this farm and hunted on the mountain for the remainder of his days. So it is not surprising that a map-maker of the day, having heard "lion" and knowing of Nathaniel, wrote the name "Lyon."

Incidentally, the first woman to ascend the mountain, in 1876, was Miss Hattie Lyon, a granddaughter of its first settler.

All this history was unknown to me when, at the age of seven or eight, I laid my plans for my first ascent of the mountain. But the same irresistible attraction that it held for Nathaniel Lyon was there for me in like strength. The view of the mountain from my childhood home was the same as that seen by the early voyageurs. To make it more tantalizing, my parents frequently took me westward to visit relatives in the town of Saranac. This brought me ever closer to the beckoning summit. From the home of my maternal grandparents, the Lion seemed but a short distance away across the fields and woods. It was my firm intention to pick a good day and walk until I reached the summit. I spoke of my plans to one of my uncles. He shattered them by telling me how deceptive the apparent distance was, and of the unknown dangers of the journey. From that day forth I was well watched. But at last there came a day when I could lay more plans with better chance of success.

It was a four-day holiday weekend in October. My friend Alice and I had talked for weeks of a trip on horseback to spend the holiday at the home of my grandmother, who lived in the hilly, partially cleared area across the river from the village of Saranac. We were fifteen. The spirit of adventure ran high. We could not sleep or eat properly for days.

Unknown to Alice, I had additional ideas of my own. Craftily I made inquiries, studied maps, and worked out my plans in secret. Experience had taught me that talking about my plans could be their undoing.

The great day arrived. We had laid out our route well and about twelve miles of it was over sand rocks, through pleasant pine and hemlock country. The roads were numerous and at first confusing until we found out that, like the roads in the old saying, they all led to Rome. All was as it should have been until that ill-fated pause in Peasleeville. Here Alice left me to hold the horses while she called on one of her friends. The folks there were just eating a bountiful chicken dinner of which they asked us to partake. But darkness was approaching so I declined. Alice argued that it was both rude and wasteful to refuse food. So while I impatiently kept our mounts in readiness, she ate her fill of chicken.

It was always my contention that the added weight of the food she had consumed convinced Alice's horse (a tough, disillusioned old westerner) that he was carrying two. Whatever his reason, his rate of progress began to slacken to a pace that would have made a snail seem supersonic. We still had four miles to travel.

The road, if you could call it that, was merely a set of fairly well-worn wheel tracks, with grass growing between. We passed one old shack in the course of the four miles. Darkness was falling rapidly and the warmth of the day had changed to the damp chill of a North Country evening.

Progress was slow and the atmosphere dismal; soon it began to snow. At this juncture, Bob's slow crawl ceased altogether. Alice urged him gently with her heels. He laid back his ears but remained immobile. She slapped him with her reins and kicked again. There was a warning movement of his derriere.

Alice was an excellent rider, but here in the darkness and snow and on the narrow, stony trail was no place for a show of rodeo horsemanship, so with admirable prudence she dismounted. With his mistress before him coaxing and pulling, Bob's morale improved slightly and he once more began to move slowly forward. This arrangement sufficed for a while, but it was not a very happy one. The traveling was uphill and very slippery with the new snow. My mount was chafing uneasily at the slow pace. A better solution rose I my mind.

"Why don't you ride behind me on King?" I suggested.

To quote from some verse in which I later recorded our adventures:

Bob's rein o'er the cantle, they snaked him along
For fear the direction he'd chose would be wrong;
But King he was youthful and right full of vim,
And carrying three was a trifle for him.

Thus we continued to the top of the long rise. Not far beyond, the lights of my grandfather's place came into view. Old Bob noticed the change of prospect and voluntarily picked up speed. We were able to arrive at our destination in the style proper for dashing young horsewomen.

The next day dawned bright and clear. Undaunted by our difficulties of the afternoon before, we decided to explore the countryside. Gladly I picked up my grandmother's suggestion that we visit her sister, who lived northward across the river in the direction of my longed-for mountain summit. The rest of the trip to the mountain was not too difficult to manage. At one point in the journey, however, we made a diversion that might have been a calamitous one.

We had been told of the old Taylor cabin, original home of some ancestor. It was just an ordinary, plaster-chinked weathered old log cabin, a common enough sight along the roadside in this part of the country. But with that special curiosity common to young girls, we felt impelled to see what was inside. Dismounting, we went in and looked about the two-room ground floor. There was nothing there. We climbed the rickety ladder and looked about the dusty loft. There was nothing there. Downstairs again, a trap door opened into yawning darkness. Not being provident, we had not brought flashlights. I asked Alice to search her pockets for a match but she had none. So reluctantly we left the cabin, without exploring the cellar.

Once arrived at the trail that led up the mountain, I casually suggested that we ride a distance along its course. This aroused no suspicion in my companion's mind. The trail proved a pleasant bridle path for nearly two miles, then gradually became too steep and stony for our mounts. At this point Alice assumed that we would turn about. It was with some difficulty that I persuaded her that we should tie the horses and walk a little distance up the trail to a point where we could see the countryside below us.

The afternoon was creeping on and this was another of October's shortening days. Alice became suspicious of my intentions and refused to go farther. But I had waited too long for this to be turned back now. Very reluctantly, but with that feeling of responsibility that the strong feel for the weak, the good for the wicked, and the wise for the foolish, Alice came along with me.

True, she came sniffily and self-righteously, her demeanor suggesting that if Providence had ordained that it be her lot to shepherd an addlepate through an unknown wilderness, well, she was a Christian and knew her bounden duty. But she did come and by the time we came to the last part of the climb, the steep ascent that ended at the ranger's cabin, Alice was reconciled.

Balboa when he first viewed the broad Pacific, or Columbus the Indies, could not have felt greater rapture than I when I put foot on that long desired summit. The air was hazy, the view limited, and the sun was dangerously low. But at last I was there and my happiness was complete.

It was not so with Alice. She had neither planned for nor longed for this event. The climb had been exhausting and she was not uplifted with that special excitement that sustains young dyed-in-the wool mountaineers.

We lingered too long on top, savoring the grandeur of this height so far above the common world. That is, I savored it. Alice regaled the observer (at that time Will Everleth) with the story of our climb.

Descending, complete darkness was not far away when we reached the spot where we thought we had left our horses. They were not there. Fear seized us. Had they got loose, and if so, had they returned to Plattsburgh or just to Grandfather's farm? We spent several terror-stricken moments in futile search when an impatient whinny from among the trees reminded us that we had tied the horses safely off the trail.

Marion Fresn was acquainted with many of the original weathered old log cabins, farm houses and camps in the vicinity of Lyon Mountain.. *Courtesy Meredith Flerlage*

By the time we were down off the mountain, the early darkness of an October evening was upon us. We were not at all sure that we could remember all the turns in the road that led to warmth and comfort. But this was farming country and we were certain that inquiries could keep us on the right way. But we little dreamed that this usually peaceful, hospitable neighborhood would be frozen into a strange hostility. At the first house where we stopped to ask the way, odd things took place. The door was opened a crack, then slammed shut. (Here it should be noted that Alice favored boys' clothing, including a disreputable man's cap.) The lights in the house dimmed, and sounds of moving furniture could be heard. Queer people, we thought, and rode on.

The next place was little better. A window was raised a bit, and to Alice's desperate plea for directions a few garbled sentences were spoken. We soon found out that my luck was better. I did not gain admittance, but for some reason, when a childish voice piped up from a small figure, the local folk were able to answer with sensible directions. But it was nearly midnight when we reached Grandfather's home. It had taken us five hours to travel what should have been a distance of eleven miles.

It was not the next day but the following one that we learned the cause of the curious hostility of the people in that part of Saranac. The morning following our climb, an escaped convict from nearby Dannemora, a reputedly vicious, long-term criminal, was captured in the Taylor cabin we had so blithely explored!

ADIRONDACK STORYTELLING

By William J. O'Hern

Until I became a teenager, it never occurred to me just how first-rate my childhood outdoor and Adirondack experiences had been.

In summertime, I'd go to my grandparents' seasonal camp, as well as tent camp, most often in the Lake country: the central Adirondacks between Old Forge and Blue Mountain Lake. My parents' destinations were various state campgrounds—rustic facilities compared to those available at the same parks today. Eighth Lake was our favorite camping spot. My mother, at 98 years old, considers the difference in one line: "It's *really* not camping today."

I see her reasoning. But then again, I look at the advertising poster and snapshots "Slim" Murdock has given me. Those family heirlooms show his father, Don A. C. Murdock, and some of the conveniences that were available at the lake for summer excursions during the 1890s. Don was captain of the two launches he operated on the upper waters of the Fulton Chain of Lakes. The *Spray* carried passengers from Sixth Lake Dam to the head of Seventh Lake, where a walk of three-quarters of a mile "over one of the finest carries in the Adirondacks" (as the poster described it) brought

Camping at Mountain View, Franklin County. ca. 1890s. It's still there, a collection of camps mostly. It's about 20 miles SSE of Malone and 20 miles due west (but not directly reachable from) Lyon Mountain. *Courtesy Special Collections, Feinberg Library, SUNY College at Plattsburgh*

them to Eighth Lake. There, the launch *Anona* carried "passengers around one of the most beautiful lakes in the whole country."

There were a canopied awning with cloth screening to keep bugs from destroying comfortable luncheon accommodations, a neat privy, and a sign reminding passengers "Don't Fail to See the BEAVER DAM at 8th Lake." It was at the end of a well-marked path through the tall pines leading to the lake's outlet. Bold black advertising proclaimed tickets were only 75 cents for the sixteen-mile round trip, which included lunch.

Thinking of how rustic a camping trip would be at the turn of the 19th century, Captain Murdock's summer excursion seems as comfy as today's flush toilets, hot running water and showers, septic dump sites for trailers, hardened road surfaces, animal-safe garbage deposits and electricity hookups. Mom might have just preferred things more rustic!

Each evening in the mountains we gathered around the outdoor fireplace. Starting a fire was a woodcraft skill I enjoyed. Nighttime fires were a treat for everyone. Along with the obvious contentment of the warmth and peacefulness of an evening fire were the much-anticipated activities of toasting Campfire brand marshmallows and hearing thriller stories, as well as trying our hands at telling tales ourselves.

Storytelling is an old mountain tradition. Tall tales found in old issues of *North Country Life* magazines, segments of Wallace's 1895 *Descriptive Guide to the Adirondacks*, and Alfred B. Street's 1869 *The Indian Pass* were not yet expensive collectors' keepsakes. The magazines and old books provided thriller-type tales of earlier times in the mountains.

Did we children know that a Mr. Scott, of North Elba, became lost while hunting many years ago? During that time he chanced upon a vein of silver that "glistened before his admiring eyes." The story from *The Indian Pass* went that Scott "secured a specimen of the treasure, which was subsequently reduced and formed into a heart; but after leaving the spot, in the confusion of intellect to which all persons are subject who are lost in the woods, he was never able to identify it; and, to this day, guarded only by the grim 'Genius loci,' sleeps unknown this Potosi of the Adirondacks."

Wow! Another silver mine tale. I'd heard about the one near North Lake. It was exciting to consider chancing upon the find while hiking.

The silver ledge was believed to be somewhere near Wallface Mountain. Some people said they thought David Henderson, who discovered the great McIntyre iron deposit near Tahawus, was searching for Scott's silver in 1826, the day before an Indian met him and showed him a specimen of iron ore. This stopped Henderson's hunt for the silver, and he immediately headed out of the pass to announce his big iron ore discovery.

Henderson stated in a letter to Archibald McIntyre of New York:

> *We found it impossible to make a complete search for silver ore this season... We followed the road-way through a clearing to the river. [He means the Ausable, since the party had just come a few miles from Elba, Essex County.]... Tuesday and Wednesday were employed in running lines and searching from near the ruins of the top of the largest burnt cobble, examining every ledge as we went along. On Thursday we came across your old camp and removed ours to within a gun-shot of it. Finished the examination of that cobble by the evening. No signs of what we wanted.*

Some feel certain that the Adirondacks holds wonders of which people are unaware. In one book about them, Wallace's *Guide*, I find written: "The Highlands of the New York Wilderness were first called the Peruvian Mountains by the early settlers, who believed that they were rich in mineral treasures." Street, in his *The Indian Pass*, asserts:

> *Natural curiosities abound throughout the county (Essex). That others are buried in the terrific forests still darkening two-thirds of the surface cannot be doubted.*

Street did not know it, but he was prophesying the legend Stan Vickers told about in "Delving into the Dark Ages," in *North Country Life's* Summer 1949 issue. Who wouldn't have a natural curiosity about that prehistoric cave? Would it ever be found again? People did search for it, as well as lost mines. There were also reports about buried treasures.

Near Ticonderoga is Rogers' Slide, a wall-shaped face of bare rock arising hundreds of feet abruptly from the waters of Lake George. Local legend has placed a hidden cave near the top of this slide as the repository of one ton of silver bars. Walled up with the bars are supposed to be mining tools, supplies and guns. A vein of silver from which the bars came is in there, too. Or, so states this awe-inspiring legend.

The story goes that two Spaniards came to that part of the Adirondacks 150 years ago or more. They carried a map that showed the slide as the main marker to the walled-up cave. After searching for days without

The log cabin, shielded by hemlock bark shingles, was not a chalet, and was not even particularly roomy, but it had a number of curious nooks and alcoves and indentations and a great measure of Adirondack outdoorsiness, and it sat back in the forest near Muskrat Creek. Great white pine trees rose close by, and the outdoor eating table held all sorts of drinks and delicious tantalizing foods—jelly and pickles, baked beans, pies, rolls, hard boiled eggs and wild game, giving each meal in the late summer an unforgettable feeling that picnic days, followed by stories of ghostly legends, would never be forgotten.
Courtesy Earl M. Kreuzer

finding the cave, they took a local trapper into their confidence and showed him the map. Even with his expert help, the cave remained undiscovered, but it was through him that the tale came out.

That the trapper was not making the story up is proven by the statements of a number of old men who had seen the Spaniards at work up on the mountain. The local Spaniards kept up the search—some do even to the present day.

While no one has ever found a single treasure, some seekers have never called it quits—including me. Throughout the years I researched the history of the Moose River Plains; I logged a lot of time traipsing untrailed sections of expansive territory. I'd heard a number of stories of "caves," a grave, and ghostly log remains of former logging camps. One particular story I learned from an old Raquette Laker who worked his entire life as George Vanderbilt's personal assistant. He fondly recalled a so-called cave somewhere between Camp Sagamore and Bear Pond where he used to stash steel traps. He called it the Bear Hunter's Cave. Although he had last used the cave in the early 1940s, his telling about it in the 1970s incessantly stirred my interest to find the place.

I was getting pretty good at finding exact locations. I had located the legendary grave site of Fred Hynes near Ice House Pond, walked onto numerous thought-to-be-obliterated logging camp sites and even located a couple of old trappers' cabin ruins complete with old relics, some of which now decorate my Adirondack room. But the Bear Hunter's Cave continued to be a mystery until an old Inleter, Bill Apager, led me to the remains of his former Red River camp.

"Yeah, I know the spot," he said of the cave. "It's over near St. James Mountain. I'll take you there." And true to his word, before the end of the summer I entered the Bear Hunter's Cave, leaving with some metal dishes and a couple of Indian-head pennies.

Collection V holds some of the thrillers I have always found enjoyable.

As for my childhood Adirondack camping experiences, I always returned home a bit more tanned, perhaps a smidgen taller, and filled with happy memories.

TO A HERMIT THRUSH

Dear bird of Eventide,
Thou lovest the gloaming best.
How tenderly dost thou greet,
With thrilling notes from thy retreat,
Birds homing to their nests.
Sweet lullabies dost thou sing,
While breezes sway their cradles high,
Of birdlings soon wrapt in sleep.
Then a hush comes o'er the woodland deep,
As night draws her curtain high.
Companions are we in solitude;
We love the mountain side
Where wonderful lights and shadows dwell.
Thy melody weaves a magic spell,
Sweet bird of Eventide.

—W. C. Rice, *York State Tradition*, after 1960

Editor's Note: W. C. Rice, known as "The Hermit of Ampersand," was fire observer on Ampersand Mountain from 1914 to 1922.

Upper Ausable Lake from the inlet. *Courtesy Special Collections, Feinberg Library, SUNY College at Plattsburgh*

DELVING INTO THE DARK AGES

By Stan Vickers, *North Country Life*, Spring 1949

Glyndon Cole was as much taken with mysterious cave locations and Adirondack ghost towns as any folklore hunter. Perhaps to stir up interest, he reprinted Stan Vickers' story about North Countryman Dick Johnson in North Country Life's *Summer 1949 issue.*

"A gold disk, believed to be some 18,000 years old and carrying on its surface the carved outline of a mastodon, may lead Kenneth Spring, archaeologically-minded Ticonderogian, to the discovery of a cave in the town of Ticonderoga, which, if an old legend is true, would supply the world with important new information on prehistoric times," began a story first reported in the *Ticonderoga Sentinel.*

Dick Johnson of Ticonderoga, owner of the gold disk, received the ancient talisman from his grandfather and, although Mr. Johnson was never able to locate the cave in which his grandparent reportedly found the mysterious disk, Kenneth Spring has taken up the search. Armed with new information from area hunters as well as his own extensive knowledge of the Adirondack country, he is confident of success.

The legend surrounding the gold disk began in the period following the Revolution, when the Johnson family left their southern New York home to settle in the wilderness country in the vicinity of Brant Lake.

One day two of the Johnson children were out berrying in the mountains with a young Indian companion. When they were overtaken by a storm, the Indian youth led them to a cave where the grandfather of Dick Johnson picked up the gold disk. Returning home afterwards, the children told of their experience, displayed the disk, and described the pictures of animals and birds which they had seen carved on the white walls of the cave.

Perhaps because of superstition or because of the usual parents' fear of the explorations of their children, the Johnson children were warned never to go back to the cave. As if in tragic consummation of the ill omen seen in the discovery of the cave, the Indian boy was believed to have been accidentally drowned shortly afterwards.

When Dick Johnson was a very young boy, his family lived in the Schroon Lake area, and he can remember his grandfather telling him of finding the cave, and showing him the disk. The grandfather gave the boy the object and promised that, when he was older, he would lead him to the cave. But before Dick was old enough to make the trip, the grandfather died.

The boy hid the coin and forgot it, but about 1953 the Johnson family had a barn torn down and workmen discovered the little piece of precious metal once again.

By this time Dick Johnson was a member of the American Society of Mineralogists and also extremely interested in archaeology. Recalling his grandfather's story as best he could, he searched for the lost cave,

Campers gather together around a blazing evening bonfire. ca. 1917. *Courtesy John Chamberlain*

believed to be located about one-half mile east of Lake Pharaoh and about one-quarter mile inside the present southwest boundary of the town of Ticonderoga. He discovered that Grenville limestone was present in that area, a white mineral which, because it is soft, would be a suitable and attractive surface for any would-be prehistoric artists.

Failing to find the cave, Mr. Johnson reported in 1937 his ownership of the coin to the Champlain Valley Archaeological Society. From the Society, Mr. Johnson learned that the origin of the almost-pure gold coin seemed to be Eurasian, probably dating back to the Cro-Magnon or Aurignacian cultures of from 11,000 to 18,000 years ago. The gold itself differed from the gold found in this hemisphere, containing a red tint as compared with the all-yellow cast of the precious metal found in the Americas.

One theory advanced was that nomadic hunters from Asia had left it here in the cave where Dick Johnson's grandfather found it.

The disk itself is about one inch in diameter and weighs three-fifths of an ounce. According to present prices [1947], it contains about twelve dollars' worth of gold.

But as one archaeologist observed to Dick Johnson after studying the disk, "If you can locate the cave from which this was taken, I wouldn't take thousands of dollars for its possession."

MURDER IN THE ADIRONDACKS

By Allan Keller, *North Country Life*, Fall 1946

Each time the hammer hit the nail, the sharp crack echoed through the wilderness; aside from that alien noise there was nothing to challenge the funereal quiet. The wind that had been whipping across Whittaker Lake died down and in its place snow fell silently.

Old Eula Davis, Adirondack Mountain guide and woodsman, was fitting a door to his two-room log cabin. It was four days before Thanksgiving of 1928, and Davis knew how the freezing winds could knife through the cracks of a sagging door. So now the old man was hurrying.

Woodsman though he was, he heard no sound to warn him that he would never live to shut the door against winter's chill. In fiction, malefactors step on twigs or frighten the denizens of the wild so they hear warning of the evildoer's approach. But here was stark reality. The snow was a carpet that cushioned every sound until a rifle cracked and old Davis fell across the threshold.

Out of the edge of the woods stalked a figure, powdered with snow and ghostlike. It bent over the prostrate figure for an instant, then straightened up and moved away into the twilight murk. The snow filtered down through the awed silence, obliterating the footsteps that no ghost could leave behind.

Four days later, New York State Troopers Ralph Fitch and L.G. Eggleston were eating their turkey dinner in the police sub-station in Speculator when Ernest Duane, a young guide and jack-of-all-trades who lived in the village, interrupted their repast. He told them of going out that morning to tend his trap line and finding the body of Davis when he stopped in at his friend's cabin.

Hours later, after a drive over icy roads and a long climb into the mountains, they came to the cabin above Whittaker Lake. By the light of their flashlights, Fitch and Eggleston saw that the shack was open and dark and that no plume of smoke issued from the chimney.

Inside was horror. In the first room were dark stains that formed a track from the outer threshold into the second room. There, beside the cold chunk stove, was the body, a rag tied like a tourniquet around the left thigh and a pencil with a broken point still clutched in the frozen fingers.

It was Trooper Eggleston who noted that the rifle bullet had entered the dead man's hip pocket, and it was the coroner's physician who probed the wound and found particles of currency, establishing the fact that the lethal bullet had pierced the guide's wallet. But his wallet was missing.

Trooper Eggleston was a new member of the force. Just out of rookie school, he was working on his first murder case. He was indefatigable in his search for some mistake made by the slayer, some misstep that had been overlooked. As soon as the snow stopped falling, he drove back up the Indian Lake road and hiked up the mountain to the Davis cabin.

The eerie silence of the clearing oppressed him. The skin on the back of his neck tingled and he found himself unconsciously looking over his shoulder as if some evil wraith were waiting for a new victim. He forced himself to go on searching—in the cabin, in the clearing and into the woods as far as a bullet from a hunter's rifle could travel.

The trooper deserved to find the spent shell of the .30-30 cartridge that killed Eula Davis. It was simple justice. Eggleston picked it up from a patch of snow among the sassafras bushes, a perfect hideaway that hugged the edge of the clearing closest to the unfinished cabin door.

A ballistics expert proved that the bullet that killed Davis had been fired from the shell Trooper Eggleston found on the mountainside, but that didn't help at the time.

Back in Speculator, other troopers made the rounds of the stores to learn if any of the dead woodsman's money had been taken in. They went to Duane's home and questioned him again about the details of his stumbling upon the body. Duane's story was flawless; his presence in the woods that morning was most natural.

Adirondack lean-to shelters were the scenes for many a spooky tale. *Courtesy Leigh Portner*

The police reasoned that the crime had gone unnoticed for four days and that a murderer who had escaped detection that long would not go running to police. Nevertheless they decided to hold the young trapper as a material witness. Duane went off to the Hamilton County jail without any rancor.

The fact that Duane was inside this citadel of the law, ramshackle as it was, had an unexpected and unpredictable psychological effect on the village postmaster and storekeeper. He waited for darkness, bundled up in a coat which had a collar so big it almost hid his face, and walked down to the police substation. He kept to the back streets of the village. Once in the station he whispered to the troopers:

"You really mean business with Duane?"

"Well, we're holding him as a material witness, and under lock and key," Trooper Fitch replied.

"Then I'll tell you what I've been afraid to say before," said the postmaster hoarsely. "Ernie Duane gave me a $10 bill Thanksgiving evening for some provisions. I didn't want to say anything first off. You know what they say about him burning down the house of folks he don't like, but with him in jail I figgered I'd tell you about the money. Here 'tis."

He handed the troopers a bill. Near the middle was a hole, circular and neat. A piece of paper torn from a mail-order catalog was pasted on one side of the bill to make the hole less noticeable.

With this for evidence and a special prosecutor named by the governor, the state proved Ernest Duane, who once served as guide for Gene Tunney when he was heavyweight champion of the world, guilty of murder in the first degree.

Sentenced to die in the electric chair, he was saved because the governor was impressed with medical testimony indicating mental instability. Duane was then resentenced to life imprisonment.

Months later Trooper Eggleston was enjoying a vacation in the Adirondacks not far from where Duane murdered Davis for the bankroll. The trooper met a farmer whose land lay between the Davis cabin and the town of Speculator. Around the campfire they fell to talking about the case.

"It's a funny thing," reminisced the farmer. "Four days before Thanksgiving morning, when they found old man Davis dead, I was looking for the heifer that had strayed into the woodlot. Who did I see but Ernie Duane, cutting cross lots down toward the village? He was too far away for any talking, so we just hollered at one another. He went on down into town and I went looking for my calf-critter."

The state trooper banged his knee with his fist.

"That clears up the last bit of mystery about Duane," Eggleston said. "He knew he'd been seen near the scene of the crime and that's why he came to us after mulling it over and told he'd found the body. Sort of outfoxed himself, didn't he?"

Mountain trekkers in1917. *Courtesy Jane Ritz*

A LEGEND OF PITCH-OFF MOUNTAIN PASS

By Grace L. Hudowalski, *North Country Life*, Summer 1950

Years ago a tinker plied his trade between "the Valley" and Lake Placid, pushing his little cart laden with shiny tins, pots, and pans from one farmhouse to another en route. The two-mile stretch through Pitch-Off Mountain Pass, with the rocky ledges towering over the narrow trail on one side and the Cascade Lakes on the other, seemed especially long in that no one dwelt in the pass. On sunshiny days it was pleasant, but when the wind blew, rocks were hurled from Pitch-off into the pass, even as today, and travel was hazardous.

One day as the tinker pushed his cart up the steep hill leading out of the pass towards Lake Placid, a terrific wind came up. And the tinker, his cart, tins, pots, and pans were blown into the lake and he was drowned.

Legend has it that on a stormy day, should you linger in the dangerous pass, you can hear the clatter of the tinker's wares as they are being blown into the lake. However, should the sun be shining, you can see the glitter of those shiny tins on the lake's bottom. Find a parking place and see for yourself!

THE MYSTERY OF THE LOST CAVE

By Glyndon Cole, *York State Tradition*, Spring 1973

A story on the front page of the *New York Times* for March 10, 1909, created a mystery which has not yet been convincingly solved. It reported the discovery—in one of the wildest sections of the Adirondacks—of a cave rivaling in size the great Mammoth Cave in Kentucky.

Discovery of the cave, according to the story, was made by Captain E. E. Thomas, a timber cruiser, inspector and sealer for the woodland's department of the Delaware & Hudson Railroad, in the area of W Mountain in Franklin County, a few miles southwest of Upper Chateaugay Lake. It is wild country, and the terrain is rough and rugged. The going here is hampered by the dense forest, the thick brush and the fallen timbers. Few have tried to penetrate it.

Captain Thomas reported that he and a Mr. Cooper went inside the caves 800 or 1,000 feet and that there seemed to be no end to the distance one could go with the proper equipment. According to his report, the opening is fifty feet wide. "The first room," Captain Thomas said, "is fifty feet long, twenty feet wide, and thirty feet high. There was a decided smell of sulfur. In the next room, which was about forty feet by twenty-five feet by twenty-five feet, we found passages branching in many directions and were unable to explore all of them. With only the feeble rays of a lantern to guide us, we several times narrowly escaped falling into pits. You can imagine how deep some of these were when I say that we had time to count to 15 or 20 before rocks we dropped into them were heard to strike."

Although this 1909 story created a stir at the time, apparently it was soon forgotten. Nothing about it seems to have appeared in the newspapers again until 1950, when the Chateaugay Record called attention again to Captain Thomas' description, but there was no further publicity until the fall of 1970. At that time, the 1950 article in the Chateaugay Record was brought to light by researchers in the North Country Historical Research Center at State University College in Plattsburgh.

Inquiries among area woodsmen brought out conflicting opinions. There were confirmations of the existence of the cave: there were also claims that no such cave existed. There seemed to be some agreement among woodsmen that a cave did exist in neighboring Norton Peak, but that it did not match the description of Captain Thomas' cave.

A number of newspaper articles about the possibility of a cave on W Mountain prompted several parties to attempt an investigation of the mountain. One explorer, according to the *Adirondack Daily Enterprise*, covered much of the eastern and southern exposures of the mountain. He concluded that if there is a cave in the area, it is located on the western or northern side, basing this conclusion not only on his failure to find it elsewhere but also on the geological slant of the rocks. Others who explored the mountain felt certain that there is a cave there somewhere, basing their opinion on their claim that the ground "sounds hollow."

Nothing really conclusive has resulted from any of these investigations. The area being so large and so difficult to traverse, only a thorough search by a sizeable tem over a period of several days can ever answer the question of whether a cave exists on W Mountain. To our knowledge, such a search has not yet been made.

Also in the fall of 1970 there were newspaper articles about the cave on Norton Peak, which, as the crow flies, is three or four miles from W Mountain. Numerous exploring parties that time and later visited the cave. The writer and his son and a friend went into the cave in September, 1972. Neither we nor any of the other parties found anything that seemed to fit Captain Thomas' description.

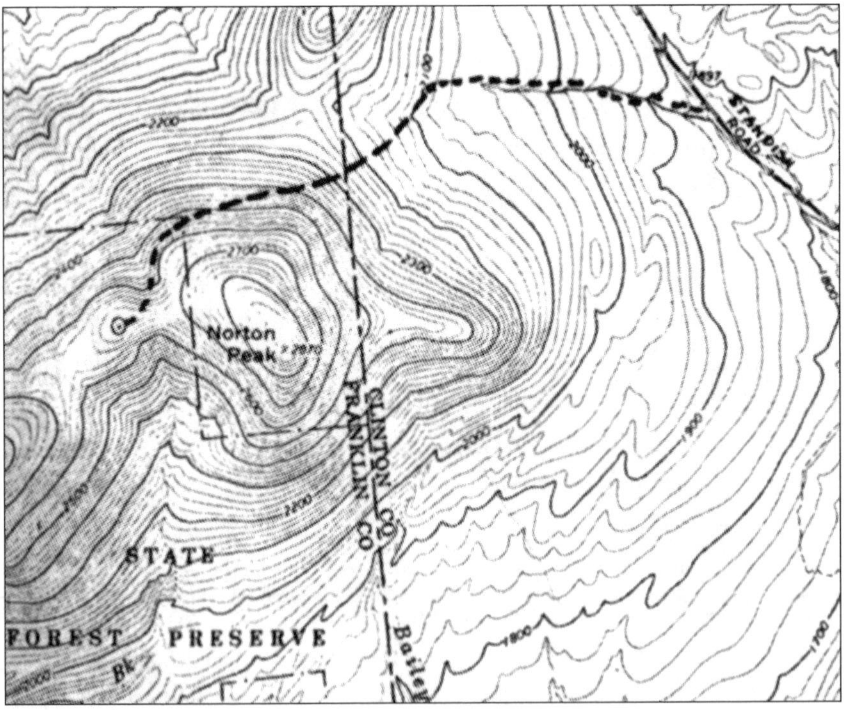

The broken line represents the trail from the Standish road up Norton peak and to the cave.

The opening, in a depression near the top of Norton Peak, was only four or five feet wide, not fifty feet. The writer's son penetrated the cave's first eight rooms, a distance of about 225 feet. The cave did seem to go on endlessly down into the bowels of the earth. We have heard of no one who has found the end of it. But no one has found rooms of the dimensions described by Thomas; no one has found deep chasms; no one has found an odor of sulfur.

Incidentally, however, this cave makes a climb up Norton Peak an interesting excursion. It is best approached from a point on the Clayburg–Standish road 2.8 miles north of the little hamlet of High Bank. From this point a trail is marked all the way, although at times it is somewhat difficult to follow. Three-fourths of the way the climb is very gradual. For a mile or so, the trail, marked with spots of beige paint on the trees, follows a brook. A short distance past the source of the brook, a trail marked with red paint crosses. Following the red marks to the left, one climbs steeply to the top of Norton Peak, the trail leading directly to one of the openings of the cave. A drop of about fifteen feet just inside the opening makes it advisable to take along a rope, and of course a good light is a must.

This writer, in talking with residents of the Standish area, discovered that they commonly refer to Norton Peak as W Mountain. As Norton Peak is viewed from the hamlet of High Bank, it does have the shape of a W. Knowing this, one might be inclined to believe that Captain Thomas also was referring to Norton Peak as W Mountain. But when one considers the marked discrepancies between the known features of the Norton cave and Captain Thomas' description of a "mammoth cave," one has to conclude that the cave on Norton Peak is not the one Captain Thomas claimed to have explored in 1909, unless his description is filled with a great deal of exaggeration.

Was Captain Thomas deliberately perpetrating a hoax, or is there really a huge cave on W Mountain which has been lost to man's knowledge and which remains to be rediscovered?

THE ANATOMY OF A LEGEND: THE LAKE CHAMPLAIN SEA SERPENT

By Connie Pope, *North Country Life*, Summer 1949

Arthur Knapp remembers seeing the Dexter serpent as a young lad. In 1952 he shared his remembrance about the legendary "Dexter Sea Monster Boys" with Glyndon Cole and Associate Editor Rowena B. Peterson. His memory adds additional lore to Pope's story.

> *In 1900 or 1901, two well-known residents of Point Salubrious near Chaumont, Dr. Amadon and Orin Pomery, set about to make a sea serpent in a class by itself. They assembled a quantity of beer kegs, bored two holes through the "chimes" at each end and passed a rope through the holes. Each keg was painted with green stripes. The head was another work of art—huge jaws, open red mouth, large white teeth, and fierce unkind red eyes.*
>
> *This monster, about 30 feet long, was anchored about 200 feet from the foot of Cherry Island. The ripple of the water let the kegs work in the ropes and the thing presented a live appearance.*
>
> *The first man to see it rowed his boat onto the shore of Point Salubrious and ran, shouting in fear. Others came to view it—but always at a respectable distance.*
>
> *Fishermen avoided the haunt of the serpent and mothers forbade their children to swim or play in the water for the rest of the season.*
>
> *"The hoax was finally discovered and the artists themselves burned their creation on the shore of Cherry Island."*

★ ★ ★

Something was out there on the lake—something anyone could see, but no one could identify; something all could describe, but none could agree to; something that appeared and disappeared at will, arousing, frightening, and mystifying the populace for more than 100 years. They called it the Lake Champlain sea serpent. Its legend rivals that of any monster known to man, ancient or modern.

It would take a book of encyclopedic proportions to record completely the serpent's documented cavortings on Lake Champlain. This account therefore will involve for the most part sightings recorded during the mid-1880s in Plattsburgh newspapers of those years.

The Champlain Valley in the 1880s offered a perfect breeding ground for monsters. Politically, the countryside was split into two camps, protectionists and free traders. Both professed to have solutions—though diametrically opposed—to all economic problems.

The industrial climate gave little relief from the confused political situation; in fact, it compounded the unrest. The lumber business had not yet recovered from the bankruptcy in 1876 of the king of lumbermen, Christopher F. Norton. The iron industry was entering a period of inactivity that would culminate in the collapse, around 1886, of ten or more major iron manufacturing companies, mainly on the Saranac and Chazy rivers. Unemployment, starting in 1883, was high and steadily climbing; whole populations were moving from inland mining and lumbering villages to lake ports and railroad centers.

Into this environment, ripe for panic, swam the serpent, first sighted by Clinton County Sheriff, Captain Nathan H. Mooney, and reported in the *Plattsburgh Morning Telegram* of July 31, 1883:

> *I looked off to the northwest, and I saw it appear again about twenty rods from us. I then discovered that it was an enormous snake or water serpent. It stood out about five feet from the water, with a long jaw, a snake-shaped head at least eight inches across at the top or flat part, and ten inches from the top of the head to the end of the jaw... Its body, which must have been twenty-five or thirty-five feet in length, was pointed to the north.*

Conditions were not precisely ideal for the sighting. The time was 4:30 PM of a late July day, described as "a very wild one, thunderstorms raging all around the sky, sending the wind to all four points of the compass, with frequent downpours of rain…the sun obscured by dark clouds… the sea rough." However, as the monster rose from the water, the clouds broke, the waves calmed, the sun appeared, and Mooney saw the creature at fifty yards distinctly enough to note round white spots inside its mouth.

Mooney's experience unleashed a flurry of similar reports, recorded or referred to in later stories. During the years 1884 and 1885, however, the monster seems to have quit Champlain's waters and for a time the *Morning Telegram* kept a running scoreboard of its foreign travels. In July 1884, the appearance of a sea serpent was reported in the Atlantic off Massachusetts, "the description of which minutely corresponds with that of our own animal." It had the head of a huge seal, no neck, a body increasing in size until hidden in the water, a wake of fifty feet. It was black in color with a white stripe running down the throat.

In September, 1884 something was seen in the Gulf of the St. Lawrence. "Is it our sea serpent in strange waters?" asked the editor. It was serpentine in form, 150 feet long, four feet in diameter, swelling tremendously with each undulation. Its head resembled a conger eel; its back sported an enormous fin and was striped like a mackerel; its jaws were immense, emitting horrible yells.

It was spotted at Iberville, Quebec, and in the Hudson River, off the coast of Maine, and further north toward Nova Scotia. In 1885, no sightings were reported; the monster remained in hiding, evidently building its mystique, for in the summer of 1886, it returned to Lake Champlain and put on such a display of acrobatics as to tax the credulity of the most gullible. Starting in July of that year and continuing through August of 1887, hardly a day went by without a serpent sighting.

Reliable, trustworthy men witnessed its appearances, for the newspapers gave space to none but those best known for honesty. They came from all walks of life—doctors, businessmen, navigators, clergymen, salesmen, schoolmen, and gentlemen. All testified to its existence, having seen it floating, frolicking, or fleeing through the waters of the lake. It appeared in every part of the lake, north to south, east to west. It was seen close to shore, in mid-channel, and twice on dry land. It looked like a serpent, like a large Newfoundland dog, like a whale, like a log, like a seal. It defied description. It was observed in the morning, at noon, in the evening, under a bright moon, and at two o'clock in the morning. Its observers shot at it, chased it, threw stones at it, attempted to pick it up, hooked it with a fishing line, flailed it with an oar, shrieked at it, and two claimed to have caught it. Each of the three newspaper editors thought he had discovered what it was. At least two rewards were offered for its capture.

The excitement of 1886 began with a sighting on the Vermont side near Dead Creek. The *Morning Telegram* gave the details in the words of a Swanton fisherman:

> *He was sporting and snorting in the morning sun. His body was out of water about fourteen feet, his head was well up and his great, red tongue kept licking his chops as if expecting a breakfast on some healthy camper; his eyes, as big as powder kegs, glowed wildly, his teeth looked like polished steel, and his horns were bright and brass-mounted; a kind of whalebone mane ran down his neck and a big buzz saw ornamented his breast. Scales as big as milk pails ornamented his sides, and his nickel-plated tail was flailing the air for bald eagles. His color was a handsome drab with white points, and his belly was old gold."*

From the tone of the story, one infers that the writer thinks it a bit far-fetched, but a month later the same paper quotes a "trustworthy statement by reliable citizens of the reappearance of the celebrated inhabitant of the deep, seen in Cumberland Bay." It appeared at seven o'clock in the morning to three gentlemen standing on the wharf of the Plattsburgh Dock Company. The day was sunny, calm and cloudless; the monster broke surface about 20 rods from its viewers. They estimated its length at 15 feet, its head at 15 to 18 inches long, its body as big around as a man. It swam with two feet of head and neck above the water and disappeared before they could take action.

Three evenings later, three gentlemen fishing off a dock almost wrote "finis" to the monster legend when one of the men succeeded in hooking it. Being unequal to the task of hauling it in, he cried for help, and his two companions set their brawny backs to pulling with him. Together they raised to the surface the head of a horrible creature, at which point the line broke and the creature disappeared. A witness, uninvolved in the struggle, corroborated the story.

In September, there were three unspectacular sightings. In October the *Plattsburgh Republican* published a history of the sea serpent, tracing its origin to Bulwaga Bay around the beginning of the 19th century. The story cited two appearances, recent and heretofore unpublicized.

The first occurred to a prominent St. Albans, Vermont, gentleman who was hunting ducks near the Mississquoi River. "It was just at daylight…when he saw but a short distance away an enormous serpent coiled up on the swampy shore and asleep…as large around as a man's thigh. He reached back to get his gun and in doing so made a slight noise when the serpent reared his head fiercely and ran off toward the tangle of undergrowth, making as much noise, as he went crashing through the bushes, as a large hound would."

The second involved a married couple taking an evening buggy ride on Cumberland Head. They had tied the horse and strolled down to the beach, where they saw a serpentine head and neck a foot and a half out of water, swimming slowly toward them. The man threw stones at the creature and drove it away.

The following week the *Plattsburgh Sentinel* offered a $1,000 reward for the capture, dead or alive, of the Lake Champlain sea serpent, the only condition being that its measurements exceed twenty feet.

The scene of the monster's exploits shifted in December to Willsboro Point, where five reliable men watched through a spy glass as it swam ten miles at a mile-a-minute clip, trailing a wake of foam the length of the steamer *Vermont*. All five men were converted from doubters to believers on the spot, according to the Sentinel.

The *Republican* verified the story by means of correspondence with a Willsboro hotel keeper, who corroborated the statement of the five "reliable men" and offered a few new yarns to add to the growing legend. He himself had seen something on the steamship lane. He described it as white, the size of the Florence Witherbee, and traveling at four times the speed. Another time he saw a tremendous sea coming north from Four Brothers Islands. It would roll, disappear, and reappear; but he failed to identify it.

Two fishermen tried to retrieve a long, colored log in Willsboro Bay; as soon as they moved toward it in a rowboat, it disappeared. A farmer spotted what he took to be a pole from his water fence floating about ten rods from his boat, and when he shifted to back toward it, the "pole" took off at the speed of a railroad train. He more than matched that speed getting home, out of breath and thoroughly frightened.

The *Republican* offered the theory a few days later that this creature might be a whale in search of new pastures. Where there was one whale, there might be others, and the paper envisioned the lakeside villages calling for legislative appropriations for whaling stations.

The serpent season of 1887 opened in May with another sighting in the Willsboro area. This time a farm boy who heard noises at two o'clock in the morning ran out to the shore and saw a mile out a serpent shape as big around as a rain barrel, making noises like a steamboat.

Two weeks later, Adirondack Murray, well-known sportsman and writer, reported the mystery solved. It was Friday the 13th. Crowds were gathered at Battery Park in Burlington to view the monster, which had been visible off and on for three hours in the bay near Juniper Island. Murray said he watched at first with the naked eye. The creature seemed at least 100 feet longer than a canal boat at that distance; his color seemed at times slatey brown, at others, glistening white. His motion was undulatory and quivering, and his speed was astonishing.

When it disappeared, Murray went for his high-powered field glass and adjusted it to the proper focus. When the monster reappeared, he discovered it to be a flock of hundreds of plovers. Their backs were brown; their wings and breasts were white. Murray's theory was confirmed by the lighthouse keeper on Juniper Island. Independent of any knowledge of Murray's testimony, he stated that the sea serpent was nothing more than a flock of birds flying along the surface of the lake.

The Murray theory appeared in the *Sentinel*, while the *Republican* and *Morning Telegram* were quick to disclaim it, citing instances which seemed to be more or less in conflict with the plover theory.

The *Republican* related the story of the daughter of a clergyman, standing on the rear deck of a steamboat sailing out of Swanton, Vermont, who "saw an animal, as described by the Willsboro witnesses, following the wake of the boat and a short distance away. She called Mr. Warren Rockswell, the pilot of the boat, who watched the animal for some time and finally shot at it, when it disappeared."

A doctor in North Hero saw from shore not five rods away from him what seemed to be a huge fish struggling in the shallow water. It rose up off the surface to a height of four feet, a cylindrical shape ten inches in diameter and dark in color. The doctor went to a nearby house for witnesses, and they returned and watched with him while the creature swam out of sight.

On the 16th of May, the *Morning Telegram* rejoined the issue with the story of a party of soldiers who were fishing off the *Garrison* and caught a creature, half fish and half animal, about fourteen inches long with a flat, arrow-shaped head, four legs, tufted, and shaped like an eel. It was identified as the offspring of a great water lizard, and the paper hinted that a brood of these vipers was being hatched in Lake Champlain.

Further disclaimers of the Murray theory came to the *Sentinel* from the Willsboro witnesses, who reported incidents of plover sightings and incidents of monster sightings, claiming that they knew the difference. One letter includes a brief reproof of Murray for serving his own interest in the yachting business better than he served the interest of truth.

The telegram quoted several correspondents who ridiculed Murray's explanation. One writer that he took said he had a powerful glass but saw no birds and wanted to know if there were birds, where they had gone when the monster disappeared a short distance from shore. Another claimed to have undisputable information that Murray had not even been present during the sighting on May 13th and actually knew nothing of it until two hours after it occurred.

Early in July the sea serpent appeared to a party of picnickers from Charlotte, Vermont. They described it as seventy-five feet in length and as big around as a barrel. The creature headed directly toward the party. Some of the women screamed; the creature turned and disappeared. A clergyman in the picnic party swore that they had with them no beverages stronger than coffee, tea, and lemonade.

Immediately a report came from a Lake George correspondent:

> *The sea serpent, lately seen by a party of picnickers...has left the lake (Champlain) and is making his way overland in the direction of Lake George. He was seen last night about five o'clock by a farmer driving to his barn with a load of hay. Chancing to look behind him...he saw a sight which he says he will never forget as long as he lives. Not five rods behind him, gliding along like a snake with its head raised about four feet from the ground, was an immense monster anywhere from 25 to 75 feet in length, with a gray and black streaks running lengthwise of its body, which was covered with scales... Its trail was plainly seen, but so great was the fear of the farmer that he would not let his men follow the serpent, which he says he has no doubt is the true and only sea serpent of Lake Champlain.*

On August 12, through the columns of the *Sentinel*, P. T. Barnum, the famous showman, offered a reward of $20,000 for the capture, dead or alive, of the sea serpent, the only condition being that the captors should preserve him and immediately notify Professor Ward of Rochester.

The serpent sightings of the 1880s closed with a report in the Sentinel that Dr. Byrum (or Byram) of Keeler's Bay, Vermont had captured it. "If not the original 100-footer, the story goes, "this answers the description in all other respects… This animal, fish or serpent, is some six feet long, will weigh from 150 to 200 pounds, is black as jet on its head, back, and sides, while its belly is white; the nose is hooked, the eyes small, and it can kick the water to a white foam. The animal was taken off Cooper's Point in the sturgeon's net. I have called it the baby sea serpent and want others to tell me what it is." There is no mention in the story that the doctor planned to claim Barnum's reward, and his captive, in length, failed to qualify for the Sentinel reward.

Whatever it was that was sighted so frequently in the 1880s, we see it no more in the waters of Lake Champlain. A more sophisticated generation watches for flying saucers. Newspapers are more concerned with civil disobedience and men on the moon; but down there in depths of Lake Champlain, who knows, the serpent may be lurking yet, waiting its time for a new appearance.

PART TWO

Campfire Stories

The original Adirondack Lodge, 1879–1903, was an immense log dwelling on the shore of Heart Lake in the center of the wilderness. Godfrey Dewey referred to it in *Told Around the Campfire* as "the apotheosis of the forest lovers' refuge, while its creator, Henry van Hoevenbergh, 'Mr. Van,' was as unusual as the Lodge itself was typical, and the Wednesday evening campfire tales, for which he was largely responsible, had a quaint flavor all their own." —*Told Around the Campfire: Henry van Hoevenbergh of Adirondack Lodge*, edited and with Biographical sketch by Maitland C. DeSormo, 1967.

Adirondack Lodge 1879–1903. Scene of many a campfire story.
Photo S. R. Stoddard. Courtesy of the Mailtland C. DeSormo Collection

PART TWO

Campfire Stories

COLLECTION SIX
Stories Told Around the Campfire

Deep woods camps, typically built between 1880–1920, once abandoned functioned as ready-made shelter for sporting people and a gathering place for nighttime story telling.
Courtesy North Elba-Lake Placid Historical Society

TALES OF ADIRONDACK FOLKS

By William J. O'Hern

"Tales" is a collection of stories that are representative of the lore that appeared in *North Country Life/York State Tradition*. Embedded within Adirondack natives' everyday living was—and still is—a down-to-earth humor.

From "the stories and experiences of the pioneers, hermits, guides, lumbermen, and village characters," wrote researcher/historian Ted Abner, who often stared "into the countenance of death itself—in the lumber woods, in blinding blizzards, in treacherous log jams while river driving, in devastating forest fires—virtually in daily living," a simple form of entertainment developed. The tradition of oral storytelling grew to become humorous. It punctuated the monotony of winter and brooding nature; it amplified commonplace happenings. Most often born from true events, successive tellings put a humorous twist to mysteries, tragedies, violent deaths, devastating community fires and encounters with wild animals. These "tall tales" included legends and lore, ghosts and monsters.

The "campfire" stories included were contributed by a logger, sailor, a school teacher, a young man who wanted to feature his great grandfather, a newspaper reporter, a holy man, a housewife-hunter, diehard mountain climbing enthusiast, a saloon keeper and a regular general store cracker-barrel character. The writers related stories that have been passed down by natives who lived throughout the Adirondacks. They form an accurate picture of the character and self-reliance of the mountain people they champion in the low rolling hills and mountains fifty to a hundred fifty years ago.

Some of the tellers of these tales were natives; others spent much time in and about little hamlets and villages of the Adirondacks. They knew the people well. I suspect that they picked up most of these stories through casual conversation at the diner, the post office, at relatives' homes, or at other gathering places. I know of one former Glens Falls librarian who told me he has filled a huge notebook of yarns he heard over the years that were swapped over breakfast at a local diner.

I would guess the stories presented in Glyndon Cole's quarterly magazine would have never been published anywhere had the interested parties not been absorbed with storing them up, recording them and finding that the publisher of the now out-of-print periodical believed in sharing them with his readership.

A few of the stories are of the tall-tale type, but most of them are within the realm of fact. Indeed, they are based on actual incidents. An example is the logger's tale about escaping certain death, and that of a hunter "back in the 1870s," when timber wolves were still plentiful in the Big Woods. A hunter, out after deer, found himself homeward bound late on a late November afternoon, "his ammunition completely expended without any worth-while result." The early tale in the Adirondacks continued with the details of the day.

"As he trudged wearily along on old tote-road through the woods, he looked over his shoulder to see that a big timber wolf was trailing him a hundred yards or more behind.

"The hunter wasn't particularly worried at first, but sometime later, when he glanced backward again and saw another wolf over his other shoulder, he hastened his steps, for he felt sure that the pack was gathering and would close in on him when it became dark. Finally the wolves drew so near and became so threatening that the hunter dashed for a good-sized tree in a clearing, climbed it hurriedly and perched himself out of reach of the animals on a limb. He believed that they would tire of waiting after a time and go away.

"The hunter was relieved when the wolves, a dozen of them by this time, actually turned tail and dashed off through the forest almost immediately, but to be sure they were gone, he waited for a half hour before he climbed down out of the tree and started across the clearing toward the main highway. He had traveled only a few steps, however, when he saw the entire pack returning on the run.

"And this time they were bringing with them a beaver."

Although each story has a definite locale, the humor common to all gives them a universal appeal.

Mother Johnson's, situated a quarter mile above Raquette Falls, about midway between Long Lake and Upper Saranac Lake, was a popular mountain hotel in the 1860s and '70s. Travelers secured meals, lodging, and hospitality and listened with interest to incomparable tall-tale tellers. *Courtesy Special Collections, Feinberg Library, SUNY College at Plattsburgh*

Each story, uncluttered by unnecessary detail, is well told. The tellers' and spinners' simple, concise style—most appropriate for "Tales of Adirondack Folks"—makes reading their work a pleasure and might well inspire a new generation to find its own stories, worthy of recording and perhaps of eventual publication in a similar anthology of personal folklore.

THAT CAMP O'MINE

I have a camp up in the woods
Where I go to rest and play.
I watch the beavers from my porch
And fish at close of day.

Of course there's just a little work;
Things need to be done, you know.
You can't let things just run themselves
And still put on a show.

I mend the roof after each rain,
And cuss the cloudy skies.
I work all day at picking fruit
So wife can make some pies.

The screens need paint, wood must be cut,
Kids broke three panes of glass.
I lug in ice and burn up trash
And don't neglect the grass.

I'll tell the boys of fish I caught;
They'll grin and say, "That's fine."
But just the same, in spite of bugs,
I love that camp o' mine.

—Edmund P. Davis, *North Country Life*, Summer 1961

Author and his wife at their camp.
Author's photo

The West Canada Creek camp was getting beat-up then. And I certainly remember the black muck lane. I remember a lot of old sportsmen and guides who sat around in the sun and talked of times past. It was special to be back there. It was joy. *Courtesy Edward Blankman (The Lloyd Blankman Collection)*

CY BROWN, WOODSMAN EXTRAORDINARY

By Barnett Fowler, *North Country Life*, Spring 1949
Reprinted from New York State *Conversationist*

Of all the tellers of tall tales that have come out of (or stayed in) Northern New York's evergreen country, Cy Brown, fisherman and hunter extraordinary, ranked among the finest. This distinctly unusual man passed away some years back, but behind him he left a vast heritage of Adirondack mountain stories.

To say that Cy's experiences verged on the extraordinary is to put it mildly, yet Cy was a man of considerable background and had a bland manner of recounting his exploits, each, they say, being delivered to natives and pop-eyed tourists as King Solomon delivered his verdicts, each ringing staunchly of truth and wisdom.

Cy was a man of exceptional physical prowess. It is reported that he once beat a streak of lightning down a tree trunk, although it is *not* reported what he was doing in a treetop during a lightning storm. He was also an ingenious fellow, and on one occasion used blackstrap molasses to cement a log raft together on Cedar River Flow. His instinct, as usual, proved uncanny; as flies were attracted to the raft, so were trout, and Cy had no trouble in scooping up barrels of them with a frying pan.

Cy died a natural death. There was a time, however, when he was threatened with a most unnatural one, and that's a story still recounted by native Adirondackers. It was the time he and a friend named Prentiss were chased by thirty ravenous wolves in the mountains north of the settlement on Indian Lake.

On a bitterly cold and clear morning, the two men were aboard a sled on an old logging road about ten miles from home. It was with a thrill of sheer horror that they heard the quietness of the woods shattered by the lonely, chilling howl of a wolf pack in full pursuit. In a flash Cy knew this was no ordinary pack; stories brought in by local hunters had pegged these wolves as being expertly led by a huge and fearsome beast of the utmost valor and daring. The whole pack had a reputation for uncanny wisdom, cruelty and fearlessness, and their leader in particular was reputed to have an appetite of immense proportions.

As he lashed the team to top speed, Cy's spine tingled with the memory of a lonely hunter treed by the pack. It was common knowledge that the wolves had obtained two beaver to gnaw down the tree, and the terrified huntsman had time to kill only ten before the pack, in a gesture of supreme derision at all hunters, ate him up and left only his pants hanging from a limb. (It is also a matter of record that five of the wolves which ate the cartridge belt later blew up.)

There was little comfort in these memories. But both men prepared to sell their lives valiantly, and Prentiss, armed with a rifle, started shooting the moment the pack hove into view. With his first shot he killed one. As the beast fell, the other 29 pounced upon it, tarried only long enough to devour it, and then resumed the chase with redoubled ferocity and appetites keenly whetted.

Cy and Prentiss knew then that these wolves were no different from others; they were cannibalistic as well as half-starved, and they would eat a wounded or dead member with as much compunction as a helpless rabbit. Neither man felt happier for this knowledge, but an idea blazed in Cy's brain. He ordered Prentiss to keep shooting the foremost wolf. Expertly his friend picked off one after another, fighting against the sway of the sled. In a short time he had killed ten, and as each one fell, the pack stopped for its quick grisly meal.

By the time the horses began to show the strain of the terrific pace, the animals had been cut down to 15, but they were as ugly and fierce as when the pursuit started. As Cy lashed the horses, Prentiss redoubled his efforts and managed to kill ten more, and as each one fell, there was a short breathing space for the horses. Finally it could be seen that the five remaining wolves, each containing his share of 25 others, were slowing up from sheer weight.

But further misfortune bedeviled the men. Prentiss discovered he had only four cartridges left. By this time the horses were again staggering,

On the way from Inlet to Eagle Bay, John remembers that the wagon driver calmed his fears that the only ghosts he ever knew about were those that lurked in the deserted village of Adirondac. *Courtesy John Chamberlain*

and application of the whip could no longer obtain more speed. The wolves were only a few yards distant, and although Prentiss drilled four more, by the time the lone remaining wolf—the real leader of the pack—was left, the horses were barely able to stand.

Cy, peering anxiously ahead, abruptly exulted. Home and safety were visible! So, however, was the wolf, although strange things were now happening in this slow motion drama. The wolf stopped frequently. Once it emitted a gigantic burp. Often it sagged wearily against trees before resuming the pursuit. And the horses—they were reduced to a weary stumbling plod.

Eventually, however, the sled drew up in front of the house. Cy and Prentiss dashed inside, Cy to reappear an instant later with a pork chop in his hand.

"Whar you goin'?" shouted Prentiss.

"I'm goin' ter fix thet thar wolf!" muttered Cy.

He approached the beast as it crept up. He noted its distended belly. He walked directly up to it and for an historic moment man and animal eyed each other. Suddenly Cy shoved the pork chop into the animal's face.

The wolf, filled with 29 of its companions, took one look at the food, groaned despairingly, and collapsed at Cy's feet.

"Died a' sheer disappointment," Cy recounted later. "On purpose, I didn't put no gravy on the pork chop."

FIRESIDE LEGENDS OF THE ADIRONDACKS

By Reverend W. N. P. Dailey, *North Country Life*, Summer 1951

The Adirondacks are rich in legends and folklore. Practically every part of the Great North Woods has its own Indian legend, or if not an Indian legend, some tale of how mysterious influences were supposed to have given a name or character to a prominent natural feature of the section.

Two of the earliest men to attempt to preserve in some form the Indian legends and other stories of the Adirondacks were Henry Van

Hoevenberg, who for many years conducted Adirondack Lodge, and S. R. Stoddard, the Adirondack pioneer, in whose *Northern Monthly* many of the legends gathered by Mr. Van Hoevenberg appeared. A feature of the life at Adirondack Lodge, until it was destroyed by the great forest fire of 1903, was the custom of relating stories around a great blazing campfire after dark. The following are a few of the stories that were told around that campfire.

Indian Pass. Indian Pass is one of the natural wonders of the Adirondacks. It is a great cut in the mountain by which Lake Placid is surrounded. Its walls, almost perpendicular, rise to a height of about 2,000 feet. The legend connected with this weird piece of nature's handiwork has it that a guide, pausing beside a mountain spring to quench his thirst, spied a bit of paper on the ground nearby. Despite the effect of rain and sun upon the writing, he was able to decipher enough to inform him that if at midnight of the 8th of September he would scale Summit Rock, the highest point in the pass, he would see to the west a hemlock tree overhanging the chasm below. To the south, in line with its trunk but a thousand feet higher, he would see the mouth of a cave. In this cave, guarded by the spirit of one of their number, he would find an immense treasure hidden there by the Indians many years before.

Returning at midnight on the 8th of September, the guide climbed to the hemlock, and looking up discovered far above his head the yawning mouth of the cavern in the side of the rock wall. He imagined he could make out a series of small cuts in the rock by means of which he could reach the spot, and drawing off his boots and socks and priming his revolver, he started. Never daring to look behind lest he should become dizzy and fall, he tightly hugged the face of the rock wall, up which he went slowly, inch by inch. In one place he had to jump to reach a projecting ledge. As he made the leap, the rock gave way beneath his feet, but he caught a stout shrub and drew himself up after hanging for a time in mid-air over the yawning chasm below. Finally he reached the mouth of the cavern, and peering in, discerned the treasure piled up on the rock floor.

At the same instant he caught sight of a great form with dark, forbidding face and flaming eyes advancing upon him. He drew his revolver and fired at it, but even as he did so, he felt himself caught up in two great muscular hands and borne, despite his struggles, to the edge of the rock platform before the entrance to the cave.

Just for a second he was suspended in air. Then his captor released his hold and the unfortunate guide shot downward like a stone. His body struck the old hemlock tree, and that, giving way, went down too, serving in a manner to break the force of his fall. When he regained his senses, he found that it was daylight. One arm was broken and his whole body mangled and bruised.

Grandfather, John "J.B." Todd, was superintendent for The Gould Paper Company. During the summer months when lumberjacks were not actively working in the woods beyond North Lake, Grandma Hazel and he would bring my brother and me to stay at Camp Seven. The lumber company camp was located at the base of Ice Cave Mountain. I remember we were often ferried up the lake on the White Swan. Rev. Byron-Curtiss ran a part-time navigation business on the lake. There were summer evenings when he would arrive at camp. Grandpa and he were great friends. We used to sit around the evening campfire and listen to them talk about all things outdoors and old time characters. One tall tale they told was about the Lopsided Side Hill Gouger—it used to scare the dickens out of me. —Dorothy Payton. *Courtesy Dorothy Payton*

His first thought was that it had all been a dream, but the pain in his arm and body, the hemlock tree on the ground nearby, and a gold ornament he still clutched in one hand told him the occurrences of the night had been only too real. The legend concludes by pointing to the fact that the uprooting of the hemlock tree has forever obliterated all clues to the hiding place of the Indian treasure, an apparently safe conclusion since it has never yet been found.

The Forsaken Village. The legend of the forsaken village is another interesting story of the Lake Placid country. As far as the facts go, the forsaken village was the little village of Adirondack, which was years ago the scene of iron ore mining operations conducted by a party of capitalists on the strength of a discovery of some rich iron ore made by an Indian in the locality.

After a great amount of money had been expended, the price of iron fell and the project was abandoned with such speed that the people of the little hamlet did not remove their household goods from their homes. Moreover, few, if any of them, could bear the cost of transporting their goods. When the work stopped, the people simply walked away and left the little village to its fate.

Legend has it that a New York businessman on vacation chanced to come upon the moss-covered remains of the little village. Entering one house, he found it perfectly furnished. Further on, he came across the office of the company by whom the mines had been operated. Even the ledgers had been left in the safe, the doors of which were open. Before he realized it, night was upon him. Deciding to make the best of the situation, he returned to the house he had first entered, and taking possession of one of the silent bedrooms, he threw back the musty bed covers and made himself as comfortable as possible for the night.

In the middle of the night he was awakened by the sound of footsteps to find a man standing in the door of his room. To the astonished city visitor, the newcomer related a tale, the substance of which was that he was the founder of the village and that his daughter, Mina, fell in love with an artist who formerly visited the place. The father did not approve of her choice and ordered the lover away. He forbade all communication between the two, and when a letter arrived from the artist addressed to his daughter the father kept it from her.

Before long the maiden became ill, and when she grew worse, the father sought for the letter to give her. He could not find it. The girl died, and the agonized parent from that time on had been doomed to search for the hidden letter. With the coming of the morning, the city man searched for the letter and at last found it in a hole in the wall. That night he placed it on the table. Again his midnight caller came and the sleeper was awakened by a great cry of joy. When he reached the table where he had placed the letter, it was gone.

The Devil-Fungus. The devil-fungus was a mysterious plant growth supposed to have had its existence in the caverns on the mountainsides in the vicinity of Lake Placed. The story told about this weird plant is that a party coming into the Adirondacks from the city for the summer included a maid and two men who loved her. One of these men, much older than the girl, was not deserving of her, but their engagement had been announced. The devil-fungus had the power to imitate the charms of a beautiful woman and to emit an intoxicating scent. The story runs that the elder man, falling beneath the spell of the devilish plant, was rescued by the younger man and that the former immediately left the woods and the youthful lovers to themselves.

WEIRD BELIEFS OF EARLY DAYS IN THE NORTH

Author unknown, *North Country Life*, Spring 1953
Reprinted from the *Syracuse Post-Standard*

Readers today are horrified at the methods employed in the Salem witchcraft cases, where a materialistic Satan was associated with the accused. Yet Northern New York is not so young as never to have practiced occult methods in criminal investigations.

Historian Franklin B. Hough relates that as late as 1815 a suspect was made to touch the corpse of his supposed victim under the belief that, if the other had committed the homicide, blood would flow from the long-dried wounds.

The case cited by Hough arose in the town of Denmark, Lewis County. In June, 1815 the body of Henry Waggoner was found in Deer River. Murder was suspected, and the coroner impaneled a jury that failed to agree. Public demand insisted that something be done. A jury of 23 persons was summoned from distant parts of the county, and the body was disinterred. Twelve of these jurors agreed upon a verdict of suicide.

Meanwhile it had been recalled that Waggoner had denounced a young man named Simpson Buck, whom Waggoner charged with intimacy with a daughter-in-law. Waggoner had intensified the bitterness between himself and Buck by appearing against the latter in a lawsuit, after which, according to public report, Buck had declared that Waggoner would not again appear against him in court.

Evidence laid before the coroner's jury by 42 witnesses established that, when last seen, Waggoner had gone to a field a mile above High

Saturday, October 25, 1924. Heading into hunting camp. "Darwin Parker and the Wolves" was a standard Adirondack tale-of-the-day that wandered farther from the truth with each retelling, and that simply made it more appealing. Modest campfire entertainment but memories aplenty. *Courtesy Town of Webb Historical Association*

Falls to hoe potatoes; that there was a mark on the skull that might have been made by a hoe; that blood was found in the field and on a fence near the chasm, and that the body was found below the falls.

After the body was recovered, Buck was accompanied to it by a group of citizens and made to touch it. No blood appeared, and whether this fact influenced the jury in its findings, Hough did not indicate.

The coming of photography developed another manner of establishing the identity of murderers. Had it proved actual, rather than occult, it would have simplified the work of homicide squads. Under this belief, the eyes of the victim retained an image of the assailant. An incident is related in Jefferson County when it was proposed that photographs be taken of the eyes of a supposed murder victim to establish the perpetrator.

Belief in ghosts or the materialization of the dead was by no means unknown among early settlers. Tales of ghosts and haunted buildings are frequent, although seldom considered worthy of inclusion in histories.

Threescore years or more ago, a dwelling stood on the Somerville Road leading toward Rosie. In one of its windows, it was claimed, the distorted features of Jack Taylor, a reputed suicide, appeared under the illumination of certain July electrical storms. Taylor, according to tradition in St. Lawrence County at the period, had shot his wife to death, fled into the swamps, and then returned, eventually hanging himself opposite the window, where his features frightened passersby in the heat lightning of early July evenings.

In the latter period of its use as a hostelry, "Aunt" Judith Black occupied a little home diagonally across the state road from the present East Hounsfield Library. Her life had been saddened by the sudden disappearance of a son-in-law, Levi Derusha, and her grandson, Johnny Derusha, as they were in route home one night after the man had finished his day on one of Tilden's "tin" peddling carts.

It was suspected that Derusha was murdered for the considerable sum of money he purportedly carried, but no body was ever found, no trace of man or boy, and no proof of foul play.

Eventually Aunt Judith was declared insane through the instigation of a neighbor, to whom, as she was taken forcibly to the madhouse, she promised to return in immortal form upon her death. Today, to "haunt you" is not considered a serious threat, but it is a recorded fact that after the woman's demise the threatened neighbor became stark raving mad, following in Judith's steps to the insane asylum.

But these were simple and gentle apparitions compared to the mammoth goblin reportedly haunting the Copenhagen area in the spring of 1900. It was getting a little late in human occupation of Northern New York for such curiosities, but this "Jabberwock," as it was termed by the press, was observed by so many travelers along the unlighted highways that notice was taken of it.

Buggies didn't carry headlights in 1900, so visions were obscured in detailing the monster, described as shaped like a frog, ghostly white, possessing fiery eyes, and capable of exuding a smell that sickened pursuers. One spectator declared it hopped easily over a six-rail fence, and another saw it merely step over. Two persons, who caught it in the rays of a lantern, discovered that its face resembled a human's, set off by two curled horns like a ram's.

If the jabberwocky left any offspring, they evidently have removed from these parts, for none have been reported recently. The brief presence of the creature along the northern edge of Lewis County added a zest to living.

MY ENCOUNTER WITH WILD DOGS

By Vivian Steves Walker, *North Country Life*, Winter 1960

The little hamlet of South Bay, located in Washington County, on the southern tip of a body of water also known as South Bay, is flanked on two sides by Mt. Diameter—notorious for its rattlesnake dens and rockslides—and East Mountain. The backdrop is a series of ridges and pinnacles that rise straight up to descend in hilly juniper-spotted pasture land and neglected woodlots. The only way out of the valley is the way you came in, for less than three miles beyond, the narrow road comes to a dead end.

I've lived in the country for thirty odd years, and up until a few years ago the most menacing creature I have had the misfortune of tangling with has been the rattler. Had anyone as much as suggested the possibility of there being bears, lynx, or wild dogs lurking in the dark niches of the vast acres of timberland surrounding South Bay, I would no doubt have dismissed the idea with little more than a shrug.

Perhaps that is why, looking back now, it seems so incredible. In fact, at the time it seemed just as incredible. But I know that it happened. I still get a little sick when I think about it.

I had hunted the Oak Ridge the better part of the day and was feeling rather smug about the four gray squirrels that made a rather prominent bulge in my pockets.

Times without number my husband had kidded me about hunting squirrels with an "elephant gun," referring to my .25-20, which I preferred to his .410. I liked the feel of the .25-20, probably because it belonged to me.

In the wilderness, a dog really is man's best friend. *Courtesy Town of Webb Historical Association*

A light snow which had fallen during the night had gradually melted under the penetrating glare of the sun. Only a few patches were still visible in the more sheltered areas.

I never carried a timepiece, but from the position of the sun I judged that it was crowding three o'clock. About three quarters of a mile below the ridge, I left the old tote road and took a short cut across a thickly wooded area. It was impossible for me to get lost here. I knew the country like the back of my hand. It proved, however, to be a laborious trek, up one ledge and down another. My legs soon ached, and to relieve the muscle strain in my arms, I shifted the rifle from one hand to the other as often as possible.

By the time I had worked my way back to the road above the Draper Place, heavy, black clouds were sailing in and the sun had become almost obscured. I hadn't heard as much as a "bark" from the squirrel department since taking the short cut, so I decided to call it a day. Tomorrow I would catch those elusive devils making their usual sun-up whoopee.

Sloane's Pinnacle lies to the east, adjoining the Draper Place. This hog's back of a triangle seems to rise straight up from two sides, with the third descending in long grassy slopes that lose themselves in a maze of scrub pine and juniper. A narrow deeply-rutted road runs aimlessly along the west side of the pinnacle through an orchard of scraggy spy trees and down over Hogan Hill into the hamlet of South Bay.

As I stepped into the road, things started happening. All at once there was the sound of a brief struggle, mingled with the agonized howl of an animal in pain. It was close by, but off to my right in a small thicket.

The cry split the air in a sharp, resonant wall that momentarily galvanized me to the spot. As soon as I had recovered from the sudden chaos, I put down the rifle and made a frantic search for a cudgel.

My husband and I had been through this routine so many times that I felt a little ridiculous at my jumpiness, and not a little friendly at our neighbor, whose "Heinz dog" we had freed from a trap so many times that I wondered whether the dog had any feet left.

I had never attempted this by myself, but the dog knew me so I assured myself that it would be simple. My husband had always cautioned, "Be sure to use a forked stick or a club." The best I could find on such short notice was an old cedar fence post.

The cries had died to a low menacing growl that sent a slow paralysis crawling up my spine. A massive clump of juniper just past the ancient barbed wire fence separated me from the trapped animal. I crawled through the fence, leaving one of the elbows in my jacket as a grim warning to the next one who might attempt a likely maneuver. I've never yet escaped unscathed from one of those man-made snares.

I halted a moment to get my breath. I started forward again and now there was a devil of a rumpus coming from the brush. I circled the juniper and was as prepared for what I saw as I am for Judgment Day.

There, under the sprawling branches of an enormous pine, stood two large dogs. Their bodies were thickset, with large paws and small, neat ears. Their coats were a faded grayish tan, and mangy-looking.

They advanced menacingly, their thick tails twitching and lashing. They were less than a dozen feet away and were swiftly closing the gap between us. I took a few cautious steps backward. To turn and run would be suicidal.

I felt the cold rough security of a tree gouging me in the back. They were almost on me now. They kept up a steady guttural grating, and the nearest one assumed a wiggling crouch, then suddenly lunged for me.

I swung the fence post with all the force that my 115 pounds could muster. I let out a yell—a yell so loud that it should have carried to the top of Double Hill two miles away.

The blow caught him in mid-air and sent him crashing to the ground at my feet. I landed a couple of chipping blows to his head before he managed to roll free of me and stagger to his feet.

Meanwhile his playmate was circling to get behind me. I was getting tired, and the sweat was pouring down my face. I was not only outnumbered, but outweighed. I shouted at it and waved the cudgel threateningly. It backed away, but started circling in the opposite direction.

I had just one thought—to keep them both in front of me. Somehow I would make out, but only if I kept them both in front of me. Something inside kept saying, "Easy does it; just take it easy; no quick moves." It was like an inner voice, but it was soothing. I felt the tenseness flow out of me.

Nothing happened for several minutes, and I wondered if they had decided to call it quits. This proved, however, to be wishful thinking, for a second later my opponent came hurtling through the air in a fresh burst of fury. His eyes were flaming and his teeth bared in a spine-tingling snarl.

I managed to sidestep the full impact of the lunge, but the tops of my snow boots were turned down and he ground off a mouthful of the sheepskin lining, nearly dragging me to the ground.

I pulled free and started backing away. The scuffle had torn up the soggy carpet of pine needles, making it difficult to keep my footing. Darkness was less than an hour away. I glanced helplessly toward the spot where my gun lay useless. The utter hopelessness of getting to it filled me with despair and a reckless determination.

One of the dogs was still pacing like an expectant father. The other was plastered with a combination of pine needles and caked mud. He was coming in for another attack. He came at me like a pile-driver and sent me stumbling backward five or six feet. I landed harder than I wanted to.

Out of my daze I saw him scramble to his feet. By the time he reached me, I had gathered myself up and was swinging wildly. The first blow struck him over the left eye, dazing and confusing him. I didn't wait for him to recover. I struck him again—once, twice, three times. He was down, but struggling wildly and blindly to get up. Blood spilled from his ears, staining the ruff of his neck a bright crimson.

Right then I became really sick—the stirred-with-a-spoon kind of sickness. I felt very tired. My eyes refused to focus properly. I grabbed the nearest tree and hung on until the landscape stopped its somersaulting.

When the turmoil had passed, I discovered that I had dropped the cudgel, but one look at the dogs assured me that I no longer needed it. My opponent had staggered to his feet and was pirouetting like a chicken stung by a rattler. His friend was attempting to give him the once over, at the same time keeping an eye on me; but he would have none of it.

He kept up a steady thrashing about, pausing every few seconds to massage first one side of his head and then the other against the ground. When his frenzy was finally spent, he retreated in the opposite direction, heaving unsteadily. His friend slouched meekly after him.

Much later, although it was only a short distance, I stumbled into the road, a disheveled package of nerves. Sweat rolled down my back, and my feet and legs felt encased in mortar. Although home was less than half a mile away, it seemed hours later that I was fumbling weakly to unlock my door.

According to this story George Shaughnessy told, a river driver slipped from a log and got into a terrible fix. Pinched between several logs he found himself squeezed so tightly that he couldn't get out. They held him fast.

The poor driver knew that he must free himself somehow or be crushed, die from drowning or hypothermia. His whole life flashed before him. Suddenly he remembered that he had received a notice that he had failed to renew his subscription to his hometown newspaper. This made him feel so powerful that he was able to leap between the squeezing logs and up out of the water without difficulty. *Courtesy: George Shaughnessy*

GREAT-GRANDFATHER AND THE PANTHER

By Doris B. Morton, *York State Tradition*, Winter 1964

Have you heard the cry of a catamount—half baby-wail, half man-in-agony scream? You know, then, the ripples of horror that chase up and down the spine, and in spite of yourself, no matter how long since you have heard it, these sensations return whenever you think of that tawny, short-haired animal, a little larger than a boxer, with a great tail that can lash as wildly and lithely as a house cat's.

Only occasionally now are panthers found in the Adirondacks, but at one time they were common inhabitants of these woods. At least my Great-Grandfather James John Albert Swan found them so.

Grandfather lived in a small community called Cobb's Hill in the southwest corner of the town of Lewis, Essex County. Within walking distance—for people walked in those early days—was the mining center of Fletcherville, more commonly known as Seventy-five. Each week Great-Grandfather commuted on shank's mare to his place of labor, where he helped in the process of making charcoal, the fuel used to smelt Mineville iron ore. Each Saturday night he hiked home again to spend the Day of Rest with his family.

The route home lay through the forest. Customarily Great-Grandfather carried home a burlap sack of groceries slung over his shoulder. One particular Saturday night he was carrying home not "the bacon," but chunks of salt pork, a staple item of the early settlers' provisions. As he moved along through the woods, doubtless dusk had settled down, for this was before the eight-hour day and daylight saving time. He became aware that he was not alone. Not the snap of a branch nor the rustling of brush, but the steady pad of paws on hard-packed earth made his hair tingle at the roots. Risking a glance over his shoulder, he confirmed his suspicions. A panther was following him!

Now Great-Grandfather was resourceful. He bethought himself of the chunks of salt pork. Without slackening his stride, he swung the burlap sack forward, plucked out a chunk, and twisting, threw it with all his

"I love to fish. I started fishing young and have never lost the enthusiasm every time I reel in a fish. I can sit on a dock for hours, patiently waiting at the prospect for that big one. It's a life-long hobby. I picked it up from grandfather along with his many Adirondack tales." —Dorothy Payton. *Courtesy Dorothy Payton*

strength backward over the path. Facing forward again, he lengthened his stride into running leaps to cover ground. As he expected, the heavy paw steps were soon thudding behind him. Again out came another chunk; another throw was made, and Great-Grandfather's race was resumed. This routine lasted until with a great burst of speed, he gained his house and shut the door.

Night definitely had fallen now, but the small yellow glow of lamp-light did little to scare the animal. With the remembrance of pork in his mouth, the catamount leaped upon the pile of four-foot wood that leaned against the ell of the house. Here, until the glow of the rising sun, Great-Grandfather and his family heard him pacing back and forth from woodpile to ell. But with the dawn the animal quitted the wood pile in search of sleep—or perhaps a drink of water for the salt pork.

Often I heard this family tale from my mother, Metta Swan Begor, who in turn heard it from her father, Horace Swan. With each telling I could feel that hair-raising tingle that Great-Grandfather must have felt.

HEARD OVER IN ST. REGIS FALLS, AN OLD LUMBER CAMP TALE

Author unknown, *North Country Life*, Fall 1947,
Reprinted from *The North Countryman*

At Santa Clara, back in the woods five miles to the south, a strapping lumberjack with a pock-marked face and hair an inch long on his chest strode into the late Eli Gokey's saloon one afternoon, dragging a full-grown wildcat on a chain behind him. The big cat was newly caught and it snarled and snapped and fought the chain. The little group of tough woodsmen, lounging in the rough chairs tilted back against the wall, or leaning on the bar, scattered to give the beast plenty of room.

Finding itself inside four walls and startled by the unusual noise and confusion in the smoke-laden room, the animal became desperate, crouched, and with outstretched claws and fangs showing, leaped suddenly at the throat of its owner.

The hairy man met it in mid-air with a crushing blow of his fist, knocking it to the floor, and then kicked it into submission as the awed spectators looked on. Then he strode on to the bar, ordered a pint of whiskey and gulped it down without taking his lips from the bottle.

As the last drops gurgled down his throat, the head of a big snake thrust itself from under the hairy man's jacket, its long red fangs showing dangerously close to his chin. He scarcely gave it a glance, however, but demanded another pint of redeye, which he downed as he had the first one and wiped his mouth on the sleeve of his jacket.

The little group of rough lumberjacks stared at the hairy one in amazement, and finally one of them asked: "Stranger around these parts, ain't you mister?"

"Yaw," the man replied. "Come from Tupper Lake. Pretty rough customers over there. Me, an' some others, they run us outa town. Allowed as how we was too sissified."

An early Adirondack campground scene. *Author's Adirondack collection*

CAPTAIN NICKLAUS SPINS A YARN

Unknown author, *North Country Life*, Summer, 1948
Reprinted from *The North Countryman*

Captain Albert Nicklaus, former member of the Columbus (Ohio) Fire Department, (who was visiting relatives in Rouses Point at the time) dropped into the office and spun the following yarn about the family of an old farmer in the huckleberry country around Altona. If it weren't for the fact that the Captain's reputation for veracity had always been unquestioned and that he attended church regularly, one or two of his statements might possibly be discounted.

"It was last summer," remarked the ex-firefighter as he settled himself comfortably in a swivel chair and hoisted his feet to the top of a desk, "that I decided to build a small log cabin on a piece of land I expected to buy just south of the village. Finding the logs proved to be quite a problem, however, until the man who was to sell me the property referred me to old Noah Slender. He lives in the town of Altona and, in addition to his logs, has a son who has quite a reputation for his great strength.

"To reach Mr. Slender's place, I was directed to go straight south from Sciota over the macadam highway to Altona and continue two miles west before turning to the left on the second gravel road outside the village; then to drive for another mile and a half and stop at the second frame house beyond the point where the walls of an old sawmill rose above a patch of blueberry bushes.

"I followed the instructions faithfully and finally came upon a man with a long gray beard pushing a plow through the stoniest field I ever saw. There were no horses hitched to the plow and I marveled at the strength of a man who could turn over the ground simply by pushing the heavy plow ahead of him in a field where the ordinary farmer would use two horses.

"I asked the man where Mr. Slender lived, and he raised the plow with one hand, pointing it down the road in the direction of a dilapidated farm house. "My dad lives there," he said.

"Driving toward the house as directed, I met old Mr. Slender, a man of 95 or more, walking down a path almost obliterated by weeds. After introducing myself, I asked about the logs and was disappointed to find that he had sold them the previous week. Then I inquired about his son plowing in the field and remarked that he appeared to be a man of unusual strength.

"The old man told me that the son had been a delicate child and that for a time he and his wife had despaired of raising him. "He was born puny," Slender said, "because of an incident a short time before birth that somewhat upset his mother."

"Mr. Slender explained that about four months before his wife gave birth to the baby, he had sold his old blacksmith shop, which had been out near the road, with the understanding that he was to move it to a new location across the highway. To do this he ran two small saplings

Mr. Sweet's traveling house on wheels. McKeever, N.Y. 1926. It was a summer of vernal green. The air was full of water flowers' sweet scents for working honey bees, green grass and the sound of whippoorwills from among the trees. They posed by the motor coach before the dinner bell rang, calling the children to return to camp from the river, through the scent of sweet wild flowers that drifted randomly through the wide Moose River valley. *Courtesy Dorothy Payton*

lengthways under the building and at a distance apart that would balance the structure properly and at the same time provide handles for carrying. Then he went up to the house to get his wife to help carry the building across the road to its new location.

"Before they got halfway over, however, Mrs. Slender said she guessed they would have to stop and rest a few minutes. He asked her if there was anything wrong and she said there wasn't except that she felt a slight stitch in her side. They got the building in position, however, and when they opened the doors found that a neighbor had driven in a pair of oxen to be shod and that he had tied them at the end of the building. Mrs. Slender had been carrying. When the boy was born, he was "puny," as Mr. Slender said, and he never did develop the strength he undoubtedly would have had to not been for this unfortunate incident.

"The old man explained the reason why the boy was plowing the stony field without horses by saying that just the week before one of the animals sprained a leg and his son had to carry it from the field to the barn, a distance of a quarter mile or more.

"When the boy was five years old," the old man remarked, "his mother sent him over to the shop to borrow a hammer for use in tacking a carpet to the floor. I happened to be using the sledge at that time so he took my extra 125-pound anvil for my wife to use as a tack hammer. It slipped once and hit her on the little finger and she had to wear a rag around it for almost a week."

"I asked the old farmer if his wife still did her own housework, and he said that she did. "Right now I wreckon, he volunteered, "she's sitting in the kitchen knitting the boy an undershirt."

"Before I left, Mr. Slender asked if I wouldn't like to meet his wife, and he took me to the kitchen door. Inside, rocking back and forth in an old fashioned chair, sat Mrs. Slender with three crowbars and a roll of barbed wire knitting that boy an undershirt."

ACCOMPLISHED LIARS OF ROUSES POINT, A CHAMPION TALE-SPINNING TOWN

Unknown author, *North Country Life*, Winter 1949
Reprinted from *The North Countryman*

From the days of its original settlers the village of Rouses Point has been quite generally recognized as champion among the North Country communities in the matter of tall tales told by its citizens. This reputation dates back to its first permanent resident, Jacques Rouse, from whom the village derived its name, and who is said to have been a most accomplished liar; through the days of the late Arthur Couture, a raconteur par excellence, and of Captain Nicklaus, the one-time Columbus fireman, who dropped in every summer to visit with relatives and to spin yarns in the local newspaper office.

There's the sea serpent, for instance, that's good for a column or two every two or three years; the Couture tale about the cattle buyer and the thirty calves; the feats of strength of old Noah Slender, from over Altona way; the story of the church-pecking woodpecker, and a hundred others. During bootlegging days the tales that went out of the village over the Associated Press and the United Press wires would have put Baron Munchausen to shame.

And now the neighboring village of Champlain, jealous, no doubt, of Rouses Point's admitted superiority in the important tall story field, gives out with a tale by one John Supernault, Sheridan Iron Works molder—a tale designed, we suspect, to steal some of the glory that is Rouses Point's.

Be that as it may, Mr. Supernault, then a private or corporal or something or other with a mechanic's rating in World War I, was ordered out on a French battlefield to repair an ammunition truck that had broken down between the lines. The enemy gunners had the range all right and shells were dropping thick and fast around the stalled vehicle.

Mr. Supernault admits now that he may have been just a little bit scared. But an order is an order, and so, with rifle in one hand and a tool kit in the other, he dashed out across No Man's Land, dodging shells and

Left to right: Randolph Spears and Dana Lincoln. Two sports writers who had another tales to tell after pulling their boat over the many beaver dams along Falls Stream near Piseco, N.Y. *Photo by Elgie Spears. Courtesy Edward Blankman (The Lloyd Blankman Collection)*

bullets and rockets, avoiding land mines and booby traps and shell holes. Miraculously he reached the truck in safety.

Ducking underneath the stalled vehicle and turning upon his back, the Champlain soldier located the trouble without difficulty. Jolting over the rough terrain had loosened a nut which had dropped from a bolt that held the gears in mesh. So Private or Corporal or Sergeant Supernault reached into his kit and found a nut to fit. Holding it between the thumb and forefinger of his right hand, he raised it up and was about to fit it to the threads of the bolt when he heard a tremendous shriek and he knew that a shell was headed in his direction.

Mr. Supernault says that he closed his eyes and said a prayer. Then there was a terrific explosion directly over his head. When he opened his eyes again, the truck was gone.

"You can imagine how silly I felt," concluded the Champlain man, "lying out there on my back in front of the whole army and holding that nut up in the air with nothing to put it on."

THE UNION SOLDIER'S GHOST

By Dorothy Pitt Rice, *York State Tradition*, Winter 1965

Our family has its own "ghost story." It has been told and retold for more than a hundred years, and like all stories, it probably has both lost something and gained something through the years of retelling, though the basic facts remain the same.

The small farm home where my great-grandparents lived was on a hill in Crown Point, overlooking miles of the Champlain Valley. Only a few neighbors lived on that road, and in order to go to church, school, or store, it was necessary to go down the "long hill" first.

It was late in the fall of this long-ago night. A cold and lonesome breeze blew through the dry leaves. There was a penetrating chill in the air, and when "Gramp" came in from the chores, he spoke of the hollowness of the air and expressed the thought that it might forecast snow.

But inside there was a feeling of warmth and security. The big lamp in the middle of the table, set for supper, shed a pleasant glow. A woodfire crackled in the stove and sent out welcome warmth. The shades were partly drawn against the darkness and the cold. The family sat down to enjoy the good, plain food and talked of the latest news of the "War between the States." This was not a happy topic, for Great-Grandmother felt a deep concern for her two young brothers, who had recently enlisted and were somewhere in the South.

As the conversation lapsed, a sound different from the crackling fire, the loud ticking of the clock on the shelf, or the bumping of a loose shutter became noticed. Way off in the distance, up the "long hill," past the Barnett place, past Marsh's farm, came the sound of a horse's hooves. Nearer and nearer and louder and louder they came until suddenly a man on horseback drove up to the window in full view of the family at the table. He was dressed in the blue uniform of a Union soldier. Leaning forward on his horse, he bent over and peered under the half-drawn

A crackling campfire invites a rousing ghost tale. *Courtesy Lake Placid-North Elba Historical Society*

shade. For a long minute he looked at the startled faces inside. Then suddenly he wheeled his horse around and rode swiftly away. Even after it wasn't physically possible to hear the horse's galloping, the sound seemed to remain for a long, long time.

The next day, still excited about the strange visit, "Gramp" inquired of his neighbors about the unknown horseman. In that time, when there were no radios or televisions for alibis, every unusual sound was carefully noted and analyzed. But the horseback rider had been neither seen nor heard by any of the neighbors. Further inquiries at the store at the foot of the "long hill" were in vain. No one had seen him or knew anything of his identity.

Shortly after this strange event, word came that Great-Grandmother's brother, Uncle Will Chapin, had been killed and was buried by the Rappahannock River.

Was the horseback rider a ghostly visitor bearing a message of death well in advance of human means to relay it?

While I was visiting a cousin a short time ago, she gave me an old family Bible she had found. As I turned the pages of this Bible, I found a letter which no doubt is the final chapter of our family ghost story. It was dated Camp Jessie, November 16th, 1862, and read, in part:

> *The report is here now that Stonewall Jackson is within two days' march of us with 60,000 troops and Burnside tite to his heels a-following him. Let him come. We are ready for him. There will be by night 16,000 troops here. They are coming all the time... Now let him come. We are ready for him. ... My love to you and Joseph and Uncle Obe and the children. Good bye, William C. Chapin.*

AFTERWORD

Mary L. Dennis

I didn't grow up in the North Country. I was a post-war child of the 1950s, and my parents were thrilled to be able to afford a nice brick colonial in a suburb of Cleveland, Ohio. Still, we seemed to spend every Sunday driving in the country, or if it was summer, basking on the wide golden beaches at Mentor Headlands or East Harbor, both on Lake Erie, both crowded and noisy. That was fine with my brother and me, but Dad and Mother always seemed faintly disappointed. When August arrived, there was a definite spring in Dad's step. Mother began making lists. I began counting the days until we'd begin packing the car—a Nash Ambassador that looked like a gigantic maroon turtle. Not an inch of space was wasted, and we pulled out early, while it was still dark. We were flatlanders heading north, the farther north the better.

"Getting ready to face a chilly day at Lake Eaton campground while my little dog Donny waits for me to get the show on the road. Mother and I slept in the car, an old Nash whose seats folded down. We were lucky we could turn the heater on every now and then at night. My brother and dad slept in the waxed canvas tent." —Mary L. Dennis.
Courtesy Mary L. Dennis

The trip took two days. We'd stop to camp the first night when Dad deemed that we were truly "Up North." We celebrated the first white birch and the first glimpse of Lake Huron, following its coast to Mackinaw City, where a car ferry took us across the Straits. Another ferry took us across the St. Mary's River into Canada. Then we had a long, rough road to our final destination—one of five rustic cabins on a huge, crystalline lake surrounded by granite hills and tall, tall trees. We thought of those mountains and isolated lakes and rushing rivers of our north country paradise as fondly as Glyndon Cole's contributors and readers did their special places in Adirondack locales like Old Forge, Lake Placid, Tupper and Saranac Lakes, Lake George, and Lake Champlain. And the two regions have a lot in common—from interesting mountain "characters" to regional legends to incredible fishing and hunting.

One year when I was around ten Dad decided we should venture elsewhere: the Adirondacks. We camped in the state park at Lake Eaton. I remember Dad sitting at the picnic table, drinking his second cup of coffee, poring over a tableful of regional materials, figuring out where we'd go that day. He loved to read and plan, and I wouldn't be surprised if one of those magazines was the Summer 1957 issue of *North Country Life*.

If it is possible to be nostalgic about the past at age ten, I was. A particular museum (which must have been the Adirondack Museum) was enough to make me wish I had lived in the "good old days." Frontier Town had the same effect. I remember how impressed my parents were as we circled up the Whiteface Mountain Memorial Highway. I don't know if that's where we saw the beer-drinking bear, or if it was on some other road, but I do remember my mother saying how terrible she thought it was to use the bear so cruelly and my father remarking that the bear's owner "had to make a living somehow up here."

The overnight lows were below freezing, so we huddled close to the fire in the evening while Dad kept us entertained with stories. He knew all sorts of myths associated with the dazzling constellations in the black sky, and he threw in a few tall tales and ghost stories too. I can still see how those close-enough-to-touch stars were reflected in the lake as the fire crackled and orange sparks flew up into the cold, clear air.

One day a ranger came along and said they were recruiting people to help fight a forest fire nearby. My brother and Dad went with the ranger, and Mom and I worried all day that they could be injured or that we might have to evacuate the campground—and then how would they find us? Instead, the fire was contained and Dad and John came back grimy and exhausted, but exhilarated. That evening, the campfire stories were about the day's adventures and all the people they had met, and how they had all "fought like brothers" to save the woods.

I've always wanted to go back to the Adirondacks, and in a way, I have journeyed all over the region—thanks to Jay O'Hern and now also to Glyndon Cole and all his contributors. All of Jay's books evoke strong memories of the north woods. I can smell the balsam, see a bear cross the road up ahead, hear the loons calling late at night, hear a log shift in the old wood cook stove. Editing Jay's work has been pure pleasure. His *Adirondack Kaleidoscope* and *Adirondack Memories* books are just that—an everfascinating, ever-changing pattern that allows anyone, anywhere to experience the North Country at its finest, most inspiring, most magical best.

Pardee's reputation was as a guide and sharpshooter. Less acknowledged was his concern for all things wild. Left to right: Unidentified man, Randoph Spears, George Pardee.
Courtesy Edward Blankman (The Lloyd Blankman Collection)

THE DOE

She stood transfixed with wonder,
The little amber doe.
Her tender nostrils quivered,
She questioned, "Friend, or foe?"

Then found a sudden answer
And trotted to the wood,
Leaving me in shadows
Lonely where I stood.

She left to seek her brethren
Beneath the twilight shade:
I left, my heart regretful,
To join a world man-made.

—Elsie Wilkins, *York State Tradition*, Winter, 1964

POSTSCRIPT

William J. O'Hern

North Country Life's long time poet, Elsie Wilkins, opened the spring 1957 issue with "Bluebird Weather," proclaiming in the first stanza her adoration of the beginning of April.

Let us go out in bluebird weather—
It doesn't matter how, or whether
You come to walk, or just to dream,
For April's dancing by the stream.

Splitting firewood soon after the snow melts—in "bluebird weather"—has always helped me clear my mind of any late winter lassitude. It's a satisfying physical task, and it's also pleasant to watch the pictures frozen in my memory—bird-wings whirring at the feeder, crocuses and daffodil shoots pushing up through last year's blanket of woodchips, white snow blossoms near the chopping block, the resident woodchuck poking his furry face from the burrow hole at the edge of the woodshed.

Wilkins continues:

. . . The woodland brooklet leaps and dashes,
For April is bathing her silver feet,
Along the bank where the willows meet.

Glyndon Cole's faithful writer is describing one of the wistful thoughts that have been going through my mind. I should soon spot the earliest bluebird scouts that arrive to check out nesting sites in advance of the larger group that will come later.

. . . O let us go out in bluebird weather
While April stays—it's now or never.

As April goes on, spring's arrival seems more and more definite. What a feeling of freedom to go outside without even a jacket! Snowshoes, sleds, skates and skis are pushed to the back of the closet, and kayak paddles, fishing rods and tackle boxes move to the front as spring unfolds in all its delicious splendor, promising that summer too is on its way.

And no matter what the season—spring, summer, fall or winter—Glyndon Cole's proliferation of poets caught in words life scenes everyday people find enjoyable.

> *...The peaks or the foothills alike make me know,*
> *True joy in real living as forward I go.*
>
> —*From "Adirondacks," by Arlina Taylor Thompson, North Country Life,* Winter 1954

A Summer Evening at Camp Oasis. I am seated on a worn sheepskin throw rug in front of a mortared cobblestone fireplace. The radiant heat is comfortable; firelight casts dancing shadows against the walls. Grandmother, seated under a flood of yellow lamp glow, is knitting wool mittens. A deep CROAK, CROAK, CROAK sound within easy earshot is coming from the wetland on the opposite bank of the river. The bullfrog's utterance is familiar. Grandpa is telling me about the day the goliath bullfrog surprised him as he bow-hunted carp that traveled the river's edge. Afterwards, Grandma tells a story about her mother (my Great Grandma Sally), when she was a young girl in England.

A Crisp Late-Autumn Morning. I am curled snugly in bed. I'm in no rush to leave the comfort of the warm quilt. Besides, Mother is telling me an imaginary story: "Do you see the circus tent and five trained dogs sitting on stools?" she asks, "and the tightrope walker?" She is pointing to a spider and its web that connect a floor lamp's apex to the outside edge of a window drape. A tightrope walker and safety net to be sure, with a bit of imagination! Ruffled material gathered in tufts along the length of a wooden curtain rod above the double-hung window unquestionably appear analogous to circus-trained poodles perched on high stools.

A Crackling, Popping, Campfire. The distinctive smell of an old-style waxed canvas umbrella tent—an everyday Adirondack campground setting.

The common denominator of these images? My family history and all the energy spent selecting stories in the development of *Adirondack Memories and Campfire Stories.*

Edward Blankman, who writes under the pen name "Luther Root" for the *Watertown Daily Times*, helped me to accumulate a complete set of all of the *North Country Life* and *York State Tradition* magazines. "They are difficult to find today; [a]...complete set is indeed rare. If you find some copies, however, there is some wonderful reading about the olden days in" the Adirondacks and throughout other regions of New York State, he explained.

In his September 18, 2010, column titled "Magazine covered charms of *North Country Life*," Blankman told readers that while G. Glyndon Cole "was teaching in Ogdensburg ...[he started] the first issue dated Fall 1946." The quarterly magazine "was about the first and most successful of the precursors of [today's] *Adirondack Life* magazine."

My belief is that humans' lives are enriched when touched by others. In Ardath Rodale's *Gifts of the Spirit*, she challenges insight in one's search for "truth, wisdom, and spiritual growth":

> *I've been pondering life changes with the generations and asking,* 'With television, computers, and busy family schedules, what kind of family history do parents teach? Do our children know their roots, where they came from, and who they are?' *Their lives need to be touched not only by the new, but by the living hearts of those people who came before. It's vitally important to study new things but also to remember what we can learn from the past. I believe we are entering a new age where people will begin to have another look at their roots as a way of surviving in a world where we are moving too fast.*

I believe Mr. Cole's magazine did just this—it allowed readers to enjoy stories of Upstate New York that were not just dry history, but the real life stories of the people who actually lived it and participated in it.

Each issue provided detailed accounts of past historical and political events, personal reminiscences, eyewitness accounts, stories of inventions and colorful characters, brave individuals as well as unusual findings, folk-tales, tall tales and yarns—each story painstakingly edited by Cole or one of his associate editors.

Some accounts of life are so real you are almost there, enduring the hardships of the early pioneers and living through the tragic days of our War of 1812, the struggles of depression times, the changes brought on by the 1930s, the gradual decline of the North Country during the 1960s, and the state's recreation improvements.

The emphasis of the magazine was on the life stories of the people, who were typical of their era, places and events. It was a tribute to the forefathers, to their thoughts, dreams and lives. Birth death, love, family, church, and home were all important in the lives of those people, and these are the threads from which each issue was composed. And of course, with their daily comings and goings, one is introduced to the various business establishments and their owners, who along with the farmers made up the economic life of the Adirondack North Country and Upstate New York.

The Present. I am at my woodland home on a frosty spring morning. The sun-drenched woodlot is filled with the light pattering sound of red squirrels and chipmunks skittering over the dry leaf-carpeted ground. Returning Canada geese are honking overhead. I often sit on the chopping block and do nothing but enjoy the warming sun and take in the woodland setting. I like to see the four deer that traipse around the clearing looking for tender spring shoots in my wife's flower beds, but I know my chopping disturbs the privacy they prefer.

Spring is arriving. Soon the traditional spring showers will splat millions of water drams, striking the asphalt shingles. I like to hear the sound when I go into the attic. It won't be long before tree frogs will announce their reemergence from their mud beds with "chirrup, chirrup." Owls hoot, whistle, shriek and bark in the distance as doves coo at the sunflower feeder.

The sounds are familiar echoes of my lifestyle; they bring to life a lot of good things stored in my mind.

Various artifacts and stacks of cassette tapes are scattered about my Adirondack room in my basement. Stored on each reel of thin, flexible plastic are hundreds of hours of interviews conducted over thirty-some-odd years of Adirondack data-gathering sessions. First-hand recollections that document a former time. Voices that transcend time for the interviewees who have passed on. Their voices reach out from the grave alongside my collection of Glyndon Cole's magazines and hundreds of other North Country books.

Today, little survives of some of the once small but thriving towns that dotted the upstate counties—at one time some of the most productive areas—now covered by a network of abandoned roads and wooded expanse. I have happened upon the burying grounds that verify the existence of those who struggled to claim a settlement from the wilderness.

★ ★ ★

Kerplunk! Splat! I finally deliver a bulls-eye on a floating leaf in bordering Groton Pond. The outward flowing ripples created by the pebble plunked into the water are the only agent of disturbance. What a wonderful characteristic of water. There is, indeed, a regal orderliness in all the glorious wonders of creation: its green forests and the wind upon the waters, the melting of ice on warm spring days, the battering wind of a summer thunderstorm, colorful, restless autumn leaves lightly whipped by a zephyr, winter snowsnakes slinking on a warm day off their boughs, open meadows and the plants and animals that live in and by water, the birds flying over the earth, wetlands and mountains and oceans, even the people in their high-tech vehicles that move upon the land.

There are these sayings: What we see all the time we stop seeing. What we hear all the time we stop hearing. I like to think I never have stopped wondering and learning about the state I live in.

The first question I asked myself, after completing *Adirondack Kaleidoscope* and *Adirondack Memories*, was, "Why stop with just highlighting some of Cole's best magazine stories? I knew he had published so many interesting things that are never going to be found in traditional history books. After all, Glyndon Cole's strove against the odds to develop a successful thirty-seven year run of magazines. The effort was a fulfillment of a long-cherished dream. It seemed almost criminal to let the remainder of his life work slip away into oblivion.

That's why I'm planning to offer two other whole anthologies to cover the Adirondack Mountains-North Country and Upstate New York.

Plans are underway now for *From Mountains to Foothills and Gathered Memories: A Celebration of the Adirondack-North Country and Upstate New York*, two upcoming releases. Both will continue the tradition of highlighting stories that appeared in *North Country Life* and *York State Tradition* magazines between 1946 to 1974.

The anthologies will feature the most engrossing articles and stories of history, people, farming, old days and ways, life and manners, community insights, the logging industry, lakes and streams, social history, upstate characters, ghost towns and outlaws, adventure, recreation, legends and folklore, forgotten things and fireside tales.

It took a native Northern New Yorker to draw together the resources to build one of the best magazines of his era. I look forward to opening a new door to Upstate New York's past.

ACKNOWLEDGMENTS

I would first like to thank G. Glyndon Cole, who gave his vote of confidence for this project when I spoke with him in March 1989. Without his support this project would never have been started. It has been a privilege to honor his commitment to regional history. A special thanks to his daughter, Carolyn Trivilino, who shared background material and rounded out my collection of *North Country Life* and *York State Tradition* magazines.

This book would never have been completed without the interest and support of a wide variety of helpful people. Enormous gratitude goes to all those who contributed to *North Country Life* and *York State Tradition* over the years, and to those who generously backed my effort to share the historical significance of Cole's out-of-print magazine.

The author extends his expression of gratitude to Daniel E. Alexander, President and Publisher, Denton Publications, Inc.; Edward Blankman; Dick Case; Maitland C. DeSormo; Alice Genthner; Samantha Gleba, Admin. Secretary of the Shriners International ZIYARA SHRINERS and *Bugle* Editor; Caroline Kehne, Editor *Lake Champlain Weekly*; Joe Kelly, editor and publisher of the *Boonville Herald & Adirondack Tourist* and host of the Joe Kelly Show on WUTR-TV; Cathleen Kittle, Bureau Director, Division of Public Affairs and Education of the New York State Department of Environmental Conservation; Rob Igoe, Jr. President, North Country Books, Inc.; Debra Kimok, Special Collections Librarian, Plattsburgh, State University of New York; Jennifer Kuba, Assistant Director, Archivist/Curator at the Adirondack History Center Museum, Essex County Historical Society; Stan Linhorst, Senior Managing Editor of the Syracuse *Post-Standard*; M. Dan McClelland, Publisher, T*upper Lake Free Press*; Dorothy Mooney; David H. Nelson, Editor, NYS *Conservationist*; John Seaman; Mike Spain, Associate Editor, *Times-Union*; Town of Webb Historical Association, and Bill Zullo, Hamilton County Historian.

A special heartfelt thank-you goes to my daughters Susan Steverman and Kerry Suppa, whose nimble fingers eased the labor of some keyboard work for their father.

The assistance of my dedicated editors, Mary L. Dennis and Neal Burdick, was invaluable. They shared the work of copy correcting as only those with their skills can do. Their insightful questions and suggestions gave me confidence to carry forward.

For permission to use material that previously appeared in Albany's *Times-Union* newspaper by Hayden S. Pearson, grateful acknowledgement is made to *Times-Union* and Mike Spain, Associate Editor.

For permission to use material that previously appeared in *The Syracuse Post-Standard* grateful acknowledgement is made to *The Syracuse Post-Standard* and Stan Linhorst, Senior Managing Editor.

For permission to reprint David H. Beetle's chapter, "The South Branch and the League Club," in *Up Old Forge Way* [cast from Beetle's original article, "Kilroy Was NOT Here"] grateful acknowledgement is made to North Country Books, Inc.

For permission to use Indian Lake photographs, grateful acknowledgement is made to Bill Zullo, Hamilton County Historian.

For permission to use *Prospect House: One-Time Mecca of High Society*, grateful acknowledgement is made to the Ziyara Shriners, A.A.O.N.M.S.

I have made every effort to acknowledge the assistance of everyone who helped. Any omission is an unintentional oversight.

CONTRIBUTORS

Glyndon Cole was closely acquainted with many of his contributors, and for them it is possible to list *biographical* notes. For others, we know nothing more than where they lived. For still others, nothing is known beyond a name. Readers are encouraged to provide additional information for inclusion in subsequent editions.

➡ **ROBERT V. ANDERSON**. Associated with Utica College of Syracuse University.

➡ **E. EUGENE BARKER**, Albany, N.Y. Worked as a landscape architect for the Office of New York State Architecture.

➡ **ETHEL BARNETT**, Crown Point, N.Y.

➡ **DAVID H. BEETLE**. His work as long-time columnist for the *Utica Sunday* and *Daily Observer Dispatch*, the *Utica Daily Press*, and other newspapers in the Gannett group, gave him wide readership. Beetle is the author of *West Canada Creek, Along the Oriskany, Up Old Forge Way* and *The New York Citizen.*

➡ **WILLIS N. BUGBEE**, Syracuse, N.Y.

➡ **REV. A. L. BYRON-CURTISS**, Utica, N.Y. Author of *Life and Adventures of Nat Foster: Trapper and Hunter of the Adirondacks and A Pass in the Mountains*. Byron-Curtiss is the subject of the biography *Under an Adirondack Influence* by William J. O'Hern and Roy E. Reehil.

➡ **RICHARD G. CASE**, formerly on the staff of the Chicago Historical Society, has been a columnist for the *Syracuse Herald-Journal* and currently the *Syracuse Post-Standard* for 50 years.

➡ **THEOBALD CLARK**, Lansdale, Pennsylvania.

➡ **G. GLYNDON COLE**, Saranac, N.Y. Teacher, school librarian, and Editor and Publisher of *North Country Life* and *York State Tradition.*

➡ **PAUL F. CRUMLEY**, Fort Anne, N.Y.

➡ **WILMA CUMMINS**. A long-time resident of Canton, N.Y., she was a homemaker and wife of the St. Lawrence University chaplain.

➡ **Rev. W. N. P. Dailey**, Pottersville, N.Y.

➡ **Edmund P. Davis**, Wanakena, N.Y.

➡ **Mary L. Dennis**, Fort McCoy, Florida. Author and Editor.

➡ **Caroline H. Fish**

➡ **Gretchen Houghton Fish**

➡ **Barnett Fowler**. Newspaper columnist and feature writer-photographer and commentator for WGY radio. Author of *Adirondack Album I*, *II* and *III*.

➡ **Marion S. Fresn**

➡ **Walter B. Gunnison**, served on the staff of the Brooklyn, N.Y., *Daily Eagle* newspaper. It is believed he was the editor. He formally lived in Canton, N.Y., and was a graduate of St. Lawrence University.

➡ **Dorothy O. Haeusser**

➡ **Gilbert Hagerty**, Lee Center, N.Y.

➡ **Arthur Hall**

➡ **Helen Ireland Hays**

➡ **Grace L. Hudowalski**, Albany, N.Y. Born in 1906, she was one of the founders of the Forty-Sixers and first president of the Adirondack Forty-Sixers. She worked as a promotion supervisor for New York State and held numerous positions in various organizations following retirement, including past president of the New York Folklore Society, lifetime historian of the Adirondack Forty-Sixers, secretary of the Adirondack Park Association, past editor of the Adirondack Mountain Club publications and editor of *The Adirondack Forty-Sixers* (1958) and *The Adirondack High Peaks and the Forty-Sixers* (1970 and 1971). Grace was the first woman to climb all forty-six Adirondack High Peaks.

➡ **Charles E. Hughes**

➡ **Allan Keller**

➡ **Dorothy LaBelle**, Historian, Town of Chateaugay, N.Y.

➡ **Dot Mills**, Chateaugay, N.Y.

➡ **Roland B. Miller**. Miller wrote many articles for the New York State *Conservationist* magazine during the 1950s.

➡ **Doris B. Morton**, Whitehall, N.Y.

➡ **HAYDEN S. PEARSON**
➡ **GEORGE E. PHINNEY SR.**, Port Henry, N.Y.
➡ **CONNIE POPE**. G. Glyndon Cole wrote this about Connie in the Introduction to his *Manuscripts for Research*: "By 1969 the collection had grown to such an extent that the assistance of another professional librarian was obviously required. At that time Miss Connie Pope was assigned as a full-time assistant. She took charge of the cataloging of books, did extensive indexing of newspapers, and added hundreds of clippings to the file. Thousands of cards were added to the catalog through her work. In addition, she did a great deal of researching, much of it during her off-duty hours, by which she acquired extensive knowledge of the history of the area, making her extremely capable in assisting users of the collection." Connie Pope was enthusiastic about local history and wrote a good deal about her findings as shown at: http://banweb.cc.platsburgh.edu/pls/banprd/polaris.results
➡ **MARJORIE L. PORTER**, Keeseville and Keene, N.Y. Associate Editor of *North Country Life & York State Tradition*, she died in 1973 at the age of 82. Up to the time of her death, she wrote newspaper columns on folklore and historical subjects, wrote and published several historical pamphlets, and was a frequent speaker before historical groups. In addition, she served at various times as Essex County historian, Clinton County historian, and Plattsburgh city historian. In July 1972 the New York State Historical Association presented her with an award of merit "in recognition of long service to local history and the folklore of the Adirondack area."

Mrs. Porter willed to the North Country Historical Research Center, State University College, Plattsburgh, her collection of local history and folklore consisting of books, pamphlets, manuscripts, notes, photographs, clippings, and more than 100 tapes and records. The tapes and records are recordings of folk songs and interviews with North Country residents. Her collected works are undoubtedly the largest in Northern New York.
➡ **BRENDA RAWLINS**, Schroon Lake Central School, Schroon Lake, N.Y.

➡ **DOROTHY PITT RICE**, Crown Point, N.Y. A life long native, Rice did corresponding for local and area newspapers.

➡ **W. C. RICE**, Rice worked as a fire observer for New York State's Department of Conservation on Ampersand Mountain. Right under the peak of Ampersand, climbers will find a bronze tablet with this inscription:

In loving memory of
Walter Channing Rice
1852 - 1924
"Hermit of Ampersand"
Who kept vigil from this peak
1915 - 1923
Erected by his sons -1930

When *North Country Life* Associate Editor Billy Burger last saw the plaque in 1950, he reported to Glyndon Cole, "It was nearly ruined by the scratches and scrawls of people who have a yen to write or carve their names everywhere they have been. One of these days some curio hound will probably jimmy it loose to gloat over with his pals at home."

"Walter Rice preceded the fire tower on Ampersand Mountain. In fact he built his own observatory, a neat little stone hut which has long since disappeared.

"While Walter Rice was on Ampersand only eight years, he had the same sense of belonging to his mountain that Old Mountain Phelps had to Marcy. It possessed him to such a degree that he must have written poems about it as he did about other things that took hold of him. Unfortunately none of these survive and little information about the Hermit of Ampersand is available. But from what little we know and from the impression he made on some of us who met him on his peak, we sensed that here was a rare combination of woodsman, philosopher, poet, and gentleman, a kind of Robert Frost on a mountain top. Too bad Henry

Van Dyke didn't meet him. They would have had a rare time together, for both were in love with a lovable mountain."

A clipping from a Saranac Lake paper, dated April 26, 1918, reveals the essence of Walter Channing Rice. He is starting up his mountain for the summer season, and this is what he tells an inquiring reporter:

"'I'm anxious to go back. People will tell me that they don't see how I could live up there all alone. But they don't understand that I have the best friends in the world up there—the wild flowers, the birds, the animals, and the many manifestations of Nature that go to make up the comradeship of the soul. The still life—that is the source of contentment on old Ampersand. Let them come up to that little world of mine and let me show them the joys that fill my existence there, and then, if they can see it all as I see it, they will no longer condole with the Ampersand Hermit.'"

➡ **LINDON E. RIGGS**, Winthrop, N.Y.

➡ **MELINDA RYAN**

➡ **FRANCES B. SEAMAN**, Long Lake, N.Y. Frances Boone Seaman was the author of *Nehasane Fire Observer*. Her publisher, Nick Burns, reports Frances "was a very nice lady and talented." Early in her life she worked as a commercial artist in New York City, drawing women's fashions for newspapers and magazines. *Nehasane Fire Observer* is about her time in the 1940s as a fire tower observer at Nehasane Park. She functioned as the historian of Long Lake for decades.

➡ **SENECA RAY STODDARD**, photographer-writer (1843–1917).

➡ **ARLINA TAYLOR THOMPSON**, Keeseville, N.Y.

➡ **FRED TORRANCE**

➡ **JOHN VAN BRAKLE**, Jamaica

➡ **HENRY VAN DYKE**, (1852–1933). Van Dyke was an American author, educator, and clergyman. He had a passion for fishing in the Adirondacks.

➡ **STAN VICKERS**

➡ **VIVIAN STEVES WALKER**, Gansevoort, N.Y.

➡ **Richard F. Ward**, Associate Professor, State University Teachers College, Plattsburgh, N.Y.

➡ **Louella Waterman**, Philadelphia, PA. & Croghan, N.Y.

➡ **Elsie Wilkins**, Utica, N.Y. contributed poetry for eight years

Bette O'Hern heading to the scene in a *North Country Life* story. *Author's photo*

In preparation of this book, the author and publisher have grammatically edited, where necessary, articles that appeared in *North Country Life* and *York State Tradition*. However, the information in those articles is presented as the writers wrote them. Should there be historical errors, the information in this book is sold without warranty, either express or implied. Neither the author nor In the Adirondacks will be liable for any damages caused or alleged to be caused directly, indirectly, incidentally, or consequentially by the information in this book.

SOURCES

BOOKS

Aber, Ted. *Adirondack Folks.* Prospect, NY: Prospect Books, 1982.

Adler, Jeanne Winston. *Early Days in the Adirondacks, The photography of Seneca Ray Stoddard.* New York, NY: Harry N. Abrams, Inc., Date unknown.

Allen, Richard S.; William Gove, Keith F. Maloney and Richard F. Palmer. *Rails in the North Woods: Histories of Ten Adirondack Short Lines.* Utica, NY: North Country Books, 1978.

Beetle, David H. *Up Old Forge Way/West Canada Creek.* Lakemont & Old Forge, NY: North Country Books, 1971.

DeSormo, Maitland C. *Seneca Ray Stoddard, Versatile Camera-Artist.* Saranac Lake, NY: Adirondack Yesteryears Inc., 1972.

Donaldson, Alfred L. *A History of the Adirondacks Vol. I & II.* Harrison, NY: Harbor Hiull Books, 1977.

Grady, Joseph F. *The Story of a Wilderness: The Adirondacks, Fulton Chain—Big Moose Region.* Boonville, NY: The Willard Press, second edition 1966.

Harter, Henry A. *Fairy Tale Railroad.* Hamilton, NY: Vail-Ballou, 1980.

Northrup, A. Judd. *Camps and Tramps in the Adirondacks,* 1880.

O'Hern, William J. *Adirondack Characters and Campfire Yarns: Early Settlers and Their Traditions.* Cleveland, NY: The Forager Press, 2005.

O'Hern, William J. *Adirondack Stories of the Black River Country.* Utica, NY: North Country Books, 2003.

O'Hern, William J. *Under an Adirondack Influence, The Life of A. L. Byron-Curtiss 1871–1959.* Cleveland, NY: The Forager Press, 2008.

Stoddard, Seneca Ray. *Old Times in the Adirondacks.* Saranac Lake, NY: Adirondack Yesteryears Inc., 1972.

Tolles, Jr.,Bryant F. *Resort Hotels of the Adirondacks: The Architecture of a Summer Paradise, 1850–1950.* University Press of New England, Lebanon, NH, 2003.

MAGAZINES AND NEWSPAPERS

_____. "Captain Nicklaus Spins a Yarn. Tall Tales Dept." Reprinted from *The North Countryman* (date Unknown). *North Country Life,* Summer 1948.

_____. "Tall Tales Department." *North Country Life,* Fall 1948. Reprinted from *The North Countryman.*

_____. "'Heaven up-h'istedness." *North Country Life,* Winter 1948.

_____. "An Early Tale in the Adirondacks." Adapted from *The North Countryman* (date unknown). *North Country Life,* Winter 1948.

_____. "Weird Beliefs of Early Days in the North." Reprinted from *The Syracuse Post-Standard* in *North Country Life,* Spring, 1953.

_____. "Journey to the Skies." *North Country Life,* Summer, 1955.

_____. "This is Tupper lake." *North Country Life,* Fall 1955.

_____. "Prospect House: One-Time Mecca of High Society." The Editor of *Ziyara Bugle* credits the following sources of information: *Adirondack Country* by W. C. White; *Central Adirondacks* by Jim Fynmore and the files of the *New York Times* newspaper. *North Country Life,* Summer, 1960.

Anderson, Robert V. "Fishing Piseco—1850." *North Country Life,* Summer, 1960.

_____."Destination: Brown's Tract." *York State Tradition,* Winter, 1963.

Barker, E. Eugine. "Mr. Hammond's Iron Towers." *North Country Life,* Spring, 1957.

Barnett, Ethel. "Recalling the Old Country Store." *York State Tradition,* Spring, 1962.

Beetle, David H. "Kilroy Was NOT Here." Reprinted from the Utica *Observer-Dispatch* in *North Country Life*, Spring, 1947.

Bellows, Ralph. "The Search for the Indian Lead Mine on Lyon Mountain." Adapted from "Letters to the Editor." *North Country Life*, Date unknown.

Bugbee, Willis N. "The Lure of the North." *North Country Life*, Summer, 1955.

Byron-Curtiss, A. L. "Forestport Days." *North Country Life*, Spring, 1955.

Case, Richard G. "In Search of the Real American Tragedy." *York State Tradition*, Summer, 1969.

Clark, Theobald. "Treasure Roundup." *North Country Life*, Spring, 1950.

_____. "Treasure Roundup." *North Country Life*, Summer, 1950.

Cook, David B. and Roland B. Miller. "Pit Burning Charcoal." Reprinted from the *New York State Conservationist* Aug.-Sept. 1952. *North Country Life*, 1959.

_____. "Silver Near the Hudson River Headwaters." In "Treasure Roundup," *North Country Life*, Winter, 1951.

Cole, G. Glyndon. "Chateaugay: Oldest Town in Franklin County." *North Country Life*, Summer, 1949.

_____. "Saranac Lake." *North Country Life*, Summer, 1956.

_____. "Saranac Lake Free Library." *North Country Life*, Fall, 1956.

_____. "The Mystery of the Lost Cave." *York State Tradition*, Spring, 1973.

Crumley, Paul, F. "Fort Anne." *North Country Life*, Summer, 1954.

Cummins, Wilma. "What Is the North Country?" *York State Tradition*, Spring, 1969.

Dailey, Rev. W. N. P. "Fireside Legends of the Adirondacks." *North Country Life*, Summer, 1951.

Davis, Edmund P. "That Camp O' Mine." (poem) *North Country Life*, Summer, 1961.

Fish, Caroline H. "Early Vacation Days in the Town of Chester." *York State Tradition*, Spring, 1969.

Fish, Gretchen Houghton. "Indian Lake." Reprinted from the New York State *Conservationist* in *North Country Life*, Winter, 1952.

Fowler, Barnett. "Tall Tales Department." Reprinted from the New York State *Conservationist* in *North Country Life*, Spring, 1949.

Fresn, Marion S. "The Lion Couchant." *North Country Life*, Winter 1954.

Gunnison, Walter B. "Memories of an Old Country Fair." *North Country Life*, Summer, 1949.

Hagerty, Gilbert. "How Eagle Lake Got its Name." *North Country Life*, Winter, 1958.

Hall, Anthony F. "A Journey Through Our Back Pages: Re-discovering North Country Life." *The Lake George Mirror*, June 14, 2013.

Hall, Arthur. "Our Town—Willsboro." Reprinted from the *Essex County Republican*, in *North Country Life*, Summer, 1960.

Haeusser, Dorothy O. "Head for the Hills." *North Country Life*, date unknown.

Hays, Helen Ireland. "Excursion to Spruce Lake." *York State Tradition*, Spring, 1971.

Hudowalski, Grace L. "The Legend of Pitchoff Mountain Pass." Reprinted from *The Ad.i.ron.dac Heven Up-h'istedness* in *North Country Life*, Summer, 1950.

Hughes, Charles E. "Crown Point." *North Country Life*, Summer, 1951.

Keller, Allan. "Murder in the Adirondacks." *North Country Life*, Fall, 1946.

LaBelle, Dorothy. "Bootlegger's Paradise." *York State Tradition*, Sprint 1970.

Miller, Roland B. "Long Lake." *North Country Life*, Winter, 1954.

_____. "Blue Mountain Lake." *North Country Life*, Spring, 1955.

Mills, Dot. "Chateaugay in the 1920s." *North Country Life*, Summer, 1947.

Morton, Doris B. "Great-Grandfather and the Panther." *York State Tradition*, Winter, 1964.

Pearson, Hayden S. "Old Plank Bridges." Reprinted from the Albany *Times-Union* in *York State Tradition*, Fall, 1963.

Phinney, George E. "The Fieldstone Wall." (poem) *North Country Life*, Fall, 1954.

Pope, Connie. "The Anatomy of a Legend: The Lake Champlain Sea Serpent." *York State Tradition*, Winter, 1970.

Porter, Marjorie L. "Blueberries, A 'Grapes of Wrath' Industry in Early Clinton County." *North Country Life*, Summer, 1952.

_____. "Redford Glass." *North Country Life*, Spring, 1953.

_____. "East Hill, Two Experiments in Social Living." *North Country Life*, Fall, 1957.

Rawlins, Brenda. "Tanning: Schroon Lake's First Industry." *North Country Life*, Winter, 1960.

Rice, W. C. "To A Hermit Thrush." (poem) *York State Tradition*, Quarterly unknown. Date after 1960.

Rice, Dorothy Pitt. "The Union Soldier's Ghost." *York State Tradition*, Winter 1965.

Riggs, Lindon E. "The Story of the Old Clock." *North Country Life*, Fall 1958.

Ryan, Melinda. "The Fabulous Loon Lake House." *York State Tradition*, Summer, 1971.

Seaman, Frances Boone. "Cold River Valley—By Canoe." *North Country Life*, Summer, 1947.

Stoddard, Seneca Ray. "Wilderness Prison." *York State Tradition*, Summer 1968

_____. *Old Times in the Adirondacks*. Saranac Lake, NY: Adirondack Yesteryears, 1972

Tolles, Jr., Bryant F. *Resort Hotels of the Adirondacks: The Architecture of a Summer Paradise, 1850–1950*. University Press of New England, Lebanon, NH, 2003.

Torrance, Fred. "Jay's 150 Years." *North Country Life*, Fall, 1948.

Van Brakle, John. "Sea Gulls in the Adirondacks." *North Country Life*, Summer, 1960.

Van Dyke. "Ampersand." Abridged from *Little Rivers* (1903) in *North Country Life*, Summer, 1961.

Vickers, Stan. "Delving into the Dark Ages." *North Country Life*, Summer, 1949.

Walker, Vivian Steves. "My Encounter with Wild Dogs." *North Country Life*, Winter, 1960.

Ward, Richard F. "Geology of the Hudson." *North Country Life*, Fall, 1959.

Waterman, Louella. "Driftwood." *North Country Life*, Summer, 1958.

Wilkins, Elsie. "The Doe." (poem) *York State Tradition*, Winter, 1964.

INDEX

CURRENT TITLES

by William J. O'Hern

Spring Trout and Strawberry Pancakes: Quirky Cures, Borrowed Tales, Camp Recipes and the Adirondack Characters Who Cooked Them Up, 2014

Adirondack Memories and Campfire Stories
Edited and with Biographical and Historical Commentary by William. J. O'Hern
In the Adirondacks, 2014

Adirondack Wilds: Exploring the Haunts of Noah John Rondeau, 2014

The Hermit and Us: Our Adirondack Adventures with Noah John Rondeau
In the Adirondacks, 2014

Adirondack Kaleidoscope and North Country Characters
Edited and with Biographical and Historical Commentary by William. J. O'Hern
In the Adirondacks, 2013

Thomas C. O'Donnell's
Life in a North Woods Lumber Camp
Edited and with Biographical and Historical Commentary by William J. O'Hern
The Forager Press, LLC, 2012

Adirondack Adventures: Bob Gillespie and Harvey Dunham on French Louie's Trail
By Roy E. Reehil and William J. O'Hern
The Forager Press, LLC, 2012

Noah John Rondeau's Adirondack Wilderness Days: A Year with the hermit of Cold River Flow
The Forager Press, LLC, 2009

Under An Adirondack Influence: The Life of A. L. Byron-Curtiss, 1871–1959
By Roy E. Reehil and William J. O'Hern
The Forager Press, LLC, 2008

Adirondack Characters and Campfire Yarns: Early Settlers and Their Traditions
The Forager Press, LLC, 2005

Adirondack Stories of the Black River Country
North Country Books, Inc. 2003

Anyplace Wild in the Adirondacks
Self-published, 2000

Life with Noah: Stories and Adventures of Richard Smith with Noah J. Rondeau
North Country Books, Inc.
Second Paperback Printing 2013

UPCOMING RELEASES

by William J. O'Hern

At Our Adirondack Table: Recipes and Stories from Mountain Camps

From Mountains to Foothills and Campfire Tales: Gathered Memories from New York's Adirondack-North Country and Tug Hill Region

Adirondack Pastimes: Camping and Sporting Adventures in the Cold River Country with Hermit Noah John Rondeau (1913–1950)

Remembering Adirondack Legend Noah John Rondeau: Following a Hermit's Footsteps Through His Final Years (1913–1967)

Gathered Memories and Fireside Stories
A Celebration of Past Adirondack-North Country and Upstate New York Life
Compiled, edited and with Biographical and Historical Commentary by William J. O'Hern

Logging in the Adirondacks: The Revolutionary Linn Tractor and Lumber Camp Stories

The Informal History of the Moose River Plains